AF556428

WOMEN IN INDIA

WOMEN IN INDIA

(An Exhaustive Study)

Edited by

Arunima Baruah

ANMOL PUBLICATIONS PVT. LTD.

NEW DELHI - 110 002 (INDIA)

ANMOL PUBLICATIONS PVT. LTD.
4374/4B, Ansari Road, Daryaganj
New Delhi - 110 002
Ph.: 3261597, 3278000
Visit us at: www.anmolbooks.com

Women in India

First Edition, 2003

ISBN 81-261-1340-5

PRINTED IN INDIA

Published by J.L. Kumar for Anmol Publications Pvt. Ltd., New Delhi - 110 002 and Printed at Mehra Offset Press, Delhi.

Contents

Contents

Preface

Women's studies is relatively a new discipline, but not an insignificant one, for studies on women, as a subject have been in the vogue for decades now. In fact, one can find even a centuries old book on one or the other aspect of 'women'. We find mention of women in our ancient religious books also.

Researchers have been engaged in studying and analysing matters related to the better half of the human beings. Hence, thousands of books on the issues concerning the fair sex. Still, one may feel, there is a dearth of comprehensive and exhaustive books on the subject. Only this feeling made this author begin a painstaking research, spread over the years, that eventually resulted in a modest work, which this volume is.

Over the past thousands of years, our society and polity have evolved and developed, and the new millennium has dawned, still the lot of one community in our land has remained more or less same — the women. They have suffered for hundreds of years, and they are suffering even now. But we must keep our hopes alive that this half portion of our social fabric would not suffer any more. At least, they deserve their rightful place in our setup—social, economic and political.

Not that no body thinks of the interests of women. Movements for the women lib are about a century old now.

There has been awakening, regarding feminine matters and gender justice, for seven-eight decades, even in India. Various governments, the alien one earlier and our own democratic one, after independence, have devoted enough attention to the problems of the weaker section, culminating into numerous reforming steps and framing of laws. However, the practical output has not been satisfactorily good. Therefore, a genuine concern about the group of 'have nots', known as women, among the academics and scholars, is quite natural.

This study is an humble effort with an aim of creating an awakening, regarding women, their issues, their problems and their future in our society and country.

This author would feel honoured, with a sense of achievement, if this work of hers, succeeds in making men sit and think about their fellow beings — women.

Editor

ONE

Introduction

A woman has to play a vital role in life and society. In fact, she plays many a role in a single life time. She is the mother, sister, wife and daughter, all rolled into one. A single woman plays these four roles in her life. First, she is daughter and sister and in that capacity, she serves her father and brothers. In the second phase, she acts as wife, which is perhaps the most important role, she plays. In this capacity she serves her husband and in laws. In due course, she becomes a mother and brings out her children. A woman normally commands three generations in one life of hers. She is the creator and protector of a family. She gives birth to a generation, develops it and thus forms the society.

In fact, society is a product of women. But, in spite of the importance attached to her personality, a woman is least respected - in the true sense of the word - in society. Over thousands of years, she has not been able to be free of shackles and chains, binding her and confining her to a limited space to move and act. That's the irony.

Interestingly, as far as law is concerned, it has always been there in existence, in one form or the other for the protection of women. All religions give appropriate rights to women, the scriptures have norms for the protection of their rights and personal liberty. But, in fact, the unfortunate lot, known as womenfolk enjoy no rights and no liberty at all. Over the ages, they have been forced to live under the dominance of men. No doubt, women have been in prominence in all eras, but they could at best be termed as exceptions. In an overall manner, the women are 'have nots' and a bad lot is tagged with them. A bitter fact in our lives.

However, one point, which all leaders, politicians, thinkers and scholars agree on is that no society, however, well organised, can ever be well oiled and set in motion properly, unless a justified status is granted to women. But, that's all. No one seems to believe in it practically. At least their actions do not depict anything of that sort. Although, the demand for women's lib or the movement for the protection of their rights is not new. It has been there for years now, yet, women's battle for justice got fresh momentum after the independence of the country and it has been in constant motion since then, in one form or the other. The struggle for securing a respectable status for women in the Indian polity and in society, has been on for the last 55 years and the efforts have been made inside and outside legislative bodies, all over the country, the national Parliament, being the natural leader. Following a long spell of fights and struggles - internal and external - and under the immense pressure of women's lib activists, at the international level, various governments began to act and the result was the creation of a National Commission for Women, besides enactment of a number of laws, protecting women, including some for granting reservation in different elected bodies, in order to provide them with a share in power at various levels.

The liberation of womanhood is nothing unnatural or any thing which should be termed as taxing on the males. The right to a personhood is a basic human right of every individual, bestowed upon by humanity and no one can deny it. Further, one has to believe that the progress of any nation is inevitably linked with the social status of woman in that particular country. But things do not move through papers only. For concrete results, we have to assert and act, with our full might and that's what is needed most. Empowerment of women can be granted through laws, but for its practical implementation, social response alone is required, which can come from within only.

In this study, sincere efforts have been made to bring, the real issues concerning women — in the context of Society and Law — to light and discuss the matter in a logical, convincing and empirical manner. A great effort has been made to view various problems of women in the right perspective, with legal aspects in view.

Truly speaking, emancipation of women is not so easy. For raising the status of a section of our society, we need a great will, social awareness, a determination and an initiative, which should come from within. First of all, we have to alarm the society and prepare it for a change. Needless to say that a change needs an awakening which comes through education alone. That is why education is the most important factor, working behind any movement or struggle for women's lib and women's rights, but, Indian women have been lagging behind in the sphere of education, for the last many centuries. Although, there has been considerable progress in the field of education of women, yet a lot has to be done for women education in India and its a long road to go. As is well known, women in India have always been on the academic scene. Our history has produced a number of female scholars during all ages. We had good female scholars, authoresses and poetesses in ancient India, we had great female scholars and ladies of letters in medieval India - the list includes names like Meera Bai - and a lot more in modem times.

Notably, the awakening among women - as in case of man - came first in Bengal, which produced good women scholars in 18th and 19th centuries, well before the commencement of general awareness at an all India level in the beginning of 20th century. Broadly speaking, the development in the educational status of women in India during 20th century can be classified into three periods viz, the first two decades, the third, fourth and the fifth decade (upto 1947) and the post-independence period. During pre-independence period, the educationists worked hard for the popularization of education among girls and women. They opened schools and colleges all over the country. These institutions changed the scenario to a great extent. Then dawned independence and the Government came on the scene and with that the educational development caught momentum. No doubt, we have achieved a lot, still a lot has to be done. Currently, if we look at the women's education scenario in India, we find this area cluttered with contradictory complexes, theories, opposed to each other and a number of streams, different from each other. But, the irony of the situation is that our country has a large mass of people, which is least interested in education. The rest are either ignorant or half-heartedly interested in education for the better half.

Here, it would be appropriate to discuss the purpose of education for women. In our country most women go for education to get married properly. Among the rest a majority receive education, as per their needs, as they want employment on the basis of their qualification. Lastly, only a small minority opts for education for academic purposes or for their enlightenment. However, there is a ray of hope at the end of the tunnel. There has been a tremendous and rapid growth in the number of women students in schools and colleges in the whole country after independence. In 1947 there were only 9.3 per cent female students at the higher level, but this figure rose to 43.2 per cent in 1999-2000. Expectedly, this must have risen during last two years, though the data are not available.

Primarily, the purpose of this study is to create an awakening among men, regarding the education and emancipation of women and among women themselves. This book, particularly provides information on women education, empowerment and mass media in a historical perspective. Women, today form an active section of the society, involved in all sorts of functions and performing all kinds of duties, shouldering man at each and every stage. As far as rights and duties are concerned, Indian Constitution has clear provisions for the same. It states: "The State shall not discriminate against any citizen on grounds only of religion, race, caste, sex, place of birth or any of them (Right to equality) etc." And, "There should be equality of opportunity for all citizens in matters, relating to employment or appointment to any office under the State". Thus, the Constitution has bestowed upon full rights to women, equal to men, for all purposes and in all spheres.

Now, women are active partners in the development of the country and work for it. In fact, women constitute a vital part of the work force in any business establishment and even in industries. Today, they are joining those professions as well, which were earlier considered to be the domain of males only. In a considerable manner they share the burden of man. Some of the scholars of women's studies have even gone to the extent to call women, the 'Work-force of India in Future'. This expression is very true.

In this book, an effort has been made to present an analysis of various aspects of women, in the context of work and development, among other things.

What is strongly felt is that the biggest factor, involved in the change of the world of work is the existence and presence of women workers in our society. The women are today, managers, secretaries, assistants, clerks, peons, mechanics, operators and even guards and sentinals.

This writer is not the first to think about or work on this subject. A few scholars have already done it, but, perhaps no one has so far dealt it as extensively and exhaustively, as attempted here.

Most probably, Mahatma Gandhi was the first to recognise the importance of the women power. He worked for the Indian women's emancipation tirelessly. He saw to it that the women in large numbers play a significant role in the movement for the freedom of the country, including Satyagraha and non-cooperation, etc. Actually, he believed that women's participation in political life would pave the way for their overall upliftment and guarantee a respectable status for them in future.

TWO

Basic Issues

For the study of status of women in India approaches are made through many groups of variables, turning our investigation, particularly the search for trends and patterns of social behaviour and attitudes, highly complex and difficult. Some of them stem from the characteristic features of our society, others from processes of change effected by modernization and development. Still some others were repercussions of the historical vicissitudes that affected India in the past few centuries, particularly the impact of a colonial regime and exposure to foreign culture. Lastly, they also reflected the influence of the struggle for freedom and social justice.

These variables are closely interrelated. It is imperative to examine the characteristics of our society with its lack of homogeneity within the basic pattern of inequalities, impact of the complex process of socio-economic and political change, instruments of social engineering, degree of social acceptance of desired goals, factors influencing women's progress, varied sources and periodisation, problem of definition and the analysis by categories.

The Preamble to the Constitution of India promises "to secure to all its citizens, justice — social, economic and political; liberty of thought, expression, belief, faith and worship; equality of status and of opportunity; and to promote among them all fraternity assuring the dignity of the individual and the unity of the nation"

While improvement in the status of women was a pledge made by the Constitution-makers and admitted by the national Government at the very outset as one of the major tasks facing the country, no comprehensive review of the achievements in this direction has been undertaken thus far.

Some laws, attempting to embody the principles underlying the

Constitution had, from time to time, passed through the Legislature. Attempts were made to introduce programmes of development, aimed at enabling women to play their role in our national life in an effective manner. Partly as a result of these various measures, and partly because of the general processes of social change which have speeded up since independence, the status of women in our country has undoubtedly undergone considerable change.

It is felt that while these changes have been considerable in the urban areas, problems continue to remain virtually unchanged in most of the rural areas. Further, with the changing social and economic conditions in the country, various new problems relating to the advancement of women which had not been visualized by the Constitution-makers and the Government in its earlier days have manifested.

Main Objectives

The objective of the study undertaken by the national government to examine the status of women was mainly: (a) to assess the impact of the constitutional, legal and administrative provisions on the social status of women, their education and employment, particularly in the rural sector during the last two decades; (b) to examine the status of women in the changing social milieu; and (c) to suggest remedial and other measures in the fields of law, education, employment, population policy etc., "Which would enable women to play their full and proper role in building up the nation".

The framework for the study was thus provided on the one hand by the constitutional provisions that have a bearing on the status of women and, on the other, by the clear objective specified, viz. enabling women to play their 'full and proper role in building up the nation'.

To attain these national objectives, the Constitution guarantees certain fundamental rights and freedoms such as freedom of speech, protection of life and personal liberty. While these may be termed positive rights, the negative rights are the prohibition of discrimination or denial of equal protection.

Indian women are the beneficiaries of these rights in the same manner as Indian men. Article 14 of the Constitution ensures 'equality before law' and Article 15 'prohibits any discrimination'. There is only one specific provision in Article 15(3), which empowers the State to make 'any special provision for women and children', even in violation of the fundamental obligation of non-discrimination among citizens, inter alia of sex. This provision has enabled the State to make special provision for women, particularly in the field of labour legislation like the Factories Act, the Mines Act, etc. These special provisions in favour of women need not be restricted to measures which are beneficial in the strict sense, and therefore, the provision upholding that a man is punished for adultery but not a women was regarded as not being discriminatory.

Article 16(1) guarantees "equality of opportunity for all citizens in matters relating to employment, or appointment to any office under the State". And Article 16(2) forbids discrimination "in respect of any employment of office under the State" on grounds only of "religion, race, caste, sex, descent, place of birth, residence, or any one of them". The obligation not to discriminate in matters relating to employment or appointment to any office under the State has thus at least normatively ensured a significant position and status to Indian women. However, the Supreme Court recently dismissed in *limine* a writ petition of a woman lawyer who challenged her being prevented from employment in the Judge Advocate General's office for a 5-year short service commission in the law branch. The reasons given by the government for barring women from applying were that 'they are required to travel by rail, road and river, sometimes for long periods at a stretch; they will have to be present in court martials where the judge, accused and witnesses may all be males, and that lady advocates are required to study the lives of soldiers (all males) in army units for several months'. The government failed to appreciate the fact that these same grounds also apply to the nursing and medical corps of the Army where women are employed.

In this context we would like to mention that during the tenure of Sri Charan Singh as chief minister, and under his instruction, the Government of the State of Uttar Pradesh attempted a direct violation of this constitutional provision. In reply to a question asked in the Uttar Pradesh Vidhan Sabha on 16 July, 1971, the State Government admitted that "in June 1970, the State Government sent a letter to the Government of India stating that women officers should not be admitted to the Indian Administrative Service. If that was not possible, then at least they should not be sent to this State".

Though this attempt did not succeed, it is a pointer that vigilance is necessary to ensure that the special provision permitted under Article 15(3) is not used to the detriment of women by legislative or executive action.

The Directive Principles of State Policy enunciated in Part IV of the Constitution, embody the major policy goals of a welfare State. They concretize, together with the chapter on Fundamental Rights, the constitutional vision of a new Indian socio-political order. The Directive Principles are declared as non-justiciable; but "nevertheless fundamental in the governance of the country", and the State is charged with "a duty.. to apply these principles in making laws" (Article 37). The Directive Principles were made non-enforceable in courts because it was felt that their fulfilment would be spread over a time dimension of a few decades. The constitutional values embodied in the Fundamental Rights needed immediate implementation; but in the case of the Directive Principles, this was not possible save at the cost of the viability of the State.

Juridically, the Directive Principles are a vital part of Indian Constitutional Law. Like the Preamble, they reflect high ideals of a liberal democratic polity; they are meant to be used by all agencies of the State as guidelines to action as major goals of policy; courts can use them as a body of values and standards relevant to the act of judicial choice-making. But the Directive Principles confer no power or legislative competence; nor can they give rise to a cause of action for which remedy is available in a court of law. The principles in themselves do not confer power, bestow rights, or create remedies. At the same time, they cannot be amended, save through the prescribed procedure. Some of them concern women indirectly or by necessary implication. A few are, as it were, "women-specific". In the first category fall: (a) the omnibus provision of Article 38 briefly directs the State to secure a just social, political and economic order, geared to promote the welfare of the people; Art 39(b) (c) and ' (f) enunciates the distribution of ownership and control of material resources of the community for the common good, prevention of concentration of wealth and means of production to the common detriment, and protection of childhood and youth against exploitation and moral and material abandonment; Art. 40 lays stress on organisation of village panchayats to promote self-government; Art. 41 specifies right to work, education and public assistance in cases of unemployment, old age, sickness, disablement and other types of underserved wants; Art. 43 spells out provision of work, a living wage, conditions of work ensuring a decent standard of life and full enjoyment of leisure, of social and cultural opportunities, and the promotion of cottage industries; Art. 44 delineates the Uniform Civil Code; Art. 45 provides for free and compulsory education for all children up to the age of 14; and Art. 47 speaks for raising the level of nutrition and the standard of living of the people and improvement of public health. (b) The Directive Principles which concern women directly and have a special bearing on their status include Art. 39(a) concerning right to an adequate means of livelihood for men and women equally; Art. 39(d) concerning equal pay for equal work for both men and women; Art. 39(e) concerning the protection of the health and strength of workers - men, women and children from abuse and entry into avocations unsuited to their age and strength; and Art. 42 concerning just and human conditions of work and maternity relief.

As previously mentioned, the Fundamental Rights and the Directive Principles are the instruments to attainment of our national objectives of justice, liberty and equality. By adopting the principle of adult franchise, it seeks to establish a democratic republic by giving the adult population direct or indirect share in government.

The special attention given to the needs and problems of women, to enable them to enjoy and exercise constitutional equality of status, along with other specific provisions relating to the hitherto suppressed sections of our society have led many scholars to describe the Indian Constitution as a 'social' document embodying the objectives of a social revolution. There is no doubt that the Constitution contemplates attainment of an entirely new social order by making deliberate departure in norms and institutions of democratic governance from the inherited social, political and economic systems. In doing so, the Constitution assigns primacy to law as an instrument of directed social change. It thus demands of the legislature, the executive and the judiciary, continuous vigilance and responsiveness to the relationship between law and social transformation in contemporary India.

The Impact

The complex processes generally described by broad terms like modernization, democratization, development, urbanization, industrialization, etc., have all affected the status of women in differing degrees. Here again, it would be pertinent to point out that it was not possible to discover any uniform pattern of this impact, since not all sections of women have been affected by these processes in like manner. It is, however, generally accepted that a change in the status of women is a good indicator of the pattern and direction of social change. If the direction of that change is towards a more egalitarian distribution of roles between men and women, in tune with the constitutional directives, then the direction-of change is a wholesome one. If, however, the various modernizing forces result in an intensification of inequalities, then we are moving away from the spirit of the Constitution. It was, therefore, important to understand the direction of these changes in order to assess the nature of their impact on different sections of our women.

The issue of social change in India is a complex one. Given the highly complex and heterogeneous social situation in the country, it is not surprising that change takes many directions, some of which are even in conflict with one another. We had to consider only those components of this change which affect the status of women. This brought us face to face with structural changes in the economy as a result of commercialization, expanding markets and technological changes in the methods of production. The combination of these forces with the growth of population has increased both poverty and wealth. Education, urbanization and wider avenues of participation in the social process have both contributed and tried to combat the increase in social inequalities that resulted from this process. We had to examine the extent of their impact on the roles, rights and opportunities open to women in different spheres of social life.

It was also necessary to consider the difference between what are called 'traditional' and 'modern' values, in so far as they affect the life of women. Here again, we discovered that traditionalism and modernity do not necessarily reflect their temporal setting. Traditional values handed down from generation to generation were modelled on the ideal behaviour of the upper classes of our society. Any improvement in the economic conditions of the lower castes or classes has almost invariably led to their adopting these values. An important component of upper caste values was the seclusion of their womenfolk and their withdrawal from work outside the home.

From the point of view of the socially lower groups, adoption of these values enhances their status in the social hierarchy. We could see the impact of this ideology operating among these groups even now. On the other hand, a considerable section of the upper class or the middle class of today has abandoned these values in favour of what is generally regarded as 'modern' ideology regarding equal rights and opportunities of women for participation in the social process. This indicates certain structural changes within the value - system and behavioural norms of the middle class under the compulsion of social change. The process of emulation of the traditional values of the upper classes by others, however, though they constitute modernity in the thinking of the latter, is a trend in the opposite direction. It is obvious that the impact of these contradictory forces is bound to give rise to certain ambiguities and confusion in the minds of both men and women in our society.

Laws for Protection

The post Independence period witnessed the enactment of a number of laws that sought to apply the principles underlying the constitutional guarantees to the sphere of social life. The reforms in personal laws governing marriage and inheritance, in labour laws ensuring, humane conditions of work, maternity benefits and welfare of workers, and in social laws seeking the protection of women and children against immoral traffic and exploitation, tried to remove the disabilities that contributed to the low status of women in our society. At the same time, the policies and programmes for economic and social development initiated by the government, attempted positive action to improve and widen opportunities for women to participate in the social processes in a more effective manner. Education, vocational training, health services, family planning, welfare and development programmes, sought to change and improve the conditions of living and the mental horizons of women.

Apart from examining these measures initiated by the government, we had to include under this category, the organised or individual efforts to bring about changes in social attitudes and norms of behaviour that were generated by the community. Most of them had started either as a part of the freedom movement, or dated back to the earlier movement for social and religious reform that developed in the 19th century. Leaders of public opinion and community organisations had sought to mobilize various groups of people to propagate measures for uplift of women's status. The ideology that emerged from these various attempts-governmental and social-have helped to shape the goals and left an impact on the minds of many sections of our society, and have played a significant role in changing the status of women.

Social Acceptance

Indicators of social acceptance of any goals set for the future must include the attitudes of men and women as well as the availability of institutionalized infrastructures that support the attainment of such goals. Examining this group of variables involved discussing the influence, cultural and religious norms, as well as the impact of modern values such as human rights, social justice, equality and participation. It also involved examining the regional differences in the cultural norms that affected women's roles and participation in the social process. This revealed the positive and negative sets of social factors which affected the success or consequent failure of the policies and instruments of social engineering, i.e. institutionalized opportunities as well as disabilities that affect women's enjoyment and exercise of various legal and constitutional rights and their performance of the multiple roles that the goals of our society call for.

Positive Factors

We had to examine the actual achievements in the fields of education, employment, health, institutionalized welfare facilities and services for development and participation in different levels and spheres of national life. It was also necessary to study the disappearance or removal of certain traditional taboos that had sought to restrict women's life to a limited sphere.

Negative Factors

We had to identify the centres of resistance to the desired change in women's status and roles and the disabilities that still hamper many groups of women at different levels of existence. In the process of this examination, we attempted to identify the lacuna or deficiencies in the instruments of social engineering that have caused the failure to overcome these negative influences.

In order to study the nature and influence of these broad studies of variables we had to depend on various types of indicators. Quantitative indicators provided by vital statistics of birth and mortality rates, sex ratio, rates of participation in economic and political life, literacy and education, provided certain broad measures and trends. None of them could, however, be studied meaningfully without a qualitative appraisal and understanding of their limitations in a field of this kind. For instance, the concept of national and State averages normally used for most quantitative analyses becomes meaningless in the context of tremendous socio-economic inequalities and variations in our society. Secondly, there is a wide gap between stated social objectives and achievements, between the legal framework and empirical improvement in education, literacy, life expectancy and political participation. These trends, coupled with the success and the position achieved by a minority of women, could mislead us to think that the status of an average Indian woman was very high. Detailed investigations, however, show that while opportunities had widened immensely at certain levels of society and enabled women to forge ahead in areas which had been completely closed to them in earlier years, this was not true for the other levels of society. The uneven rates of development between regions, communities and sections of our population often make analysis by quantitative methods baffling. It was, therefore, necessary to utilize other methods and techniques to assess these different levels of social reality.

Problems to Cope with

Determining the starting point for our enquiry posed a dilemma. The constitutional provisions could provide only a framework of abstract principles. We needed a concrete framework against which the changes and their directions could be measured. On Independence data was available in a concrete form, but it was found that this was not possible in other cases. Trends in population, employment, and changes in social roles, responsibilities, challenges and burdens had begun much earlier than Independence. It was also obvious that any understanding of the motives of the Constitution-makers would be impossible without a background of the freedom and the reform movements that affected the status of women. It was important to look back as well as to the future to discern a proper perspective for the study of the present, since a society in the process of rapid transformation cannot be measured except in terms of both past and future.

Before going into the diverse aspects of the status of women in India, it is essential to offer an operational definition of the term status and to also consider other allied and interlinked categories. Status refers to a position in a social system or sub-system which is distinguishable from and at the same time related to other positions through its designated rights and obligations. In the pure sociological sense, status does not imply rank or hierarchy but denotes only position vis-a-vis others in terms of rights and obligations. But as each status position in a particular structure can be viewed in terms of superiority and inferiority, i.e. in terms of power, privileges, advantages, and disadvantages, the notion of status involves comparison and grading. In assessing the status of women we shall follow the comparative approach as well.

At this juncture we need to adopt a broader perspective and understand that status denotes relative position of persons, groups, social strata, and a range of identified social categories. Men and women acquire their identities through groups, strata, and categories; as such it is imperative to take note of them in assessing women's status in India.

Each status position is expressed in terms of a role. Role denotes a set of expectations and obligations associated with a particular status position within a group or social situation. The expectations and obligations entailed by a role are in terms of activities and qualities. Each individual occupies a number of distinct statuses within a society and therefore he/she performs a variety of roles. Further, around each particular status position centres a role-set.

It is useful to make a distinction between ideal role behaviour, expected role behaviour, and actual role behaviour. Processes of change are responsible for considerable divergence between these three aspects of a role. Performance of multiple roles in varied social situations often leads to a change in the role perception of individuals. Changes in the actual role performance over a period of time influence the expected role behaviour, and gradually there are changes in the ideal role behaviour. But this process is characterized by unreasonable expectations of others and by the incompatibility between the various roles that an individual has to perform in a given situation. This is particularly relevant for women in India.

In respect of some institutionalized disabilities, women as a whole can be compared to men as a whole, for differences between the status of men and women are important in cognitive mapping as well as in ordering interpersonal relations. The presence of ascriptive norms in respect of sex-linked statuses are universal with wide variations in achievement avenues open to them.

As pointed out earlier, a woman, like any person, occupies many status positions at a given point of time and plays a number of roles, such as those in the kinship system, family system, and the wider social system. Her status in society is usually not determined by any one particular status position held by her, but by her composite status which results from the merging of various statuses. To this should be added her consciousness of her own status.

There are multifarious principles of status differentiation operating simultaneously—place in ritual hierarchy, financial position, independent job, education, political participation, and so on. A woman of the labour class enjoys a certain degree of autonomy in the house, but she has a low status in the wider setting. Similarly a housewife in a well-to-do home may be enjoying an overall high status, but she may be a distinctly inferior partner in the house. In investigating the position of women, various institutional settings have to be taken into account.

Status is realized through roles. Hence the best way to assess the status of women of any group or category, or in any subsystem is to analyse the roles women are being called upon to play and the manner of their performance. This also brings in the structure of rights and opportunities provided to them by the State and by social and cultural institutions which do not necessarily or always reinforce each other.

Examination of the groups of variables indicated earlier made it clear that the status of women in the Indian context cannot be defined simply. General concepts like equality, role differentiation, legal, social and political rights, dependency or independence, are not applicable to all sections of our population. Since a very large section of our society still continues to be under the influence of traditional standards, we had to juxtapose the role conception, norms and values in all their wide variety in traditional society, against the new dimensions in women's status and roles introduced by the Constitution and the processes of social change.

Traditional India has seen a woman only as a member of the family or a group—as daughters, wives and mothers-and not as an individual with an identity or right of her own. The radicalism of the Constitution and its deliberate departure from the social position or accomplishments, will allow women to function an a equal citizen and an individual partner in the task of nation building.

While motherhood is an important social and biological function, the Constitution implied that this could no longer be regarded as the only significant role for women. A gap between traditional social attitudes and institutions, and the new roles that women are expected to play in the political, social and economic spheres, creates problems and imposes constraints on women's ability to perform such roles. We had to identify the exact nature of these disabilities and constraints.

Roles Examined

An examination of the expected and actual roles and the constraints that affect women's performance of these multiple roles made it imperative to examine these constraints at different levels of society. Any meaningful analysis of restrictions imposed by social attitudes and norms, possession or lack of necessary equipment, for example, education and other employment skills, political awareness, etc., was only possible by studying women in different categories. Our experience showed that while Indian society can be categorized by castes, communities and classes, for our purpose the most relevant broad categories were as follows: (a) Women below the subsistence level, whose problems and constraints are radically different in nature from those suffered by women in other sections of society; (b) Women who move continuously between security and subsistence, and often descend below the subsistence level with the disappearance of their means of earning or livelihood; and (c) Women firmly above the security line.

Values and Goals

The first of the guiding principles and criteria are the values and goals put forward in the Constitution, namely equality and social justice for all.

Equality is an article of faith in our Constitution and guaranteed by specific Articles. We could, therefore, treat this as a settled fact, for which no discussion was necessary. Our investigation, however, proved that there was still considerable ambiguity as well as ambivalence in the general understanding of the need and implications of sex equality in society and employment in our country.

The history of the discussion on women's rights, both in the Constituent Assembly and in the Central Legislature over the Hindu Code Bill in the period immediately after Independence, indicates that attitudes towards women's equality vary sharply. As long as the discussion was on abstract principles, as was the case during the debate on Fundamental Rights in the Constituent Assembly, there was no dissenting voice to challenge or even to provoke a discussion on this historic decision. When it came to applying the same principles on established preserves of traditional male privileges, such as the right to property and the unchallenged dominance of the husband in family life, the reactions of the same body were very different. One group accepted both the concept of equality and its implications for society. The second group accepted the concept in theory, but was not prepared to practise, or follow up its implications. The third group rejected the concept outright as totally inapplicable and undesirable for Indian society. It is believed: (i) Equality, of women is necessary, not merely on the grounds of social justice, but as a basic condition for social, economic and political development of the nation; (ii) In order to release women from their dependent and unequal status, improvement of their employment opportunities and earning power has to be given the highest priority; (iii) Society owes a special responsibility to women because of their child-bearing function. Safe bearing and rearing of children is an obligation that has to be shared by the mother, the father and society too; (iv) The contribution made by an active housewife to the running and management of a family should be admitted as economically and socially productive and contributing to national savings and development; (v) Marriage and motherhood should not become a disability in women's fulfilling their full and proper role in the task of national development. Therefore, it is important that society, including women themselves, must accept their responsibility in this field; (vi) Disabilities and inequalities imposed on women have to be seen in the total context of a society, where large sections of the population: male and female, adults and children, suffer under the oppression of an exploitative system. It is not possible to remove these inequalities for women only. Any policy or movement for the emancipation and development of women has to form a part of a total movement for removal of inequalities and oppressive social institutions, if the benefits and privileges won by such action are to be shared by the entire women population and not be monopolised by a small minority. (vii) If our society is to move in the direction of the goals set by the Constitution, then special temporary measures will be necessary, to transform *de jure* into *de facto* equality.

THREE

Socio-Cultural Problems

Practically, an enquiry into the status of women cannot be conducted outside the social framework. Thus the problem was studied keeping in mind diversities and inequalities prevalent in our society through the ages.

Therefore, the images of women in our religious traditions, the role of social reform movements, the descent, marriage and family in the various provinces of India, changing milieu and role of women and their special problems like prostitution, women in prison, aged and destitute women have been discussed in order to understand the status of women in the Indian society and their prospects in proper perspective.

Any attempt to assess the status and problems of women in a society should start from the social framework. Social structure, cultural norms, and value systems are important determinants of women's roles and their position in society. They influence social expectations regarding behaviour of the two sexes, both as individuals and in relation to each other. Social traditions are a major influence in shaping attitudes as well as behaviour patterns of human groups; emerging trends of society cannot be viewed in isolation from them.

The response of the structural forms to the forces of change in other sectors of life is not easy to predict. Social structure can stimulate certain trends of change, but at the same time it can also prove to be an impediment in their path. Changes in the normative structure and in the organisational forms of society do not take place in unison; the difference in their pace often creates a hiatus.

Thus we find that reforms in law and educational policy do not always make the desired impact because of the normative and structural unpreparedness of the society to accept their goals and means. In respect of the status that is accorded to women by law and by the Constitution we notice that there is a gap between the theoretical possibilities and their actual realization.

Religion, family and kinship, roles and cultural norms delimiting the spheres of women's activities obstruct their full and equal participation in the life of the society and the achievement of their full potential. The new role and responsibilities and status visualized for Indian woman will thus have to relate to the living realities of the social and cultural contexts of their present position. Therefore, our main endeavour will be: (i) To analyse the institutional complexes and basic conceptions which would be helpful in explaining the present position of women belonging to various categories, groups, and strata operating in various spheres; (ii) To examine some of the myths about the natural capacities and disabilities of women and, in consequence, about the roles suited to them; and (iii) To discuss some features of our social order which reflect and affect the status of women. This would include dowry and other avoidable marriage expenses, prostitution, female suicide, female infanticide and destitution in female population.

These are essentially social phenomena which are directly related to the position of women in our society and hence constitute our important concerns. We propose to examine them in their social and cultural contexts and suggest lines of action wherever possible.

In this chapter the terms upper or higher castes, middle level castes, and lower castes are used. This has been done to conform to Indian social reality in which there exists a ritual hierarchy of castes. Although this hierarchy is not a clear cut one, in terms of closeness of status and a broad commonality of customs and practices, it is possible to conceive of three levels of castes.

In many ways the necessity of changes in role relationships and in the treatment of women in various subsystems indicates a positive need for attitudinal changes. Hence, it is necessary to think of ways and means to bring about these changes in values and attitudes and perceptions of the people.

It is obvious that for an adequate description of the social and cultural scene and for an assessment of their social status, women of India cannot be treated as a homogeneous group. Broadly speaking, in our highly complex and extremely diversified society, women in different religious groups, caste levels, economic strata, and those belonging to tribal, rural and urban areas merit separate consideration. Differences in customs and norms and in conditions of their operation across groups and categories make it imperative for us to adopt this approach.

In an effort to grasp and portray the social and cultural reality and arrive at a cogent understanding of the present status of women in India, we take note of what is present in the people's consciousness as also of what is indicated by the logic of sociological understanding.

In the first section we examine the influence of religion in shaping and sustaining certain images of women. The second section deals with the forms of social organisation that exert the greatest pressure on women's roles and status, namely descent and kinship systems, marriage, and family organisation. The third section examines some of the constraints on women because of the distinction between men's sphere and women's sphere such as, those springing from division of work and seclusion and segregation of women, and the problems of adjustment that arise due to processes of social change. These are connected with the multiple role of women as home makers, wage earners, and participants in the wider society. The fourth section discusses certain special problems of women such as prostitution and suicide.

In Reference to Religious Traditions

Indian society consists of communities professing diverse religious faiths. Because of the secular character of the polity and criminal and civil laws, the State does not make any distinction on the basis of religion, but because of the continuation of various systems of personal law, and special protection for minorities provided in the Constitution, religion does receive some recognition.

In starting with a discussion on religious traditions it is not implied that religion is of paramount importance in understanding the relative statuses of men and women or that all categories of social facts which need to be understood in this connection are rooted in religion. That religion itself is born and nurtured in a certain type of social structure cannot be denied; nor can it be denied that religion imparts legitimacy and is functional to sustaining certain kinds of social structures.

At the same time, when a religion is superimposed on the substructures of certain sections of a society, it calls for and necessitates many compromises and adjustments. Religious systems and principles of social organisation cut across each other. For analytical purposes only, therefore, discussion of religion is separated from social structure and the various social institutions.

Religion provides ideological and moral bases for the accorded status and institutionalized roles of women in a society. The social restrictions on women, and also the people's notions about their proper roles in the domestic and extra-domestic spheres, are largely derived from the religious conceptions of a woman's basic characteristics, her assumed 'virtues' and 'vices', her proverbial strengths and weaknesses, and the stereotypes regarding her nature and capacities. Each religion has a treasure of myths and legends which through descriptions of events and activities emphasize certain values.

Religion has a definite role to play in the crises of life, i.e. the points of transition in an individual's life such as birth, initiation, marriage, and death. The social and religious aspects of these occasions are intermingled in all communities. It is an accepted fact that there are definite social mechanisms which help an individual to internalize the values, norms, and behaviour patterns rooted in religion.

A continuity of conceptions regarding women's stàtus and roles is assured in the process of socialization in which women play a prominent role. A comparison of the fundamental notions regarding women in the major religious traditions reveals a direct conflict between them and the idea of the equality of sexes which is one of our guiding principles.

It is true that scriptures and sacred texts provide scope for diverse interpretations and value emphasis at the hands of different authorities and at different periods of time. Religion has a dynamic character and is shaped and reshaped by historical processes and the interaction with popular religion. In India, Islam and Christianity had to compromise with local customs since their followers remained under the influence of pre-conversion social and religious traditions.

Similarly, Hinduism has always absorbed both the "Great Tradition" and the "Little Traditions". According to Reffeld (1956) :

"In a civilisation there is a great tradition of the reflective few and there is a little tradition of the largely unreflective many. The great tradition is cultivated in schools or temples, the little tradition works itself out and keeps itself going in the lives of the unlettered in their village communities. The tradition of the philosopher, theologian and literary man is a tradition consciously cultivated and handed down; that of the little people is for the most part taken for granted and not submitted to much scrutiny or considered refinement and improvement. The two traditions are interdependent. Great tradition and the little tradition have long affected each other and continue to do so."

Through different periods of history orthodox Hinduism has produced strong reactions and has resulted in the establishment of new religions or sects, such as Buddhism, Jainism, Sikhism, Veerasaivism, and Vaishnavism, and the nineteenth century reform movement like the Brahmo Samaj and Arya Samaj. These have to be viewed in the context of the direct or indirect effect that their preachings and activities have had on the status of women.

Hinduism

Hinduism has a long history and many facets attached to it. During the centuries of its existence, the image of women has undergone many changes. It is said that women in the Vedic period enjoyed a high status. They had the right to study the Vedas and to offer sacrifices and enjoyed considerable freedom in marriage. There was no bar on the remarriage of widows or women remaining unmarried.

This is not, however, true of Hindu women today. The women of the later ages pictured in the epics, the Pitratios, and the Dharmasastras have travelled a long way and can be seen in some ways even in the modern age. The image of women is not consistent and coherent, but her expected rights and duties are fairly clear. It is not our intention to trace and analyse the deterioration or ups and downs in the position of Hindu women through the various periods of history. What we are primarily concerned with is to identify the traditions which continue to affect the status of Hindu women in modem times.

Hindu society, with its well-defined strata, cannot be said to have nurtured to the same degree and at all levels, the values, ideals, and norms propounded by a religion having a continuity of thousands of years. There has been a continuous interaction between the Great Traditions of the literate and Little Traditions of the masses, and the percolation of the ideals, models, and values contained in the corpus of religious literature of Hinduism.

This work has been carried out through the rendering of myths and legends in regional languages and by institutions like Hari Katha, Ramlila, Kirtan and Bhagavat.

In Hinduism a woman is described by a multitude of derogatory attributes. She is called fickle-minded, sensual, seducer of men; given to falsehood, trickery, folly, greed, impurity, and thoughtless action; root of all evil; inconsistent; and cruel.

She must not study the Vedas or perform any sacrifices; knowledge of the Shastras is forbidden to her. There is no provision for a woman to become a regular Sanyasin. A woman is grouped with the Sudra, and along with them is called Papayoni, i.e. of sinful birth or one preordained to a low station in life.

There are exhortations that a woman should be kept under control. "In childhood a woman must be subject to her father, in youth to her husband, and when her lord is dead, to her sons. A woman must never be independent." This dictum of Manu along with Tulsidas's well-known stanza in which he groups women with drums, morons, Sudras and cattle as objects fit to be beaten have influenced the attitude of the Hindu masses towards women.

There is no overall appraisal of a woman's personality in the lore of Hinduism. She is viewed only in specific roles. With the conception of marriage as the true destiny of a woman and with her important obligation to bear a son, the roles of wife and mother emerge as the proper roles for a woman.

The cult of the mother-goddess, whether accepted as an important trait of the pre-Aryan matrilineal cultures or borrowed from the tribals, seems to have had some influence on the status of women. A woman in mother's role has been elevated to a very high position in Hindu religious literature. She has been given high praise and a son has been asked to give respect to her.

The *Mahabharata* says that mother excels in her greatness ten fathers and even the whole Earth-There is no guru like the mother. A sanyasi is supposed to go beyond any kinships, and if he happens to come across his parents, the biological father touches the feet of his sanyasi son, but even this sanyasi is expected to touch the feet of his mother.

The close and sustained association of the child with the woman's body is emphasized in a number of ways. By idealising the quality of sacrifice in a mother and by eulogising her motherhood, religion binds a woman to the home and to her role of creating and nurturing. A young virgin before the onset of menstruation and the mother of a son are the two images which evoke veneration.

There are numerous laudatory references to the female sex in these roles in the religious texts which are hardly in consonance with her limited rights laid down in the Dharamashastras. Under the impact of images created and sustained in Hinduism, women are regarded, on the one hand, as the embodiment of purity and spiritual power, while on the other, they are viewed as being essentially weak and dependent creatures who are in need of constant guardianship and protection of men.

There is strong emphasis on a faithful and uncomplaining wife. The ideal woman is the devoted wife who is willing to suffer all kinds of adversities for the sake of loyalty to her husband. The dominant characteristics of well-known characters of Hindu mythology - Sita, Savitri, Ahilya, Draupadi, Gandhari, Mandodari, Damyanti to name a few are loyalty to their husbands, steadfastness and chastity. This has been the essence of a woman's role as wife. Her husband is her lord and master. She has no separate existence. As Ardhangini she is her husband's partner in Dharma, Artha and Kama.

As a part of Dharma she has to respect and look after her parents-in-law and other members of her conjugal family, look after the home and take care of guests and servants. As the statement of Draupadi runs, "the husband is a woman's God; it is through her husband alone that a woman, obtains progeny, enjoys comforts and luxury, attains fame in this world and heaven in the next. She serves her husband and performs Vratas for his welfare. She gives up cosmetics when her husband is away." Bhishma in *Mahabharata* states the following attributes as the best feminine virtues: fidelity, forgiveness, absence of guile, piety, and truthfulness. These virtues please Laxmi and bring rewards. Parvati says that there is no other God for a woman but her husband, and by serving him she attains heaven. She must be kind even to an unkind and irrational husband and obey him.

Thus, not only marriage but the services rendered to one's husband are of paramount importance to a woman. So much so, that it is said that for women there is no other religious rite but to serve their husbands. It is testified in the Puranas that a woman by serving her husband in thought, word and deed secures with much less trouble the same spiritual and heavenly worlds that her husband does with great effort and trouble. Expectation of immolation on the deceased husband's pyre (Sati) by the widow was the extreme limit of the notion that a woman's worth is nil without her husband.

For Moksha, women are grouped with Sudras and uneducated Brahmins. Devi Bhagavata Purana states that since women and Sudras, are unable to study the Vedas, the Puranas are compiled for their benefit. The Bhagavata Purana states that the *Mahabharata* was composed for women and Sudras, who are debarred from listening to the Vedas.

After the emergence of Bhaktimarg, the path of devotion which did not need complicated knowledge and elaborate rituals, some women attained eminence and it provided an honourable way of partial asceticism, sometimes even complete asceticism for women.

In Hinduism, a strong patrilineal social structure along with features like the giving away of the girls in marriage, importance of the son for continuity of the line, authority and superiority of the male, significance of virginity, etc., have been sanctified with the help of Sanskaras. The significant ideas contained in the Vedic or Puranic texts used for Sanskaras have their influence in varying degrees at various levels of Hindu population.

Marriage and motherhood are the most honourable and religiously valuable achievements for a Hindu woman. The critical significance of marriage, of the continuity of the married state, and of motherhood for a woman is dramatically expressed and emphasized in the observance of special Vratas. They are observed for ensuring long life and welfare of the husband, for the realization of the culturally coveted goal of getting married and of getting a suitable partner for life, and for securing special protection of sons.

Their content in terms of the type of worship, the nature of fasting may differ from region to region; but a degree of self-denial, invocation of some deity or sacred object, commemoration of the ordeals of some mythological female figure constitute their core features. Renewal and distribution or exchange of objects which serve as diacritical marks of the married state such as vermilion, glass bangles, and black beads is also customarily done on such days.

Some Vratas are meant to be observed throughout life, some for a particular period; some by unmarried girls; some by married women. To mention a few: a special worship of Goddess Laxmi on particular days; yearly commemoration of the steadfastness of Savitri who followed the God of Death and brought back her husband alive; annual worship of Parvati who performed difficult penance to win the heart of Siva; Varalaxmi puja prevalent in the South; Karwa Chauth observed in North India; Jayaparvati observed in Gujarat; Mangala Gaur or worship of Goddess of Tuesday in the month of Savan in Maharashtra, a special Vrata in Bundelkhand called Suhagle (observed for the sake of suhag or Saubhagya, i.e. the good fortune of having one's husband alive). Some of these have their sanction in the great Sanskritic tradition while others are rooted in regional beliefs.

Most of the Vratas observed by a mother for the welfare of her children are meant to be observed by those who have a son. Women having only daughters do not observe them. The differential value of son and daughter is apparent.

Internationalization of values of steadfastness, self effacement, service and playing a secondary role is effected through these Vratas, which are observed even by many educated and sophisticated women. This may be either because of the strength of their beliefs; or because of their socialization which they cannot shake off or because of the expectations of the family for whom this is an inalienable aspect of a wife's or a mother's role. Tremendous importance is attached to these observances for newly married women.

The converse of this notion of marriage as women's destiny and the married state as the most desirable, is the idea of inauspiciousness and loss of the right to full participation in socio-religious life associated with widowhood.

In contrast, a Hindu male has no fasts to observe for the wife's long life and welfare. The husband wears no distinctive marks signifying the married state and does not incur any inauspiciousness at the death of his wife. Religion, as a system of beliefs and rituals, undoubtedly accords an inferior and dependent status to Hindu woman. The common blessing to a woman 'May your husband live long' is self-explanatory.

Although the strict code of conduct prescribed for widow is no longer operative in its most restrictive and oppressive aspects, there are certain disabilities associated with widowhood. She is debarred from active participation in auspicious occasions. Besides, the items of decoration associated with the married state, she is expected also to discard colourful clothes, glass bangles, wearing of flowers and attractive jewellery. Plain white colour is associated with widowhood, and by implication is forbidden traditionally for the Sumangali, i.e., one whose husband is alive.

The widows of Bengal, who abstain from fish and the Kammas and the Reddy widows of Andhra Pradesh who give up meat are not yet extinct. Among the Brahmin and also among such non-Brahmin communities who do not have the custom of widow remarriage, there are a number of ways for restricting the life of a widow so that she gets little pleasure out of life and her natural desires are suppressed. A distinct contrast between the status of a widow and a Sumangali is characteristic of India as a whole.

Even among such groups which traditionally allow widow remarriage, the disabilities associated with widowhood are present though not in same degree of severity. In Hindu and tribal India a woman is entitled to marry with full rites only once in her life. Her subsequent unions, though approved by society, are solemnized by a very simple ceremony or may often be given recognition after a simple feast.

Women with such secondary unions suffer from a few specific disabilities in regard to performance of particular roles in the rituals of marriage and worship of deities. This again indicates the significance of marriage for a woman and the vulnerability of her purity. No such disability characterizes a man; he can marry a virgin any number of times with full rites and ceremonies. Even though the Widow Remarriage Act was passed in 1856, Hindu society still has not come to accept widow remarriage without reservation. For the majority, widowhood continues to be associated with the handicaps.

Grave impurity is associated with menstruation and childbirth. Severe restrictions over menstruating women in respect of association and participation in domestic, extra-domestic, and religious activities found in the texts have been strong among the Brahmin and upper caste groups, but have been operative among other sections especially in the sphere of religious ceremonies.

This notion of periodical impurity of women is one of the important bases for the conception of inferiority of the female sex as compared to the male. A woman is usually in charge of routine domestic worship; but nowhere is she found to be in charge of worship at the shrines and temples. Even Kali and other female deities are to be worshipped by a male priest. It should be noted that this exclusion of women from officiating at community worship is not a direct result of their lack of knowledge of rituals which may be needed for worship, since in many kind of worship no such knowledge is required. Periodical impurity appears to be the basis for the exclusion of women from this role.

The Bhakti movement which arose during the medieval period, denounced complicated rituals, and asserted that God could be worshipped not only through knowledge and rituals, but also by devotion. The devotional hymns composed in the languages spoken by the people brought this movement close to women, whose ignorance of Sanskrit had often deprived them from sharing the religious practices and experience of the men. This movement placed God within the reach of all, irrespective of caste or sex.

The history of the Bhakti movement reveals that it brought great solace to women and presented an alternative way of life to many individual women. Some even attained sainthood. Meerabai,

Muktabai, Janabai, Vishnupriya are well known names in Bhakti literature whose compositions are popular to this day For widows and neglected women, devotion provided an austere way of life and a certain justification for living. Neither a Brahmin nor a husband is needed to reach God.

Combining work and Bhakti, Veerasaivism was, at the time of its inception, a democratising movement. The corpus of religious lore of Veerasaivism consists of *vachanas* (sayings) of 200 to 300 saints. Out of these about 50 are women.

Marriage, which is not strictly a religious ceremony, is not considered as an obligatory ritual nor is it regarded as a hindrance in the path of devotion. Divorce and remarriage were allowed. Veerasaiva saints emphasize harmonious relations between husband and wife and frown upon the violation of marital fidelity by either of the two. A sin is not considered indispensable. Spiritual attainment and higher level of religious experience are possible for women also. They are known to have participated in philosophical discussions and missionary work. They are, however, not allowed to become Gurus.

Islam

In their relationship with the divine, men and women stand on a footing of equality in Islam. Woman, like man, is an individual who can pray to the Almighty, and can hope for redemption. A non-ascetic religion, Islam does not consider woman as an impediment in the path of religion, nor does it consider her as the root cause of man's downfall. The Quran is replete with-injunctions aimed at bettering the lot of women who in the pre-Islamic societies had held a very inferior and servile position.

However, in spite of the fact that Islam provided a much higher status to women than was commonly recognized in earlier societies, the social standards of the time were very different from those accepted today, and therefore the Muslim Shariat Law as it has developed over the centuries, places women in a disadvantageous or an inferior position in many respects.

Many of these disadvantages arise from interpretations of

the Quranic verse or the sayings of the Prophet in the light of the cultural norms prevailing in medieval times. Sometimes, traditions of the Prophet were even invented to validate later cultural norms which were being adopted under various types of influences. A few examples may be mentioned here.

In regard to witnesses, it was said that if a second man is not available, two women should be called so that if one errs, the other will remember. This was perhaps a safety device in view of women's extremely limited understanding of financial, commercial, and trade relationships, but it was also used for curtailing the women's right to a minimum in respect of offering evidence in criminal and civil cases.

In Islam a woman is as much a believer as a man, and (except in certain bodily conditions such as menstruation) has an equal right to undertake religious duties like praying and fasting. But a woman cannot be priest, nor can she lead the prayers. She has no place in the formal religious organization and legal affairs of the community. She cannot be appointed a Kazi.

Modesty, decorum and chastity were emphasized in the Quran, and the women were advised not to display their ornaments of beauty. This led to conflicting viewpoints about the veiling and seclusion of women. It was thought proper to keep the women away from the gaze of outsiders.

Among Indian Muslims, *burqa* and use of covered vehicles have been common devices for keeping women away from the gaze of outsiders. The matrilineal Muslim women of Lakshadweep and Kerala have however moved about without a burqa but with the head covered. It appears that the veil and seclusion of women have been more characteristic of the upper and middle strata of society, more so in urban areas.

The burqa is now becoming more of a lower middle-class phenomenon and a status symbol amongst the working classes to indicate a rise in their social status. It is otherwise decreasing due to a number of factors such as education, economic pursuits, and the forces of modernization generally. But it still continues to be a social reality and much religious feeling is associated with it.

Women's seclusion in Islam made them lose one of their important privilege that is, participation in communal prayers. It also lent extra support to a series of restrictions - women should not converse with other men, they should not talk loudly, letting their voices be heard by other men, they should not receive guests without the permission of the husband, and so on. Women can join in the prayer at the mosque for which there is a separate and secluded area reserved for them.

Marriage in Islam derives its legitimacy from the Shariat and is a contract. There is no ban on widow remarriage and divorce is allowed. Marriage is not religiously obligatory for a woman. But the contract of marriage gives unequal rights to man and woman.

Besides, the prevailing social customs are much more powerful in determining the social attitudes towards marriage, widow remarriage and divorce than the religious injunctions. As an example, religion provides for the free consent of both parties in the *nikah*, but in practice, it is a mere formality, so far as the girl is concerned. Similarly, widow remarriage and divorce are generally frowned upon, especially among the middle and the upper classes, even though they are permissible in Islam.

The rights of repudiation of the marriage contract is with the husband. Polygamy is permitted in Islam. A wife, therefore, has a distinctly inferior status. The institution of marriage-guardian (details of which differ according to different schools of law) places a woman in a subordinate position. Religion makes the husband the family head and expects the wife to obey and serve him.

Mehr (dower) is meant to be a security for the wife against the possibility of divorce at the husband's free will. It is doubtful, however, as to how many women are in a position to assert their claims to *mehr* in the event of a divorce or widowhood, particularly in the communities among whom the marriage contract need not be in writing.

Women's rights to inheritance, provided in Islam, are significant especially in view of the fact that they were meant for a patrilineal social structure. Islam introduced shares for wife, daughter, mother, sister and grandmother, the general rule being that the female was to inherit half of what the corresponding male would inherit. However, the women's right to hold or inherit property, is not often upheld in practice. This is largely due to their seclusion, absence of education, and the prevalence of customs and conventions which, in the Indian cultural setting, go against women's rights.

With regard to education, although Islam has made acquisition of knowledge an obligatory duty for every Muslim, in the case of women, it is largely restricted in practice, to enable them to offer prayers and to recite the Quran. Only the girls of the elite class have had access to some private instruction.

It is to be noted that in India, towards the end of the last century, Maulana Abdul Hayy-Lakhanavi was requested for a juristic opinion based on the Shariat whether a Muslim girl should be allowed to learn writing. Though it was supported with the help of a tradition of the Prophet, a diffused kind of feeling against women's education has continued and has received strong support from such customs and norms as seclusion of women, the desirability of their subordination to male authority, and the insistence on their performing assigned tasks in the domestic field.

The two practices that have been most detrimental to the status of women in Islam have been Talaq or unilateral divorce and seclusion of women. It is largely seclusion that has kept women backward in respect of education and health and prevented their participation in economic and social fields and has been a hurdle in the way of realizing their property rights. It has made them heavily dependent on men for the business of living and hence also for achieving any progress.

Christianity

In India, Christianity is represented by communities of various denominations. In each of these communities the practice of the tenets of Christianity has been influenced, in varying degrees, by historical and contemporary sociocultural factors. This has resulted in overshadowing, suppressing, or reviving and bringing into focus the essence of the teachings of Christianity regarding the status and role of women.

The myth of creation which says that Eve was created after Adam to act as his companion and help-mate accords a secondary place to woman in domestic and social life. She has to be subordinate first to her father and then to her husband. The mythic image of Eve as one who tempted Adam to eat the forbidden fruit has put a permanent stamp over women as tempters and seducers and has given the husband the right to control the wife.

The Indian Christians believe that the wife belongs to the husband and it is because of this notion, with its roots in religion, that among some dowry-giving Christians a man is supposed to have a right over ornaments and property received by his wife from her parents.

Marriage in Christianity, however, lays emphasis on the establishment of a mutual relationship between husband and wife and on their duty towards each other. This is powerfully expressed in the following pronouncement which forms a part of the marriage rites: "Man shall leave his father and mother and shall cleave to his wife; and they shall be one flesh."

These words are interpreted to mean that the nucleus of family organisation is the mutual relationship of husband and wife; the ultimate authority and responsibility is not placed in the extended family or the patriarch. This outlook accords a better status to the wife than the others which regard marriage as an alliance between two families and transfer of the girl from one family to another.

Our investigations show that even in some Indian Christian communities, like the various groups of Syrian Christians of Kerala and Catholic Christians of Mangalore who practise joint family system to some extent, the daughter-in-law is not relegated to the background. She can move about with her husband and it is recognized that her primary relationship is with her husband. Her status is much better than the status of a daughter-in-law in patrilineal families of the upper caste Hindus. Though the father is the recognized head of the family, the mother has her own sphere of work and influence. Although the central authority in the home is vested in the male, mutual responsibility of husband and wife is recognized.

Christianity forbids polygamy. The establishment of monogamy stands out as the one enduring factor which has raised the status of women in Christianity However, the concept of permanency of marriage which is considered a divine sacrament with no place for divorce has affected the women's status in both ways among the Catholics and some other groups. Along with the security of home and the certainty of not being separated from her children, she also has to be subjected to the husband's authority and is deprived of legal rights and independent existence. Divorce is recognized by the other groups, and is permitted according to the Indian Divorce Act of 1869.

The Bible lays great emphasis on the image of woman as a strong and steady influence for the good. Her notable qualities are: capacity to work with hands, kindness, wisdom, love and charity for the needy outside the home, and capacity to run her household in a manner that children get care and affection and the husband finds relaxation and peace.

In Christianity, both men and women are believed to have been created by God in his own image. Thus a woman is as much entitled to strive for her salvation as man. In fact, every other role in her life is subordinated to this role. She is a spiritually sovereign human being and this right vested in her may not be violated in marriage. She has an individual moral independence and responsibility.

In Christianity women have been entitled to study and learn religion and to attend and participate in all religious ceremonies. She has a right to become a nun. Thus, in one aspect of life, viz., in matters pertaining to the spirit and the practice of religion, Christianity accepts equality between men and women. Everybody is baptised in the name of Christ. However, women have never been given full ecclesiastic responsibility in the Church organization. Even in those Churches where women hold subordinate offices, ordination of women was not permitted till recently.

Today the situation varies all the way from Churches like those of the Syrian Christian who do not permit women to hold any office in the church, to the Methodist Church which accepts the ordination of women for complete priesthood.

The acceptance of the notion, common to all Christians, that by helping each other one can attain salvation and the emphasis laid on the virtues of service, love and charity provide a woman honourable careers other than marriage. Marriage is not a woman's sole destiny although socially it is most desirable.

We do not find the practice of child marriage among Christian communities, and widowhood is not a curse. A woman is not confined to the home. Her participation in congregational prayers, absence of purdah, no rigid insistence on segregation of sexes, monogamy, emphasis on husband-wife relationship, value of charity, and service to others - all these features of Christianity place women in a relatively better position than in other religions.

There is little wonder that in India in the later nineteenth and early twentieth century, Christian girls were way ahead of others in education and employment. The first educational and vocational institutions for women were established by Christian missionaries and though many of them were open to non-Christians they gave special concessions to Christian girls.

The Christian girls, not subjected to many injunctions and taboos, were in a better position to derive benefit from these institutions. As there was no taboo against their working outside the home, some of them also took up jobs. It is generally known that in the late nineteenth and early twentieth century women teachers, inspectresses of schools, doctors, and nurses in India were largely from among the Christians.

Some of the teachings of Christianity are found to be overshadowed or misused by the customs and values of particular converted groups to the detriment of women's status. However, the basic notion of inferiority of women not softened by any distinct elevation of her sex-linked roles has left Christian women to fight against the slavery of the home and against their large scale confinement to less prestigious jobs in the men's world.

Jainism

Except in Kerala and parts of Karnataka, the Jains are patrilineal and are governed by the Hindu personal law. Kinship ties and joint family living are strong. Because of recruitment from diverse culture areas, the Jains internally differ in their customs and practices, which often overshadow or even override religion.

As a way of life Jainism lays great stress on self-denial, restraint of passion, and a life of renunciation for both men and women. As a socio-religious organisation the Sangh comprises both monks and nuns as well as both male and female lay followers.

A woman has a legitimate position in the congregational life. She can occupy a position of leadership in which she deals with matters of practical concern and not with instruction. But the female ascetic appears to have suffered from certain handicaps in scriptures. By and large religious learning and renunciation are allowed to women who have a full right to aspire for Moksha.

The sects differ in their view of whether a woman can attain liberation as a woman or her soul has to be reborn as a man (as women have certain physical disabilities and mental weaknesses) in order to attain liberation. However, since according to Jainism no one is likely to attain liberation in the present age, this controversy does not have much practical significance.

In the religious context it cannot be ignored that in ascetic manuals and sermons there is severe condemnation of a woman who is looked upon as a tempter and seducer and is called tricky, deceptive, hypocritical, fickle, untrustworthy, and treacherous. This has been done with the specific purpose of warning a monk to keep himself away from women so that he is not swayed from strict celibacy in word, thought and deed. No such derogatory characterization of man is needed to keep women on the path of self-restraint in Jainism.

Jainism prescribes suitable patterns of moral conduct for ascetic as well as domestic life. Although actual customs and practices of the Jains often depend on their environmental setting and thus manifest differences between north and south, east and west, certain basic features of the faith have definite influence on the status of women. As there is no religious obligation of *Pindadana* to ancestors in Jainism there does not appear to be any premium on the birth of son.

In the patrilineal setting, however, boys have been claiming superiority over girls in respect of the right to inheritance and succession. For a daughter it has been customary to get Kanyashulka or some kind of compensation. Nor is marriage obligatory for a girl in the same sense as it is in Hinduism, for the religious path is open for her. Marriage is not a religious institution and so the customs differ from area to area, but basically a wedding is a simple ceremony. Jain women also use diacritical marks to denote their marital status. Marriages are arranged by the parents and they tend to do so in restricted circles which are something like sub-castes.

Polygamy is not forbidden. There is no sanction for widow remarriage, for a life of self-restraint is generally valued. Divorce and widow remarriage are, however, found customarily practised among certain sections. But a widowed woman does not easily lose her position. She can lead a pious life of Shravika within the family setting. A widow is obliged to lead a simple life but with the adoption of a pious way of life she could become an object of reverence. She could also become a nun. Thus widowhood is not exactly a curse in Jainism. But differential treatment of the sexes in this respect is clear.

In the context of the family, chastity in women is greatly valued and several stories in Jain scriptures are woven round this theme. Motherhood is respected but a childless woman does not find her future absolutely dark.

In Central and North India, the Jains follow a certain degree of segregation of sexes. Kinship ties are strong and women have constraints comparable to those of their high caste neighbours. The brunt of maintenance of regulations related to purity and to food falls on women. In the changing milieu, the religious prescriptions are mainly observed by women.

Buddhism

Buddhism recognized broad parity between man and woman in matters of religion; both the sexes being charged alike with the duty of upholding Dharma. Women are allowed to become nuns. Nirvana is possible for both men and women.

Thus, Buddhism as a liberal reaction against orthodox Brahmanism elevated the status of women. But after a modicum of equality, the scales have been tipped in favour of the monk. This is clear from such evidence as : a statement that the merit accruing from a donation to the Sangh of monks is more than that accruing from a donation to the Sangli of nuns, the rule that women cannot preach to the order of monks, and the rule that a Bhikumi, even though older, should bow down even before a younger Bhikhu.

Buddhism does not consider woman as evil or as one solely responsible for sensuality in the world. Yet she can be an obstruction in the path of deliverance. Woman is physically weak and dependent, but mentally as good as man.

A girl can remain unmarried by becoming a Bhikhuni. From widowhood also there is a respite in renunciation. However, the ideal propounded for women in society is not materially different from the one upheld by the orthodox Hindu view. She has to serve the man. Mother as a self-sacrificing and benevolent figure is very much present in Buddhist thought. Despite her intellectual parity, woman is definitely considered as inferior to man in the monastery as well as in society.

In Ladakh, Lahaul and Spiti where Buddhism prevails, at least in theory, men and women are considered mentally on a par with one another. But in practice the position is quite different. Of the two types of nuns in the Buddhist order, the Bhikhuni (with 300 rules of conduct and treated more or less equal to male counterparts) and the Samenara (with only ten rules to obey) today, we find only the Sainenara who generally live with their families, and are treated like honoured servants. They are given higher seats, but their job is to perform household chores. In this area there are very few nunneries. Even senior nuns are considered inferior to monks.

Because of the prevailing practice of polyandry in these regions, girls are often forced to become nuns. Since the communities in these regions practice the customs of bride-price as well as divorce and remarriage, the Buddhists also follow them.

The birth of a boy is not specially felicitated. This is presumably so because the girl is a productive worker and brings gifts at marriage. Because a son is not needed by the parents for the last rites and Pindadana, in the same way as the Hindus, girls are not lower in status than the boys.

The position of women in these areas appears to be better than that of the women in the plains, but it is difficult to ascribe this to Buddhism as such. The main reason perhaps lies in their participation in the economy. Buddhism leaves most of the areas of worldly life to be managed by the people according to their customs and traditions.

In the newly emerging areas of activity like education, medical service, and political participation men are coming forward more than women. The preaching and organization of religion is in the hands of monks.

Sikhism

Sikhism condemns formal ritual, idolatry, and superstition, and emphasizes simple devotion to God. In the pursuit of religion both men and women have a place as individuals. "That tongue alone is blessed, that utters words of God's devotion". Sikhism emphasizes the householder's ideal and demands respect for women as men's helpmate and sharer in his domestic life. It does not look upon woman as an agent of sin and evil; nor does it regard her as an object of pleasure.

Guru Nanak asks women to have a pure way of life and not indulge in extravagances of wealth. Association of impurity with the cosmic natural processes like birth is condemned. Man is exhorted not to condemn woman who is his companion and of whom are born great men and all men.

For the purposes of devotion there is no difference between men and women. In social life, however, Sikhism did not concede equality for women. Her kinship and domestic roles are emphasized. She has important roles to play as wife, mother, sister and daughter. The qualities that women are asked to develop are love, obedience, contentment, and sweet temper. A woman should be in harmony of temper with her husband. Mother's role and wife's roles are brought into relief in the tales of the wives of the Gurus.

Sikhism was adopted by people belonging to different Hindu castes mainly in the Punjab. In this religion, there are several clearly defined rules regarding personal habits, but not many well-laid out injunctions covering institutions like marriage and family that could have imperatively changed people's staunch beliefs and actions.

We, therefore, find that social customs defining woman's roles and constraints over them are not common to all the Sikhs. In this respect there are important differences from territory to territory and from group to group. The differences in the rural and urban settings are also significant. The Jat Sikhs continue to follow their original Jat customs.

In matters such as divorce, separation, remarriage, widow's position, women's rights of ownership and inheritance and seclusion of women, people generally tend to follow ~he customs and practices of their original caste or regional culture.

Importance of kinship and of the family ties, with the idea of the transfer of the girl in marriage from one family to another, have a prominent part in shaping role relationships in the family. The Sikhs are governed by the Hindu Personal Law which exists side by side with the customary law of particular groups.

Zoroastrianism

In India there are less than 100,000 Parsees, who follow Zoroastrianism-one of the oldest religions of the world. Migrating to India over 1300 years ago, the Parsees adopted Gujarati as their language, and while retaining most of the customs and elements of their religion, they could not escape some influence of the indigenous populations. After the coming of the British, they were among the first to take to the Western style of life and to English education.

Zoroastrian women enjoy a position of honour in the family and in the society. The evils of polygamy and child marriage, which had crept in under Hindu and Muslim influence, were fought and removed by the Parsee Panchayat in the 19th century. The Parsee Marriage and Divorce Act and the Parsee Succession Act were passed with the strong support of the leaders of the Parsee community.

In Zoroastrianism women are entitled to both religious and secular education. Boys as well as girls go through the investiture rites. Marriage is solemnized and sanctified by a religious ceremony, but it is a contract. It is always monogamous. Consent of both the boy and the girl is essential for marriage. Religious tradition does not approve of child marriage, and today, as in ancient days, the minimum age of marriage for girls is fifteen. If circumstances demand, a girl can marry against the wishes of the parents. Dissolution of marriage, for proper reasons, is allowed. The practice of remarriage has always been there. A Zoroastrian woman is an equal partner in marriage and family, and enjoys respect as mother and wife. Parents of both the bride and the bridegroom contribute to the setting up of a new household. A woman has inheritance rights both in her capacity as a daughter and as a wife. A widow does not have to forego the inheritance of husband's property if she remarried.

Zoroastrianism traditionally imposed menstrual taboos demanding segregation and non-participation in religious activities.

Though no longer stringently practised these restrictions are operative in the context of rituals. Women can preach but they cannot became priests. Only since 1935, the Parsee Panchayat has started admitting women into it as members.

There is one disability which women suffer compared to men, but it is more a function of patriliny, combined with a non-proselytizing religion. The child of a Parsee father and a non-Parsee mother, whether in wedlock or out of it, can be initiated into Zoroastrian faith by the Naojote ceremony. But neither by religion nor by law can a child of a Parsee mother and a non-Parsee father be received as a Zoroastrian.

The dwindling numbers of the community are to some extent due to this discrimination as marriages between Parsee women and non-Parsee men are on the increase. The community is unable to stop such marriages, for girls have great freedom of movement, but it certainly has tremendous reservations and resentment so far as their marrying outside the community is concerned. Conversely, a Parsee boy's marriage with a non-Parsee girl is accepted with greater grace, although the non-Parsee wife is never accepted in Zoroastrianism, which is not a proselytizing religion. Parsee girls marrying a non-Parsee by the Special Marriage Act are claiming a right to remain a Parsee and visit the fire-temple but the Parsee Panchayat has not yet decided the issue. It may, however, be mentioned that these girls do not lose their inheritance rights in intestate succession.

Tribal Faiths

Tribal religions in India do not constitute a homogeneous system. What is attempted here, therefore, is to identify some significant elements of these faiths and examine the place of woman in respect of them.

Another factor is the presence of Buddhism in some tribal population such as the tribals of Himachal Pradesh. Further, the people of Lakshadweep who are Muslims have been declared as Scheduled Tribe and Jaunsari people now included in Scheduled Tribe are Hindus.

Moreover, in States like Madhya Pradesh, Bihar, and Orissa many tribal groups who have been influenced by the neighbouring

Hindu population return themselves as Hindu. There is a substantial proportion of tribal population in these States, and if all of them had declared themselves as belonging to tribal religion, figures in the column of 'Other Religions' would have been different.

It is, however, important to note that those tribals who return themselves as Hindu or Christian do not completely discard their tribal customs. Majority of them hold their beliefs, worship the tribal deities and conduct rituals, etc., according to tradition.

The social structures and cultural systems of the tribes are reflected in their system of beliefs and ritual practices. Tribal religion is matter-of-fact and materialistic. The purpose of propitiation or homage and of manipulation of supernatural powers is mostly to avert misery and destruction in interpersonal relationship and maintenance of structural principles.

Religious activities can be classified into (a) of the family, (b) of the group, and (c) of the village. Women have a role only in the first set. They may be responsible for keeping the domestic fire kindled and for routine looking after of the place assigned for gods and ancestors in the house; but in the periodical or special worship of lineage ancestors or deities and clan deities, women have no place; at the most they play the role of helpers in making preparation for rituals.

Matrilineal communities like the Khasi are an exception; among them the youngest daughter has an important role to play in relation to lineage ancestors and deities. The Garo also have priestesses. However, it needs to be mentioned that even in many of the matrilineal communities priestly functions and handling of matters pertaining to transgression of taboos are in the hands of men. In most tribal communities priesthood is a male prerogative. Knowledge of ritual formulae rests with men. In a few tribes like the Saora of Orissa, and the Irula and the Paniyan of Kerala, women function as *shaman* (diviner and curer), but female priesthood is almost absent.

Horror of menstrual blood is universal in tribal India and leads (a) to exclusion of women from holding any positions of ritual importance, and (b) to their association with malefic supernatural powers. Witchcraft, which is considered dangerous, is largely associated with women, in both tribal and rural India. It is believed to be some kind of an unavoidable malefic power which gets transmitted from another person, commonly one's mother in some vulnerable circumstances. During the periods of menstrual flow, pregnancy and post-natal impurity, women are held to be specially vulnerable.

Rites of passage are definitely male weighted. So also are the sacrifices and various devices for increasing the fertility of the soil and cattle, and rites to please the elements of nature.

In some tribal communities women suffer from severe disabilities in the religious sphere. The Toda debar their women from having anything to do with the buffaloes and their products. Their rituals are centred round the buffalo and women are completely excluded. Among the Kota also women are strictly forbidden to associate themselves in any way with the funeral and other rituals. Santhal women are also not allowed to participate in communal worship nor can they eat sacrificial meals. In fact, a Santhal woman is not considered a full-fledged member of the society.

In the maintenance of community discipline and public morality which is the function of the Panchayats or Tribal Councils, women have no role. Even the Regional Councils set up after independence in some tribal areas, have resisted the efforts of few women to obtain any position on these bodies.

While their position in religion and rituals is definitely lower than man, women's participation and contribution in economic activity results in considerable freedom in norms of social behaviour. The average age of marriage is higher among tribal women than among other communities. In choice of partners, rules of divorce and remarriage, most tribal women enjoy greater freedom, though the influence of Sanskritisation has reduced this in some communities.

Reform Movements

The broad aims of these movements in the social sphere were specially emphasizing caste reform or caste abolition, and improvement in the rights and status of women and generally against social and legal inequalities. It involved an attack on certain social institutions and practices like child marriage, position and treatment of widows, seclusion and the denial of women's rights to property and education, the roots of which lay in the religious traditions of different communities.

The impact of British rule, English education and Christianity propagated by missionaries resulted in a number of movements for social change and religious reform in the 19th century. According to Gopal Krishna Gokhale in Rao & Singh (1934): "The first impact of Western teaching on those who received it was to incline them strongly in favour of the Western way of looking at things and under this influence they bent their energies, in the first instance, to the re-examination of the whole of their ancient civilization or their social usages and institutions, their religious beliefs, literature, science, art as also in fact their conception and realization of life."

Leaders of the reform movements therefore realized that it was difficult to separate social reforms from religious reforms. Though some of the earlier leaders like Ram Mohun Roy had believed that it was possible to reform all religions together, bringing out the basic unity that underlay all religious faiths, such attempts met with resistance, not only from the orthodox sections of different religious communities, but also from the policy of the ruling power which believed that the security of British supremacy in India depended on keeping the different religious communities separate from each other. This policy was particularly aided by the existence of different systems of personal law, closely related to the religious and customary traditions of the communities and castes which the British helped to perpetuate.

Historians of the Indian social system have always emphasized a characteristic feature of this stratified society which, while retaining its basic framework of inequalities and divisions, had by and large displaced considerable capacity for adapting itself to processes of social change. Much of this process of adjustment and adaptation took place because of regional diversity in cultural norms and the realization by religious and community leaders that without such adjustment it would not be possible for their particular traditions to survive in the Indian context.

Different religious faiths like Islam and Christianity compromized with existing socio-cultural traditions in different regions and communities. The British system of recording and providing official recognition to principles and practices of social organisation at a period of time however introduced an element of resistance to this process of natural adjustment and change.

It was therefore inevitable that the movement of social reform should develop within the folds of each religion rather than as a unified movement for the transformation of the society as a whole. The most important of these movements that developed within the Hindu society were the Brahmo Samaj, Prarthna Samaj and the Arya Samaj.

The Brahmo Samaj: Brahmo Samaj was founded by Ram Mohun Roy in 1825. Concerned with religious issues, it opposed the dogmatic structure of religious tradition. It also attempted to remove certain restrictions and prejudices against women rooted in religion. These included the abolition of child marriage, seclusion of women, limited inheritance rights, polygamy, etc. The Samaj emphasized the need for educating women as the best instrument to improve their position.

Under the leadership of Keshab Chandra Sen, the Brahmo Samaj became more concerned with improving the position of women. Provision was made for educating women at home and government assistance was enlisted for this purpose. A new magazine was started to publish articles of special interest to women and to provide an opening for their literary aspirations. In 1862 an inter-caste marriage was solemnized under the auspices of the Samaj. Opposition of orthodox Hindus to the legality of such marriage resulted in the passing of the Native Marriage Act (popularly known as the Civil Marriage Act) in 1872 which permitted inter-caste marriage and divorce, prohibited polygamy and prescribed 14 and 18 years as minimum age of marriage for a girl and boy respectively.

The Act facilitated the sweeping social reform advocated by Keshab Chandra Sen, particularly the abolition of caste distinction.

In 1879 the more radical section of members founded a separate wing - the Sadharan Brahmo Samaj. They started a women's association in which key positions were held by women. They propagated education and social interaction between men and women and careers for women outside the home.

It is generally believed that the influence of the Brahmo Samaj was confined mainly to Bengal and North India, but there is evidence to show its extension to South India also. At the end of the 19th century coastal districts of Andhra Pradesh were exposed to the influence of the Brahmo Samaj. But it was primarily a reform rather than a religious movement. As these districts had seen a great deal of missionary activity, and the conversion of caste Hindus to Christianity, Brahmoism expectedly gained the greatest ground here. This was because the Brahmo Samaj was not a proselytizing movement. Rather, it sought to integrate the untouchables within the Hindu fold. Brahmo leaders were active in providing education and in inculcating a social consciousness.

Venkatratnam Naidu adopted girls from the Scheduled Caste and arranged their marriages to high caste boys. Other leaders included K.Y. Pantulu, Unnavalaksh Minarayana, Ramjee Rao and Chilakamarthi Lakshmi Naresimhan.

The Prarthna Samaj: Founded in 1867 the Prarthna Samaj remained principally a movement of western India. It propounded belief in one God, supported Bhakti and opposed idolatry While as a body it did not take any formal stand on social reform except sponsoring education for women, some of its leading members were active in the women's cause. Talang was a founder member of the Bombay Widow Reforms Association which arranged the first widow remarriage in 1869. Ranade and Bhandarkar were among the participants when Shankaracharya was challenged to a public debate to decide whether or not the Shastras sanctioned widow remarriage.

Ranade acted as the spokesman of the educated people and moderate reformers strengthened the hands of the government in passing the Age of Consent Bill in 1891. Founding of the National Social Conference in 1887, with the specific purpose of bringing together annually the representatives of various associations, was a big achievement of Ranade in the women's cause. Two leading Prarthna Samajists, Bhandarkar and Chandavarkar, agreed to be Vice-Chancellors of the Women's University started by Karve in 1916.

Both these movements made a forceful effort to prove that Hindu religious tradition was certainly not the source of legitimacy for the pitiable condition of women. Under the influence of liberal thought of the West, they recognized the individuality of women. But essentially they aimed at making women better wives and mothers and were keen to bridge the gap between the levels of understanding of the males (both husband and son), who had the benefit of modern education, and the women of the family.

The Arya Samaj: While the Brahmo Samaj and Prarthana Samaj were the products of the reaction of a section of urban, western educated elite, influenced by Western liberalism, the Arya Samaj was a dissident religious movement which rejected Hindu medieval religion with its idol worship and the post-Vedic caste society. This was founded in 1875 by Dayanand Saraswati. Essentially revivalist in character, the Samaj also stood for the reform of the caste system and tried to raise the status of women in several ways. It advocated revival of the Vedic society in its pristine form. Its influence spread mainly in the Punjab and United Provinces among the middle and higher castes. Though mainly an urban movement, its influence extended to semi-urban and rural areas also.

Dayanand Saraswati emphasized compulsory education of both men and women and spoke of *purdah* as an evil which came in the way of courage learning and broad-mindedness. He propagated prohibition of child marriage by law and approved the remarriage of child widows. He was, however, opposed to divorce or to remarriage of widows in general. While he prescribed similar education and religious initiation for boys and girls, he emphasized the need to maintain sex distinction in schools and among teachers, prescribing a minimum distance of 3 miles between boys' and girls' schools. This emphasis on education was continued by the Samaj even after his death, and a number of institutions were established. The Arya Kanya Pathshalas, which gradually developed into colleges have contributed greatly to the cause of women's education. In the later years, leaders of the Samaj broke away from his disapproval of widow remarriage and contributed to improving the position of widows. The Samaj did not make any distinction in marriage rites of virgins and widows.

Its repudiation of the caste system, however, did not extend to demanding its abolition, nor did the Samaj mount a campaign against untouchability. The followers of the Arya Samaj tended to follow the pattern of arranged marriages for their children as well as the rules of endogamy. While there is no objection to intercaste marriage, most families tend to establish marital connections within the caste group, sometimes with Sanatani, families of the same caste. In consequence, the reformist character of the movement has tended to recede. On the other hand, the emphasis on the home making roles of women, whose primary duty is to love and serve their husbands, and children in the traditional way has limited its contribution to the cause of women's emancipation.

The Muslim Reform Movement: Like the parallel movements among the Hindus there were movements of reform within the Islamic community too. Regarding the position of the women, however, reforms were delayed, partly because modern education entered the Muslim community much later, and partly because the seclusion of women was defended by leaders of the community more persistently. "The practice of polygamy, however, registered a marked decline due to prevalence of modern ideas and decline in material prosperity."

A progressive movement to improve women's educational opportunities began to develop from the last years of the 19th century, under the leadership of a few visionaries like the Begum of Bhopal, Sheikh Abdullah in Aligarh, Justice Karamat Hussain in Lucknow and others of their ilk; a large number of books and journals appeared which carried enlightenment to the newly educated Muslim women.

Many reformers tried to revive widow remarriage, which had become strictly taboo among the respectable classes, due perhaps to the prevailing social ideas. Criticism also started against the custom of denying to the daughters a share in their fathers' property as a violation of the tenets of Islam. Failure to eliminate seclusion, however, defeated many of the aims of these reformers and the status of Muslim women still remained far from one of equality in spite of these reform movements. Among the urban educated middle-classes, however, these ideas contributed to some change in the position and treatment of women within the family.

Other Movements: Similar movements to improve the position of women emerged among other communities and different regions. Behramji Malabar was the main spirit behind the Age of Consent Act of 1892. The depressed condition of women in all communities made it difficult for them to fight for their own rights. A few outstanding exceptions faced great opposition from their communities. Pandita Ramabai, having incurred the wrath of the orthodoxy by marrying out of caste, ultimately turned to Christianity to aid her campaign to improve the condition of women. Dhan Korbai suffered great hardship for marrying after widowhood. Vidyagouni Neelakant faced bitter opposition to obtain education.

The changes envisaged by these reformers were only partial. They aimed to change the position of women within the family and the domestic framework and did not foresee any radical change in the social structure. Education, raising the age of marriage, widow remarriage, the abolition of seclusion and rights to property were essentially attempts to improve the woman's position within the family framework and to ensure for her a degree of dignity and independence.

None of these movements aimed to make the woman an equal partner of man in the societal roles outside the family. The movements were also limited in their appeals; while the Brahmo Samaj and Prarthna Samaj appealed only to a limited section of Western educated urban Indians, the Arya Samaj, Ramakrishna Mission and other revivalist movements appealed to a wider group, including the urban lower middle-class. The general impact of all these movements has been most pronounced on the urban middle-class. Some of the ideas projected by them, namely disapproval of child marriage and ill-treatment of widows, education and better treatment of women within the family, ensuring to them a position of greater dignity, have become a part of the general cultural heritage of this section of Indian society.

Being elitist in character and limited in approach, they have never tried a proper investigation of the problems that weighed on women outside the middle-class. Education, though valuable, could not reach the masses. The universal, oppression on all women however lay in their subordinate and subjugated position in society, which sanctioned such treatment. Its removal called for a restructuring of the social organisation which the reform movements, by and large, did not aim for. The two social ideas which really threatened the basic structure of Indian society during this period were 'women's emancipation', and 'mass education'. Since the reform movements were not prepared to identify themselves with such extreme, radical ideas, their efforts to emancipate women, could be only limited in effect.

It has to be remembered that the most towering personalities in the movement for improving the lot of women came from individuals who were indifferent to the religious aspects of the reform movements. Iswar Chandra Vidyasagar and Jotiba Phule wanted to free Indian society not only from religious superstitions, but from the social inequalities that oppressed all the weaker sections, including women. It was however left to Mahatma Gandhi and, the freedom movement to place the movement for women's emancipation in its proper perspective, as a part of the larger movement for social transformation and eventually their emancipation and empowerment.

FOUR

Legal Protection

In our Constitution, the women have been granted equality of status with men. Founding fathers of the Constitution made it quite clear that in independent India women will enjoy equal opportunities in every walk of life. But large masses of women in India have remained unaffected by the rights guaranteed to them by the Constitution and laws enacted since independence. In this chapter an examination of the subject in its various dimensions has been undertaken in order to understand the legal problems of women and then possible future prospects.

One of the main characteristics of modern society is a heavy reliance on law to bring about social change. This is particularly true of countries which had been under foreign rule for centuries and attained independence after a long struggle. Inequalities and exploitation, generated or intensified by colonial regimes, cannot be eliminated by freedom from foreign rule only.

The tasks of social reconstruction, development and nation building-all call for major changes in the social order and to achieve this legislation is one of the main instruments. It can act directly, as a norm setter, or indirectly, providing institutions which accelerate social change by making it more acceptable. The introduction of compulsory education can be sited as an example.

Like other colonial countries, independent India has also relied heavily on legislation in its effort to usher in a society where there will be no discrimination or inequality. It has sought to protect the interests of those who suffer from social and political disabilities by penalizing the practice of untouchability, eliminating caste distinctions, and so on. By clearly emphasizing the principle of equality and removing all legal discrimination inter-alia between sexes, our leaders have shown their acceptance of the view that to achieve freedom there must be complete liberty for women, and "all legislative traces of inequality of women without exception must be removed".

Stress on removal of discrimination and special protective legislation for women was necessary because the British policy in the field of family law has a crippling effect on Indian women. Whatever the motivation was, the British adopted a policy of letting Hindus be governed by Hindu law and Muslims by Muslim law in matters of family relations. This policy of relying on age old personal laws has been described as "another act of enlightened policy," but the aim was to encourage the feeling of separateness and prevent the unity of the two communities.

This policy achieved such success that modification of most of these laws has proved difficult even today. Coupled with this was another policy of non-interference or rather non-intervention in family law on the plea that 'as the British legislature cannot make Mohammedan or Hindu religion, so can it not make Mohammedan or Hindu Law'. This led to stagnation with the result that the two systems could neither absorb nor adjust to socioeconomic changes. Social tensions inevitably arise in situations when "law does not answer the needs arising from major social changes".

In early 19th century, due to efforts of our social reformers, some marginal adjustments were made in response to humanitarian considerations and social demands. Although female infanticide had been banned earlier, the most significant was the legislation which penalized the practice of Sati. The groundwork for this had been laid for a very long time, and this was an example where legislative legitimacy was given to an accepted social norm. The then Governor General, Lord Bentinck, referring to the proposed legislation, said that the government would be following and not going ahead of public opinion.

In 18th and early 19th centuries, the prevalence of child marriage leading often to early widowhood, was one of the major concerns of the social reformers. Their tireless efforts to curb this social evil finally resulted in "The Hindu Widows' Remarriage Act in 1856. Such social legislation stopped after 1857.

The social reformers realized that in the face of the government's refusal to legislate on social matters, the only way open was to spread education more widely among the people, particularly women. This, they felt, would help to eliminate some of the inhuman practices and also act as an incentive to women to organize and demand legislative changes.

As the national movement intensified, the early 20th century saw some activity in the legislative field. The plight of widows without any means of their own, depending entirely on the family, led to the passing of the Hindu Women's Right to Property Act in 1929, followed by another in 1937. These laws, while making the widow less dependent financially during her lifetime, stopped short of giving her any substantial rights of ownership since her right to property was only for life.

The success of the policy of division can also be seen from the fact that though demands for changes in the Muslim law to improve the position of women were also gaining momentum, the reformers of the two communities did not work together. A significant change that was made as a result of all the agitations for improvement among the Muslims was granting the right of divorce to Muslim women in 1939.

A by-product of the policy of non-intervention in family law had been the diversification (due to customs) among the major personal laws in different parts of the country and varied interpretations of the sacred texts. These differences had hardened over the years. Among the Muslim schools of law-there were others besides the Sunni and Shia schools. This was partially remedied by the Shariat Act of 1937, which brought all Muslims under the Act and practically abrogated the customary practices which had grown over the years. Among the Hindus, where there were two major schools-Mitakshara and Dayabhaga-and other sub-schools, lack of uniformity posed a serious problem.

The demand for major changes, no longer marginal ones, grew as a result of the untiring efforts of Gandhiji, who did not want women to suffer from any social or legal disabilities. The inferior position of women in all matters-guardianship, inheritance and divorce-had an effect on the personality of the women. Under Gandhiji's leadership, the demand for improvement and modification of the law grew, and ultimately the government was compelled to move. A committee was constituted under the chairmanship of Sir B.N. Rau, whose terms of reference included suggestions for change and the Codification of Hindu Law, so that all Hindus would be governed by the same law. Even though the report was ready and Gandhiji's exhortation that 'women should not suffer from any disability or discrimination', had influenced India's national leaders, the resistance to change was so great that no effective steps could be taken for many years.

Only after Independence, under the leadership of Pandit Nehru, could this matter be taken up. Even so, the law had to be passed piecemeal owing to the resistance from those who believed in the status quo. It is significant that the same body, sitting as the Constituent Assembly, adopted the equal rights clauses in the Constitution without any debate, while functioning in its capacity as the Central Legislature and blocked the Hindu Code Bill, which attempted to provide only partial equality to women.

Women's participation in the freedom movement had greatly helped in the acceptance of the idea of their equality and the need for their emancipation. As a result, with independence, Indian women achieved political and some social rights and did not have to struggle for them like women in many other countries.

But legislation cannot by itself change the society. To translate these rights into reality is the task of other agencies. Public opinion has to be moulded to accept these rights. The judiciary and the executive also have a major role to play in this. But this effort has not always been forthcoming. Sometimes the judiciary has interpreted new legislation strictly but failed to give effect to the principle underlying the legislation, as for example, in dealing with cases of bigamy or the right of women to work. The executive branch of the government has seldom made an effort to set up the machinery to educate the people about the socioeconomic changes. The mass media used for publicizing certain measures taken by the government has been conspicuously silent about social legislation. If legislation reflects the social values of a country the degree of women's emancipation is the natural measure of the general emancipation in any given society. It is, therefore, necessary not only to pass legislation, but also to see that it is implemented. In the following sections, an effort has been made to point out the areas where the law is lagging behind the principles, which have already been accepted by our Constitution.

Full equality of sexes can hardly be possible in a legal system which permits polygamy, and a social system which tolerates it. Though the institution of polygamy has prevailed traditionally in India, in the last five or more decades, it is on the wane and most marriages are today monogamous. The spread of Christianity with its concept of marriage "as a union for life of one man with one woman" marked the first step towards the legal recognition of the principle of monogamy. The advanced communities in the country like the Parsees and the Brahmos opted for the principle. The Parsee Marriage and Divorce Act, 1865 provided that any marriage during the lifetime of the wife or husband was void. The Indian Christian Marriage Act, 1872 lays down the condition that, neither of the persons intending to be married shall have a wife or husband still living. With the enactment of the Hindu Marriage Act, 1955, which lays down the principle of monogamy for all Hindus, 88 per cent of the Indian population are legally governed by the principle of monogamy.

The only personal law, which has remained impervious to the changing trend from polygamy to monogamy, is the Muslim law. Most Muslim countries such as Turkey, Iraq, Iran, Syria, Tunisia, Indonesia and Pakistan (including Bangladesh, which was then a part of Pakistan) have introduced reforms of varying degrees to correct the abuse of polygamy, but no legislative effort has so far been made in India to ameliorate the hardship caused to the Muslim women by the continuance of the institution of polygamy. According to an Urdu editor "...The law of polygamy is not an invention of the Muslims, but a part of the comprehensive religious code granted to them by God. And the Muslims have been exercising this right of theirs since the time of the holy Prophet to this day. To tamper with it would definitely amount to interference in religion. If some Muslim or non-Muslim administration force monogamy on Muslims, it would be a case of gross injustice; and the Muslims will oppose it as a religious duty." 'In UP we found a positive hostility to any reform in the Muslim law, particularly among the educated middle-class. Among the poorer classes of the same state, we found a desire to have monogamous marriages and blunt denunciation of the inequities of polygamy In Kashmir, the women uniformly and emphatically demanded that polygamy must be banned."

The seeming indifference on the part of the government in leaving only one section of the citizens to be governed by a law permitting polygamy and other inequalities was sought to be explained by the then Minister for Law and Justice, Mr Gokhale, when he said, "we believe that while we should do everything possible to build up and cultivate the consciousness for reform, the urge and the demand for the reform must come from the community itself".

Marriage is regarded as a contract under the Muslim law for the purpose of procreation and legalizing of children. Some eminent jurists like Fyzee and Danial Latifi have, therefore, advocated the device of standard contract of marriage, which would provide inter alia for stipulation like "The husband shall not take a second wife while the first marriage subsists, and if the husband has married or gone through a form of marriage with another woman after the date thereof", the wife shall have the power to divorce. As in Islamic law, marriage is regarded as a contract, the prevailing opinion of the jurists is that, generally such contracts become enforceable in courts.

Two subsidiary views exist regarding the technique : (i) to propagate the standard form of contract and leave it to the volition of the parties to enter into such contracts, and (ii) to provide an amendment to Section 2 A of the Shariat Act inter alia that "every contract of marriage shall be deemed to include, unless otherwise expressly provided, the terms set out", which would contain a provision that the husband shall not take a second wife during the subsistence of the marriage.

The critical question for consideration is : What are the consequences of a breach of the contractual stipulation on the part of the husband that he would not contract a second marriage during the subsistence of the prior marriage? Fyzee says that: (a) restitution may be refused to the husband; (b) certain rights as to dower may arise; (c) the wife may have a right to divorce; or, in an extreme case (d) the marriage itself may be dissolved.

Thus, the effective right of a Muslim wife having a standard contract is to get the dissolution of marriage or a right to live separately from the husband. This fails to provide a substantive relief to the first wife with children. As the second marriage is not invalidated, the position of the husband is not prejudicially affected due to the financial implications arising out of the step. The deterrence of the criminal sanction when a person intends to contract a second marriage is absent. Further, the solution of standard contracts is ineffective, in case of fake conversions to Islam from other religions to circumvent the prohibition against bigamy. The remedy is out of step with the position in the other personal laws in India and should be rejected.

The first approach to reform Muslim law relating to polygamy is to abolish it altogether. In Turkey, polygamy was abolished by law. The Turkish Civil Code lays down that no person shall marry again unless he proves that the former marriage has been dissolved by death, divorce or by a decree of nullity. The Turkish Family Law of Cyprus also provides that a marriage shall be declared invalid where at the date of the marriage, one of the parties is already married. The Tunisian Code of Personal Status in Article 18 provides: "Plurality of wives is prohibited. Any person who being already married and before the marriage is lawfully dissolved, marries again, shall be liable to imprisonment for one year or for a fine of 240,000 francs or to both even if the second marriage is in violation of any requirements of this law. The Muslims in the erstwhile USSR and the Peoples Republic of China are also governed by the rule of monogamy.

It deserves to be emphasized that in Tunisia the justification for the abolition of polygamy had its basis on a re-evaluation or re-interpretation of Islamic principles. Professor Anderson points out the following, distinctive grounds: The first was the broadly based argument that there were certain institutions, such as slavery and polygamy, which were acceptable at a certain stage in human development, but which were repugnant to the civilised conscience today... The second argument was... that the Verse of polygamy itself allows plurality of wives only on two conditions, one of which is that the would-be polygamist should have no fear whatever, of treating them with less than equal justice. But experience, the President said, had proved that no man other than a prophet was capable of such a feat especially in contemporary conditions.

The second approach is to regulate the husband's right to contract a second marriage by rendering it necessary to obtain judicial or official sanction for a bigamous marriage. In most countries where Muslims constitute a majority of the population, this approach, with variations, is favoured. Iran, Iraq, Singapore and Syria provide that permission of the court is necessary for a bigamous marriage of the husband, The laws provide that in granting the permission, the courts should satisfy themselves about the financial capacity of the husband to maintain more than one wife. Some of these laws provide for additional grounds to be fulfilled like the capacity to do equal justice to the co-wives.

On the other hand, Sri Lanka, Pakistan and Indonesia confer the power to regulate bigamous marriage on institutions other than the regular courts. For example, Section 6 of the Muslim Family Laws Ordinance of Pakistan states that no male can contract another marriage during the subsistence of an existing marriage except with the previous permission of the Arbitration Council. The Arbitration Council may grant the permission if it is satisfied that the proposed marriage is necessary and just. If a person contracts another marriage without such permission, upon a complaint being made, he is liable for punishment which may extend to one years' simple imprisonment or a fine of Rs 5,000 or both. The legislation in Sri Lanka prescribes for the prior notice of the intended marriage and the display of the notice in the mosques and at the residence of the parties, that is, the husband, the first wife and the prospective second wife. In Indonesia, the Family Law Regulations of 1947 enjoin the marriage officials to clarify and explain the position of a bigamous marriage under Islamic Law and legal conditions and obligations relating to it, to the person intending to contract a bigamous marriage.

David Pearl studied the impact of the Muslim Family Laws Ordinance (1963) in Quetta (Baluchistan), Pakistan. Two points relevant for our consideration emerge from his study.

According to the first: "many men risk the penalties inherent in Section 6 (5) (a) and (b) of the ordinance, and marry a second wife without bothering to apply to the arbitration council for its approval."

The second relates to classification of marriages in the Muslim Law. A marriage is valid (*sabih*) if all the conditions and formalities relating to marriage have been properly fulfilled. A valid marriage confers on the wife the right to dower, maintenance, etc.; and creates reciprocal rights of inheritance between the husband and wife. Among the Sunnis, a marriage that is not valid may be either void (*batil*) or irregular (*fasid*). A void marriage does not create any rights or obligations among the parties. The children of the union are illegitimate. An irregular marriage has no legal effect before consummation and it can be terminated by words showing intention to separate. The children of the union are legitimate but the irregular marriage does not create mutual rights of inheritance between the husband and wife.

Pearl points out that the distinction between valid, void and irregular marriages was not eliminated and, therefore, "it was remarkably easy.. for a girl under 16 to be married, or a man to ignore Sections 6 & 7 of the ordinance".

While the desirability of reform in Muslim Law is generally acknowledged, as mentioned, the government has taken no step towards changing the law for over two decades on the view that public opinion in the Muslim community did not favour a change. But this view cannot be reconciled with the declaration of equality and social justice. We are therefore of the opinion that ignoring the interest of Muslim women is a denial of social justice. The right to equality, in our view, like the right to free speech, is an individual right.

An analysis of polygamous marriages among Muslims in India classifies them into four groups: (a) The largest number of cases are of husbands who abandon their wives (and frequently children as well) and go off and marry somebody else. Frequently, the second wife remains ignorant about the earlier marriage and the children; (b) Where the wives, finding the marriage unbearable have left their husbands, who, in order to avoid paying the deferred Mehr, refuse to divorce them; (c) Wives who, because of economic dependence, acquiesce in the second marriage; (d) Where a person of another religious persuasion deliberately adopts Islam to contract a marriage which could not be permitted under his own system of law.

The adoption of monogamy as a rule among the Hindus under the Hindu Marriage Act, 1955 has been criticised and an opinion has been expressed in favour of "carefully regulated bigamy." According to Derret (1970): It is a serious question whether the sympathy which the public and courts seem to harbour for bigamous unions has no solid basis which we ought to recognise. It is argued that a carefully regulated bigamy i.e. popular marriages in cases of infertility, mental instability of the wife , and other cases where the good sense and humanity of the husband and his family recoils from divorcing her or annulling the marriage would not only be in accord with traditional Hindu religious sentiment and practice, but also much more realistic. It would savour less of "shop-window-dressing" with which the Hindu Code is charged. There is a small part of India which at present has controlled bigamy for Hindu husbands, namely the former Portuguese India (Goa, Daman, & Diu)... This appears to work extremely well, and the parliament has had the good sense not to interfere with the modified Hindu Law still in force in those territories... Moreover, it was the opinion of Mahamahopadhyaya Dr. RV Kane, that polygamy should be tolerated for some classes on purely economic grounds... It is the health and happiness of Hindus that counts, and the rash abolition of polygamy in a euphoric moment is not working out satisfactorily

As this view gives a misleading impression of being in the interests of women and as it is likely to be advanced in the context of Muslim Law also, it needs to be rebutted in full. We are not aware of a sympathy for bigamous unions or an opinion in favour of them in the absence of a systematic survey. A survey made some years ago showed 85 per cent of the men and 96 per cent of the women to be in favour of compulsory monogamy. While judicial decisions have rendered difficult, the enforcement of the penal provision against bigamy in Section 17 of the Hindu Marriage Act, 1955, it would only be fair to say that this stemmed not from a sentiment in favour of bigamy, but from a deep seated judicial attitude that penal provisions should be construed strictly. The economic grounds, in our considered view, equate women with beasts of burden and cannot be accepted. It is doubtful whether the advocates of controlled bigamy will also favour controlled polyandry as a general rule on the same grounds.

Long before the passing of the Hindu Marriage Act, monogamy in preference to controlled bigamy existed under the Marumakattayarn

Law in the State of Travancore-Cochin and in the Malabar District of the Madras province. It was introduced in the province of Bombay in 1946 and in the province of Madras in 1949.

We are of the firm view that there can be no compromise on the basic policy of monogamy being the rule for all communities in India. Any compromise in this regard will only perpetuate the existing inequalities in the status of women.

While bigamy has been made an offence and the second marriage should be void, bigamous marriages are still prevalent among Hindus. Apart from the figures available in many of the states, a large number of such marriages exist. In Manipur, even though the women were very bitter about the wide prevalence of this practice, they were compelled to accept it as divorce or prosecution of the husband resulted in social ostracism.

The Government had failed to enforce the law. Even Government servants, who are forbidden under the Government Servants' Conduct Rules, were practising polygamy. The Committee was also informed that a Resolution in the Legislative Assembly calling upon the Government to enforce the law had been defeated by an overwhelming majority. It is interesting to note that most women of Manipur earn to support their families. In spite of their economic independence, they have been unable to assert their social and legal rights. Quite a few of them were living with their co-wives, some had separate establishments, but all of them contributed a part of their incomes to their husbands. Little social stigma seemed to be attached to such a situation.

In West Bengal, a training centre in Sriniketan for promoting self-employment had a number of women discarded by their husbands who had married a second time. We met two co-wives, whose husbands discarded them for a third wife taking the training. Similar cases were brought to our notice in some parts of Andhra Pradesh, Bihar, Uttar Pradesh and in the rural areas of Madhya Pradesh.

Under the present law, only an aggrieved person can initiate proceedings for bigamy, which means the husband or the wife. In the case of the wife, the complaint may be made on her behalf by one of her family members. Quite often an economically dependent woman who is also uneducated has neither the knowledge nor the means to go to court. Many of them are reluctant to appear in court and face social ostracism as brought our very clearly by justice Sachar: We also cannot shut our eyes to the practical difficulties and problems faccd by an Indian girl... Instances are numerous where Indian women have gone through a literal misery of marriage for years rather than go to a court of law and expose themselves to public gaze. The attitude of the parents and relations in most of these cases is also unsympathetic.

Where social customs prevent a woman from appearing in public, the law permits some other person to make the complaint with the permission of the court. The question to be considered is whether the right to initiate prosecution for bigamy should be extended to persons other than the girl's family in all cases, in view of the general reluctance of her family members to lodge a complaint against the son-in-law or brother-in-law. The necessity of obtaining prior permission of the Court would provide adequate safeguard against undue harassment. In small towns and villages a social worker could fulfil this role admirably.

In our opinion such a provision is necessary to prevent the current widespread violation of a most salutary provision of the law which very clearly lays down the social policy of the country.

The existing penal provision against bigamy is further defeated in a considerable number of cases because of a technical construction placed on Section 17 of the Act. The Supreme Court in Bhaurao vs. State of Maharashtra held that the offence of bigamy was not proved unless it was established that the second marriage was celebrated with proper ceremonies and due form. This conclusion was arrived at on the basis that the section used the word 'solemnized'. They observe: The word 'solemnize' means, in connection with a marriage, 'to celebrate the marriage with proper ceremonies and due form' according to the Shorter Oxford Dictionary. It follows, therefore, that unless the marriage is 'celebrated' or performed with proper ceremonies and due form, it cannot be said to be 'solemnized'. It is therefore essential, for the purpose of Sec. 17 of the Act, that the marriage to which Sec. 494, I.P.C. applies on account of the provisions of the Act, should have been celebrated with proper ceremonies and due form.

As the law requires no specific ceremonies of marriage according to custom, it becomes extremely difficult to determine which ceremony or ceremonies were really essential. Whether the construction put by the court will subserve the policy and purpose of the Act, or the social objectives of the legislation was never in their contemplation.

The result of this interpretation is that a difficult burden is cast on the prosecution to show that the second marriage is performed with all due formalities. This burden in many cases cannot be discharged owing to the fact that second marriages during the subsistence of a prior marriage, are seldom performed with the usual pomp and show.

Even if it is not so, this judicial interpretation facilitates widespread evasion of law. As pointed out by Professor Derrett, the existing position will give rise to two types of devices being followed to evade prosecution for bigamy. First, a person intending to take a second wife, may deliberately undergo a defective form of marriage, to defend himself against a prosecution launched by the first wife or her relatives. Second, the relatives and friends of the second wife may commit perjury and say that the marriage is not properly solemnized and the first wife or her relatives would not be in a position to rebut it.

Shri M.B. Majumdar suggested that the words "solemnized" may be replaced by the words "contracted". But given the contemporary judicial attitudes, inherited from the English legal system, whereby the policy and purpose of an Act often are sacrificed to a literal construction of the Act, it is doubtful whether the suggested amendment will change the situation materially.

We recommend that words "solemnized" should be replaced by the word "goes through a marriage." Further, an explanation should be added to the section that an omission to perform some of the essential ceremonies by parties shall not be construed to mean that the offence of bigamy was not committed, if such a ceremony of marriages gives rise to a de facto relationship of husband and wife.

As already mentioned there is often an inhibition against prosecuting a husband for his second marriage in the present social context. The easier remedy is to prevent such a marriage taking place, if there is prior knowledge of its impending celebration. The following two cases will show that though bigamy, including the attempt and abetment of it is an offence, the position is not as clearcut as we would like it to be.

In Sankarappa vs. Basamma, the Mysore High Court held that the Hindu wife is entitled to a perpetual injunction restraining her husband from contracting a second marriage; that the suit is clearly permitted by Section 54 of the Specific Relief Act, 1877 (Sec. 38 of the Specific Relief Act, 1963).

On the other hand, a Division Bench of the Patna High Court in Uma Prasad Singh vs. Smt Radha Devi takes the view that a remedy by way of injunction against a second marriage is not available under the provisions of the Hindu Marriage Act.

The case seems to have been argued only on the basis of the Hindu Marriage Act, 1955 and the question of remedy under the Specific Relief Act, 1963 was not referred to by the parties or by the court. The only point for consideration is... Where the suit as framed and filed by opposite party 1 could be maintained under any provision of the Hindu Marriage Act, 1955.

Though the two cases can be clearly distinguished and there is no real conflict, it is desirable to clarify the matter. We recommend that a provision be introduced in Section 6 of the Hindu Marriage Act to the effect that nothing contained in the Hindu Marriage Act shall prevent a court from granting an injunction against a proposed bigamous marriage under the Act or under the provisions of the Specific Relief Act, 1963.

Another major social evil, sought to be curbed by legislation is child marriage. The disastrous effects of such marriages have been discussed already. One of the few areas where our social reformers had taken the initiative, even in the 19th century, was to curb this evil by legislation. The first legislation was the Civil Marriage Act which laid down the age of marriage to be 14 years. But as only a very small section of the people married under this Act, the problem continued.

One of the adverse consequences of child marriage, as realized by the reformers, was early consummation, with disastrous effect on the health of the young wives and their children. An effort was made in 1891 to prevent early consummation by the Age of Consent Act which prohibited consummation before 12 years. Due to lack of publicity and propaganda there was no impact of this provision. In 1925, the Age of Consent was raised to 13. This was the forerunner of the Sarda Act of 1929.

It was realized that legislation, while one of the major instruments of social change, is not sufficient by itself to fight against deep-rooted prejudices and traditional practice. Thus, the legislators compromise this by leaving the validity of child marriage untouched by making such practice a penal offence. Parents of children, those 'Performing, conducting or directing' as also the adult bridegroom, were all liable to punishment in varying degrees. The Act was further amended leaving untouched the structure of the earlier Act. The impact of this legislation and the present position regarding child marriage have been discussed already.

Apart from the Sarda Act, the various personal laws have their own minimum age of marriage. Not only do they vary in regard to the minimum age, but also in the consequences of violation of the law.

The Hindu Marriage Act, 1955 lays down as one of the conditions, the completion of 18 years and 15 years by the bridegroom and the bride respectively. Though passed in the post-independence era, the Act remains silent about the effect on the validity of the marriage and continues the earlier penal policy in cases of violation. Most writers hold the view that the validity on the marriage is not affected and this is also supported by judicial decisions.

The Parsee Marriage and Divorce Act 1936 on the other hand, lays down that no suit shall be brought to enforce a marriage between two Parsees or any contract connected with the marriage, if at the date of the institution of the suit the husband has not completed the age of 16 years and the wife 14 years. The Christian Marriage Act, 1872 provides that for a valid marriage under the Act, the age of the male shall exceed 16 years and that of the female 13 years. For a valid marriage under the classical Muslim law the parties should not be minors, that is, the parties should have attained puberty. Puberty is presumed in the absence of evidence to the contrary, at 15 and 19 in the case of girls and boys respectively.

Only the Special Marriage Act, 1954, a post-independence

legislation which provides for a secular marriage irrespective of the religious affiliation of the parties, contemplates the solemnization of marriage between adults under this provisions, as it fixes the minimum age at 21 and 18 for males and females respectively.

The legal position noted above brings forth an important feature, namely, a lesser age of marriage is prescribed in the case of girls. No doubt, throughout the world, the laws generally provide for a lesser age in case of girls. For example, in the USA only eleven States prescribed the same minimum age for boys and girls. The remaining thirty-nine states permit girls to be married at a lower age than boys. As pointed out by Konowitz : "It (early marriage for women) can lead to premature removal from socially productive enterprise or lost opportunities."

When the legal age of marriage in case of a female is below the age of discretion, she cannot be expected to form an intelligent opinion about her partner in life. The policy of law which permits the marriage of a girl before she is physically and mentally mature, is open to serious question. As reported by the Pushpaben Committee, child marriage is one of the significant factors leading to the high incidence of suicide among young married women in India. Therefore, increasing the marriage age of girls to eighteen years is desirable.

In this context, it is necessary to point out an anachronism that exists in the Muslim law that governs some sects. After attaining puberty, a Muslim male in all sects and a Muslim female belonging to the Hanafi and Ithana Ashari Shirte sects can marry without a guardian. But a Maliki, Shafi, or Daudi or Salaymani Bohra virgin cannot marry without a guardian and her only remedy is to change over to the Hanafi School and marry according to its tenets.

In two recent decisions, viz. Muhammad Haji Kammu vs. Ethiyumma and K Abubukker vs. Marakkar, The Kerala High Court struck a different note which mitigates this hardship. The parties in both cases were Shafis. In Abubukker's case, the mother who was divorced, sought the consent of her ex-husband to the daughters, marriage which he refused. On the marriage being solemnized, the father filed a suit for a declaration that the marriage was invalid as his consent was not obtained. The lower court declared the marriage to be invalid even though the girl was already pregnant. Reversing the decision of the lower court, justice Pillai stated that under the Maliki and Shafi law the marriage of an adult girl is not valid unless her consent is obtained, and communicated through a legally authorised *wah* (guardian). As the father refused his consent, she could constitute any other relation or Kazi (in this case the Kazi) to act as her agent.

In our opinion a change in the law to remove the existing disability in these sub-schools and to bring them in conformity with the Hanafi law is necessary.

As mentioned earlier the policy of the Child Marriage Restraint Act or other statutes is not to invalidate child marriages, but to punish their solemnization. The offences under the Act are, however, non-cognizable, and no woman is punishable with imprisonment.

There are large-scale violations of the Act particularly in the rural areas. The non-cognizable character of the offence is a serious hindrance to the effective enforcement of this law. The State of Gujarat amended the Child Marriage Restraint Act by making it a cognizable offence. Provisions have also been made for the appointment of a Child Marriage Prevention Officer. These changes have been welcomed by the Pushpaben Committee.

We recommend that all offences under the Child Marriage Restraint Act should be made cognizable, and special officers appointed to enforce the law.

Another effective approach to this problem is to render such marriages void. But in the present social and economic conditions, such rigorous measures may create more problems than it seeks to solve. We suggest, therefore, that it should be envisaged as a future goal.

As immediate measures to deter child marriages and to alleviate their consequences we suggest the following: (a) to provide the girl the right to repudiate the marriage on attaining majority on lines similar to the "option of puberty" under Muslim Law; Note: A Muslim girl married during her minority is entitled to a dissolution of marriage if the following facts are established: (i) that she was given in marriage by her father or other guardian before she attained the age of 15; (ii) that she repudiated the marriage before she attained the age of 18; (iii) that the marriage was not consummated.

In our view the right to repudiate the marriage on attaining majority should be made available to girls in all communities whether the marriage was consummated or not. (b) A general legal provision analogous to Section 38 of the Parsee Marriage and Divorce Act, 1865 which provides that "no suit shall be brought in any court to enforce any marriage between Parsees, or any connected with or arising out of any such marriage, if, at the date of institution of the suit, the husband shall not have completed the age of 16 years, or the wife shall not have completed the age of 14 years." Under the Egyptian Civil Code, a marriage in contravention of the rule relating to age of the parties (completion of 18 years and 15 years in case of males and females respectively) though not invalid per se will not be registered. Under Article 99 of the Code such a marriage will not be recognized by the Court for the purpose of granting any relief, except a claim relating to legitimacy of issues.

We recommend legislation prohibiting courts from granting any relief in respect of a marriage solemnized in violation of the age requirements prescribed by law, unless both the parties have completed the age of 18 years.

Compulsory registration of marriage operates as an effective check on child and bigamous marriages, and also offers reliable proof of marriage. It ensures the legitimacy and inheritance rights of children. Section 8 of the Hindu Marriage Act, 1955, enables the State Governments to provide for compulsory registration of marriages and any person contravening the rule may be punished with a fine which may extend to twenty-five rupees. However, it has been stated that failure to register a marriage will not affect its validity. Laws which provide for the voluntary registration of Muslim marriages are in force in the States of Assam, Bihar, Orissa and Bengal.

Among the Parsees and Indian Christians, the registration of marriages is compulsory. Registration is also compulsory for marriages solemnized under the Special Marriages Act, 1954. Section 16 of this Act permits voluntary registration of marriages celebrated under other laws. The ultimate object should be to recognize registration as the sole and conclusive proof of marriage, irrespective of the religious rites under -which it was solemnized. It may be mentioned here that India has neither signed nor ratified the United Nations Convention on Consent to Marriage, Minimum Age for Marriage and Registration of Marriage. Explaining the position of India on ratification, the Indian delegate stated "the Convention would impose an obligation to introduce legislation, and since that might not be feasible at the present time, he must reserve his Government's position on the question of ratification."

We regret that for over a decade no attempt has been made to introduce legislation to implement the objects of the UN Convention. This attitude indicates a casualness and lack of concern of matters affecting the status of women. We recommend that registration should be made compulsory for all marriages. We have a clear precedent for a uniform measure in the Registration of Births and Deaths Act.

The dimension and ramifications of the dowry system in its present form have been discussed in the previous Chapter.

We are compelled to record our finding that the Dowry Prohibition Act 1961, passed with the ostensible purpose of curbing this evil, if not of eradicating it, has signally failed to achieve its purpose. In spite of the rapid growth of this practice, there are practically no cases reported under the Act. During its tours of all the States, the Committee was informed of only one case that was pending before the court in Kerala, in which the father had filed the complaint only because of the ill-treatment meted out to his daughter.

During the debate on the Dowry Prohibition Bill, one MP observed. "But I feel the whole problem will be solved - very easily and more quickly, not by legislation, but by rousing social conscience. As soon as our women get economic opportunities and economic freedom, as soon as avenues of employment and other opportunities are opened to them, as soon as they become independent of their families, possibly there would not be any occasion for this law to operate."

The eradication of this evil by rousing social conscience is seemingly an attractive approach. The Committee's findings, however, indicate that there is hardly any evidence of social conscience in the country today. In Indore, at a fairly large meeting, the Committee was told of the case of a girl who was burnt in the legs and in the back by her in-laws as she had not brought an adequate dowry. The acceptance of this situation was indicative of society's indifference to this social evil. No one at the meeting mentioned the need to report the case to the police or even of socially boycotting the family. Many such cases were brought to our notice, but nowhere did we hear of any social censure being exercised.

An increase in economic freedom and job opportunities for women, to the extent that the practice of dowry becomes obsolete, under the existing economic conditions, will be a very long process. The educated youth is grossly insensitive to the evil and unashamedly contributes to its perpetuation. In our opinion, therefore, a stringent enforcement of the policy and purpose of the Act may serve to educate public opinion better.

A very small but significant step could be taken by the Government, by declaring the taking or giving of dowry to be against the Government Servants Conduct Rules. Such a lead was given earlier to prevent bigamous marriages and giving or taking of dowry should be similarly dealt with.

The major cause for the failure of the Dowry Prohibition Act, 1961 is that an infringement of the provisions of the Act is not made a cognizable offence. That the offences under the Act should be made cognizable was in fact suggested during the debate in Lok Sabha.

But the offence was not made cognizable, as it was apprehended that this might result in the harassment of citizens by the police and lead also to undue invasion of the individual's right of privacy.

In fact, the policy of making the offence noncognizable completely nullifies the purpose of the Act as it is unrealistic to think that the father of a girl who had paid the dowry (and who alone is in a position to produce evidence of the fact that dowry was stipulated and given) would prefer a complaint against the interests of his daughter after her marriage.

The offences, under the Act, should be made cognizable. We are fortified in our conclusion by the recommendation of the Pushpaben Committee, to overcome the fears regarding harassment by the police and encroachment on the right of privacy. It is suggested that the enforcement of social laws like the Dowry Prohibition Act, the Child Marriage Restraint Act, should be entrusted to a separate administration with which social workers and enlightened members of the community should be associated.

In addition, two ancillary provisions should be incorporated in the Dowry Prohibition Act, 1961. It has been pointed out that one of the 'major loopholes' in the existing legislation is that anything is allowed in the name of gifts and presents.

Therefore, any gifts made to the bridegroom or his parents in excess of Rs. 500 or which can be so used as to reduce his own financial liability should be made punishable.

The practice of displaying the dowry by parents of the bride or the bridegroom, as discussed earlier, is prevalent in some parts of India. This naturally tends to perpetuate the practice as others follow suit.

In order to make it more effective, an evaluation of the impact of the amended Dowry Prohibition Act should be made after every five years. It will help in plugging loopholes which facilitate the evasion of this law. The next step should be to set a ceiling even on the gifts that may be made to the bride. This will help to improve the situation further because it has been found that gifts given to the bride are often only a guise for dowry since generally she has little or no control over them, once she entered her inlaws' house.

FIVE

Education for Social Change

Needless to say that women constitute almost half of the human race. Education has been recognized as an essential agent of social change and development in any society. Hence to think of harmonious development without educating women is an impossibility. Moreover it has been rightly said that to educate a woman is to educate the whole family.

Therefore, the emphasis with regard to women's education should be to equip her for the multiple roles as citizens, housewives, mothers, contributors to family income and builders of the new society.

In realisation of the importance of education, in general, and the need for equality in opportunities for the intellectual development of men and women, successive Five-Year Plans have consistently placed special emphasis on the acceleration of women's education. The emphasis with regard to women's education has all along been to equip her for the multiple roles as citizens, housewives, mothers, contributors to family income and builders of the new decades of planned development — to enrol more girls in schools; to encourage girls to stay in schools; to continue their education as long as possible; and to provide non-formal educational opportunities for women. The Draft Fifth Five-Year Plan has declared that the outlays for the education of girls will be stepped up. The fulfilment of the constitutional directive in respect of providing free and compulsory education up to the age of 24 years has been included as one of the components of the Minimum Needs Programme.

These efforts have had a significant impact on the progress of women's education in India. For example, there is a primary school within easy walking distance from the home of almost all the children.

This has resulted in an increase in the enrolment of girls in classes I-V as a percentage of total enrolment in these classes from 28.1 in 1950-51 to 37.6 in 1973-74. In respect of classes I-VIII, IX-X/XII and university education also there has been an appreciable increase in the percentage of girls' enrolment to total enrolment, between the years 1950-51 and 1973-74. In fact, girls' enrolment is observed to be growing at a faster rate than those of boys.

Despite these encouraging trends and marked progress made in respect of women's education, the education status of women is still far from satisfactory for the following reasons: (a) Literacy among women is generally lower than that among men. According to the 1971 Census data, only 13.4 per cent of women in this age group of 25+ are literate. (b) Enrolment of girls in classes I to V is only 66.4 per cent of girls in the corresponding age group, i.e., 6 to 11 years; while in respect of boys the relevant percentage is 100.2 (c) Drop-out rate is also very high in classes I to V. A recent study has shown that the drop-out rate especially accentuated in the case of girls from rural areas and from the less privileged sections of society, is as heavy as 42.85 per cent between classes I and II. (d) In classes VI to VIII, percentages of enrolment of girls and boys to the total girls and boys in the relevant age group (i.e. 11 to 14 years) are 22.2 and 48.3 respectively. (e) At the secondary stage, i.e., classes IX to XI/XII girls enrolled constitute only 12 per cent of girls in the relevant age group 14 to 17 years as against 31 per cent in respect of the enrolment of boys in this age group. (f) Enrolment of girls in Post-Matric classes constitutes only 2.3 per cent of girls in the concerned age group 17 to 23 years; while the enrolment percentage of boys in this age group is 7.5.

Girls and women in India have thus not been able to take full advantage of the available opportunities/facilities for intellectual development. This is mainly because of several social and cultural factors in addition to various other reasons. Action plans and strategies for women's education should, therefore, aim at neutralizing the effects of the factors which have retarded the progress of women's education in India. With a view to facilitating the formulation of such a plan of action, in what follows, some of the major reasons which have operated against girls/women in taking full advantage of educational opportunities /facilities, are listed below: (a) General indifference to education of girls. (b) Social resistance arising out of fears and misconceptions that education might alienate girls from traditions and social values and lead to maladjustments, conflicts and non-conformism. (c) Early marriage and social inhibitions against girls pursuing education after marriage. (d) Prevalence of child labour among girls belonging to weaker sections and the hard domestic chores which some of the unmarried girls, even in the middle-class families are required to perform. (e) The prevailing notion that the sole occupation of women is to bear children, look after her husband and children, and thus be restricted to domestic work.

Promotional and Motivational Measures

(i) School timings should be flexible, as many of the girls in this age group are required to help their mothers in routine domestic chores. (ii) Adoption of multiple entry and part-time courses are recommended. (iii) Incentives like mid-day meals, scholarships, free school uniforms, free books and study materials, stipends, awards, etc., should be extended to all girls in the rural areas and slums in the urban areas. (iv) For school drop-outs of girls, pre-vocational training programmes should be organized on an extensive scale to cover all girls in the rural areas and in the slums of urban areas. The objectives of such training should be to render them self-sufficient in home management, and help them to achieve economic independence. With this in view, such training programmes should include courses in sewing, knitting, cooking, nutrition, minor repairs of the house, motherhood, child care, etc. (v) For the non-student girls in this age group, the objective should be to provide adequate preparation in life through a combined three-year course in general education and vocational training. Vocational training should be on the lines of pre-vocational training mentioned above. (vi) Such training programmes should be extended to all girls in the rural areas. In the urban areas, preference should be given to girls in slum areas and destitute girls.

Administrative and Structural Measures: (i) Separate girls' schools or separate sections should be started where the social/ cultural environment demands them. (ii) In co-educational schools special attention should be given to the provision of adequate toilet, rest and recreation facilities, separately for girls. (iii) State Governments which have not yet made high school education free for girls should do so on a priority basis. (iv) Multiple entry system and part-time education may be provided. (v) All courses of training in vocational and technical schools at the secondary stage should be open to both boys and girls. There should be no discrimination in this regard. (vi) Liberal incentives in the form of book allowances, book-bank facilities, etc., should be extended to encourage more girls in rural areas and backward areas to pursue secondary education. (vii) Separate hostel facilities should be provided particularly in rural areas and residential scholarships should be offered. (viii) The curriculum should be more diversified taking into consideration the various occupational opportunities available to women and the interests and aptitudes of girls.

Alternative Measures: (i) Condensed courses of education started in 1958 were found very useful. Under this scheme women in the age group 13-30 years who have had some schooling are prepared for middle school, matriculation or equivalent examination within a period of 2 year duration. The minimum age limit here should be reduced to 15 years. This scheme should be extended to cover all rural areas and weaker sections of the urban community. (ii) The condensed courses should be organized for smaller groups, say 5 to 7 persons, using the community resources like girls' high schools and girls' colleges. (iii) Apart from imparting general education, condensed courses should also aim at imparting job-oriented training with the active cooperation of existing vocational training institutions. (iv) Correspondence courses and self-study programmes may be introduced. (v) Efforts should be made to cover at least about 215 lakh of girls in the age group 15-30 under the condensed courses programme during the Fifth Plan period. (vi) Fourth Plan introduced a programme of functional literacy with the objective of imparting elementary general education and vocational training related to the functions performed by men and women in the rural areas who never attended schools. This programme should be expanded to cover all rural areas. (vii) Apart from imparting general elementary education and knowledge about farming techniques, the curriculum for women should include courses of training in occupational skills like kitchen, gardening, food processing, poultry keeping, animal husbandry, household arts like cooking, nutritional values of foods, locally available, sewing, knitting, etc., and motherhood, childcare and family planning as also electronics and such like fields. (viii) Similar programmes should also be designed for girls in this age group and under this category, belonging to urban areas.

(a) Education for Girls at the Higher Education Stage: Action plans in this area should aim at: (a) making higher education available to the less privileged sections of the society, particularly girls from the rural areas; and (b) making the curriculum more relevant and responsive to the cultural and occupational needs of women.

The following action plans may be taken up for consideration:

Administrative and Structural Measures: (i) The general policy here should be to discourage separate institutions for women and to promote co-educational facilities. However, in areas where separate institutions are required to promote education of women, they may be permitted on the merits of such cases. (ii) Vocational counselling and guidance services should be organized in a more meaningful way to help girls - in colleges and universities, opt for suitable courses relevant to their talent, interests and needs. (iii) Incentives like scholarships, freeships, etc., should be provided to enable girls from rural areas to pursue higher education. (iv) For girls belonging to weaker sections, in addition to freeships and scholarships, bursaries should also be provided-to meet their expenses on food and lodging. (v) Provision of self-cooking facilities in hostels for girls should also be considered. (vi) Girls pursuing higher education should be provided easy access to text books and other reference material through book bank facilities. (vii) Girls should be encouraged to enter professional courses. If necessary, reservation of seats for girls in professional courses may be considered. (viii) Diversification of courses at the junior college level and undergraduate level should be undertaken on a priority basis, with a view to preparing the girls for the various employment opportunities open to them.

(b) Education for Girls Drop-outs

Girls in this age group drop-out of educational system for various reasons. Marriage is one of the reasons which force girls in this age group to discontinue further formal education. Economic hardship is another reason which forces some girls to drop out and seek jobs, with a view to supporting their families. Social prejudices and cultural attitudes also force some of the girls to leave the formal educational system. For girls in this category, therefore, the policy should be to extend non-formal educational facilities on a large scale.

The following actions are suggested: (i) Facilities for part-time self-study and correspondence courses should be expanded on a large scale to enable working girls and non-working, married and unmarried girls to enhance their educational qualifications. (ii) In addition to courses leading to degree/diploma, short courses in specific subjects through summer schools/session, ad-hoc programmes like seminars, laboratory work, workshop experience, etc., should be organized for working girls, with a view to upgrading their professional skills and qualifications. Facilities for further education not necessarily leading to a degree, but for upgradation of knowledge and skills could be provided. (iii) While the initiative for organizing such programmes should be taken by the Central and State Governments, the employees should also be increasingly involved. (iv) Pre-examination training facilities should be organized on a large scale for educated women from the rural areas and those belonging to weaker sections with the objective of equipping them to successfully compete in examination for public jobs. (v) Entrepreneurship development programmes should be organized separately for educated women in the age group 18-30 years with a minimum of matriculation level of education.

The objective of such training programmes should be: (a) to make them aware of the various opportunities for self-employment; (b) to motivate them to take up self-employment; (c) to impart needed skills/ training; and (d) to promote achievement motivating among them.

Effective Set-up Required

To make various action plans successful and to achieve a real breakthrough in women's education, there is need for a matching and effective administrative set-up, both at the Central and State levels.

With this in view, the following suggestions are made: (i) In the Union Ministry of Education and Social Welfare, a special unit/cell may be set up to be in charge of women's education, to review and initiate follow-up action. (ii) In each State education department, a senior officer should be placed in charge of girls' education in order that it may receive adequate emphasis, execution and coordination. (iii) As the district is the operational unit for all educational programmes and as the needs of girls vary in extent and kind from area to area, within a district, a separate cell for girls' education, formal and non-formal may be created within the purview of the district educational officer at the district headquarters. (iv) School supervisory system should be staffed with more women. (v) A suitable machinery may be set up at the Centre and the States to help in the formulation of plans for women's education - formal and non-formal - to monitor, coordinate and evaluate progress of women's education from time to time, to create public opinion in favour of women's education, etc.

Value of Education

Emphasis on different arguments justifying the value and necessity of education from the point of view of the individual as well as society has varied according to the historical needs of any society in different stages of its evolution. The first argument regards education as a value in itself, since it develops the personality and the rationality of individuals. The assumption here is that society, recognizing the innate value of rationality and learning, accords a high status to the educated. The second argument emphasizes the usefulness of educated persons to society at large. Their knowledge, by serving a social purpose, raises their status in society. From the point of view of the individual, education provides the necessary qualification to fulfil certain economic, political and cultural functions and consequently improves his socio-economic status.

With the recognition of the need to direct the process of social change and development towards certain desired goals, education has come to be increasingly regarded as a major instrument of social change. According to the Education and National Development Report of the Indian Education Commission: The realization of the country's aspirations involves changes in the knowledge, skills, interests and values of the people as a whole. This is basic to every programme of social and economic betterment of which India stands in need .... If this 'change on a grand scale' is to be achieved without violent revolution (and even for that it would be necessary) there is one instrument, and one instrument only, that can be used: Education.

One of the expectations from this directed use of education is that it will bring about reduction of inequalities in society, on the assumption that education leads to equalization of status between individuals coming from hitherto unequal socio-economic strata of society. It was on this argument that the Universal Declaration of Human Rights included education as one of the basic rights of every human being. The Constitution of the UNESCO directs its effort to achieve 'the ideal of equality of educational opportunity without regard to race, sex or any distinctions, economic or social'.

The history of the movement for improving women's status all over the world shows emphasis from the beginning on education as the most significant instrument for changing women's subjugated position in society. Increase of educational facilities and opportunities, and the removal of traditional bars on entry of women to particular branches and levels of education, came to be supported by all champions of women's emancipation from the 19th century onwards. Social reformers in India, whether they were modernizing liberals or revivalists also emphasized the crucial importance of education of women to improve their status in society.

However, when we look into their justification for this departure from the tradition then prevalent in the country, we notice certain significant omissions. According to the reformers, the main purpose for educating women was not to make them more efficient and active units in the processes of socio-economic or political development, but to make them more capable of fulfilling their traditional roles in society as wives and mothers. The opposition of the orthodox conservatives was countered by the argument that women's education would strengthen the bonds of tradition and the family as the chief unit of social organization. In their view, the denial of education and early marriage prevented the development of the personality and rationality of women. Stunted and crippled personalities affected the harmony of the family atmosphere, weakening the bonds of the family. Education for women was regarded as a means to improve their status within the family, and not to equip them to play any role in the wider social context. The absence of any economic compulsion was, in fact, the main reason for the slow progress of women's education in this country.

Because of their reluctance to interfere in social matters, the colonial authorities generally supported this purely humanitarian and limited view of women's education. The problem of reaching education and health services to the women of this country led to a realization of the need for women teachers and doctors. Since this was impossible without training women in these professions the importance of these two vocations outside the familiar roles had to be incorporated in the programmes for women's education.

In the discussions on women's education in the post-independence era, a new dimension appeared due to the acceptance of equality of women and their need to play multiple roles in society. According to the First Five-Year Plan (1951): The general purpose and objective of women's education cannot, of course be different from the purpose and objective of men's education.... At the Secondary and even at the University stage women's education should have a vocational or occupational bias.

According to Report of the Secondary Education Commission, Government of India, 1953: In a democratic society where all citizens have to discharge their civic and social obligations, differences which may lead to variation in the standard of intellectual development achieved by boys and girls cannot be envisaged.

Report of the Committee on differentiation of Curricula for boys and girls: In the progressive society of tomorrow, life should be a joint venture for men and women. Men should share the responsibility of parenthood and home-making with women and women in their turn should share the social and economic responsibilities of men.

The emphasis on education equipping women to carry out their multiple roles as citizens, housewives, mothers, contributors to the family income and builders of the new society is consistent with the trend of discussions in international agencies on women's education as a basic ingredient for improvement of their status.

In spite of the growing recognition of importance of women's education, traces of the earlier view which supported it mainly as an equipment for their roles as wives and mothers without conceding any position of equality with men in other spheres of life, can still be found not only in the opinions of individuals, but even in the statements of official agencies. According to the Report of the University Education Commission (1949): Women's and men's education should have many elements in common but should not in general be identical in all respects, as is usually the case today. A woman should learn something of problems that are certain to come up in all marriages, and in the relations of parents and children, and how they may be met. Her education should make her familiar with problems of home management and skilled in meeting them, so that she may take her place in a home with the same interest and the same sense of competence that a well trained man has in working at his calling.

An understanding of this ambivalence between the traditional and the new attitudes on women's education is essential for examining the progress of women's education in this country, because it has an impact on academic planning, allocation of resources and development of values in society for both men and women. It lies at the root of all discussions regarding differentiation of curricula between the two sexes and continues to affect social attitudes regarding women's education, its social use and women's roles in society. This in turn has an impact on the class composition of women who are recipients of education. The achievements or the failures in the use of this instrument for transforming women's status have to be measured by these social indicators as well as quantitative ones like enrolment out-turn, number of institutions and teachers, literacy rates and total stock of educated women at different levels and in the light of the stated national objectives. According to the National Policy on Education (1967): The educational system must produce young men and women of character and ability committed to national service and development. Only then will education be able to play its vital role in promoting national progress, creating a sense of common citizenship and culture and strengthening national integration.

The Formal Education System

The Constitution of the Republic of India guarantees equality of opportunity to all citizens irrespective of race, sex, caste and communities and directs the States to "Endeavour to provide within a period of ten years from the commencement of this Constitution for free and compulsory education for all children until they complete the age of 14 years". The Indian Education Commission in its Report (1966) regretted the failure to achieve this target. It emphasized the crucial importance of fulfilling this directive in the coming decades. In view of the immense resources needed for this purpose, the Commission recommended phasing of this programme in the following manner: (i) by providing five years of effective education to all children by 1975-76 and seven years of such education by 1985-86; (ii) by making part-time education for about one year compulsory for all children in the age group 11-14, who have not completed the lower primary stage and are not attending schools. The aim, will be to make these children functionally literate and stop all further additions to the ranks of adult non-literates; and (iii) by efforts to liquidate adult illiteracy.

The following review will indicate that even the targets recommended by the Education Commission have not been achieved, particularly in the case of women. The enrolment targets set for the Third Plan by the National Committee on Women's Education (1959) were equal numbers with boys in the age group 6-11, at least half that of the boys in the age group 11-14 and least one-third that of boys in the age group 14-17. Statistics reveal that the targets for the age groups 6-11 and 11-14 have not been reached even at the end of the Fourth Plan. The expected proportion of one-third in the age group 14-17 set for the Third Plan has however been exceeded slightly by the end of the Fourth Plan. The Fifth Five-Year Plan notes that in spite of substantial progress in the expansion of educational facilities, the targets laid down for both elementary and secondary education registered a shortfall in enrolment, while those in higher education were exceeded. But shortfalls have been particularly large in the case of elementary education, more so in the case of girls.

Educational experts now admit that the delay in the achievement of the Constitutional directive is mainly due to the slow progress of education among girls, Scheduled Castes and Scheduled Tribes. The discrepancy in the progress of education between boys and girls may be seen in the marked difference in the percentage of boys and girls of the corresponding age groups enrolled in primary, middle and secondary schools.

The foundations of the formal system of education, sponsored and supported by the State, and divided into three well-defined stages (primary, secondary and university) and two main streams (general and vocational) were laid during the first half of the nineteenth century. It was created essentially for men with the ultimate objective of utilizing them as government servants. In the initial years girls had little or no access to it, partly because society at that time could not imagine them as government servants. However, as the formal system of education began to spread, the role of education as a liberating influence came to be recognized and increasingly accepted. Thus began the advocacy of the access of girls and women to the formal system of education spearheaded by national leaders, missionaries and a few enlightened officials. It received little response. Only a few thousand girls, mostly belonging to urban upper and middle-class families entered, the formal system of education between 1850 and 1870. As women teachers became available and social forces like: a rise in the age of marriage, urbanization and the demand for educated wives began to gather momentum during the last hundred years, this movement steadily grew and today the total enrolment of girls in the formal system of education at all stages and in all streams, is more than thirty-two million.

The movement naturally began in the cities, and then spread to the towns and villages. It began among the Christians, Anglo-Indians, Parsees and upper caste Hindus. Wealth played an ambivalent role; while middle-class families were generally more favourable to the education of girls, some of the richer and more aristocratic families. remained aloof and do so even today.

The mass awakening during the freedom movement, and the role that women played in the struggle had a great impact on women's education, and it began to increase at a much faster pace. In 1854, the total enrolment of girls in the formal system was only about 1,97,000 all in primary schools. But over the following nine decades, it grew significantly.

The expansion of women's education began at the primary stage and was mostly confined to it for quite some years. In 1947, there were 83 per cent of all girls who were enrolled in primary schools (about half of them in class I only). Expansion at the secondary stage was slow to start and slow to spread. In 1947, only 7 per cent of the girls enrolled were in secondary school. However, contrary to what happened in Western countries, the admission of women to Indian universities presented no problem. Calcutta University permitted women candidates to appear for the Entrance and B.A. examination as early as 1877 and 1878 respectively. Bombay University followed in 1883. The first two women graduates of Calcutta received their degrees in 1883, the year of the University Silver Jubilee. Congratulating them and the University for 'this memorable event', the Vice Chancellor described it as a paving stone to "A general recognition of the right of the women of this country to education, and of the duty of the men of this country to provide it from them." Even with the removal of the ban, the spread of higher education among women remained slow. In 1947 the total enrolment in higher education was only about 23,000 which was 1/2 per cent of all girls enrolled in the educational system.

Since independence, the education of women at various levels has expanded more rapidly, but is still far from satisfactory.

During the year of independence, i.e., 1947-48, the total number of boys enrolled at various levels of the educational system was 1,11,34,665 while the girls were only 35,50,503 indicating an excess of 75,84,162 boys over girls.

Current Position: In classes I-V, the total enrolment is 244 lakh or 66 per cent of the total population in the age group 6-11. One girl out of every three is thus still out of school. What is worse, the drop-out rates are very high: of every 100 girls enrolled in class I, only about 30 reach class V. In classes VI-VIII, the total enrolment is 45.37 lakh or only 22 per cent of the total population in the age group 11-14. Only one girl out of 5 is at school in this age group. As universal education in the age group 6-14 is the national objective, it is obvious that considerable headway is still to be made in the expansion of education for the age group 6-11 and especially for the age group 11-14.

The enrolment of girls at the secondary stage at present is 23.4 lakh or 12 per cent of the total population in the age group 1417 (as against 31 per cent for boys). The proportion of girls enrolled now drops down to 1 in 8. Secondary education, even now, is largely confined to the upper and the middle classes, urban areas. In the rural areas, it mainly utilized well-to do families, particularly from the middle-classes.

At the university stage, the total enrolment in general education, i.e., in Sciences, Humanities and Social Science is about 9 lakh or about 1.3 per cent of the age group 17-23 (about 31 girls for every 100 boys enrolled). A stagewise analysis, however, shows that the proportion of women to men is higher at the postgraduate than at the undergraduate level and is showing a rapid increase. In professional education, women have substantial enrolments in teaching, medicine, and fine arts; but their enrolment in other courses like commerce, law, agriculture or engineering is still very small. Higher education is mostly confined, even more than secondary education, to urban upper and middle-classes.

The National Committee on Women's Education had reviewed the progress of women's education before, during and after independence and concluded that in spite of the direct action taken by the States for this purpose after independence, "the education of women has not made satisfactory progress between 1947 and 2000. Even today there is a very wide disparity between the education of men and that of women and only 36 girls are under instruction for every hundred boys at schools. The targets fixed for the First and Second Plans even tend to widen this disparity and the education of women has made very slow progress in rural areas where it is needed most."

The Committee had, therefore, strongly recommended "that the education of women should be regarded as a major and a special problem in education for a good many years to come and that a bold and determined effort be made to face its difficulties and magnitude and to close the existing gap between the education of men and women in as short a time as possible; that the highest priority should be given to schemes prepared from this point of view; and the funds required for the purpose should be considered to be the first charge on the sums set aside for the development of education." Following this recommendation, efforts to bridge the gap between boys and girls in education were stepped up from 1960. The growth rate of boys and girls enrolment at different levels in the next quinquennium again indicates slackening of the efforts.

It is to be noted that the rate of growth is much higher in the university and the vocational stages than in the primary and secondary stages. Interpreted in the context of Indian social conditions, this indicates that the expansion of women's education is much faster when the beneficiaries are from the urban middle class.

While educational statistics have always tended to use enrolments as the main indicator of measuring progress, in the Committee's experience this suffers from certain limitations. Since the quantum of grants for all educational institutions is linked to enrolment figures, there is an inevitable tendency to attach undue importance to mere enrolment. These statistics do not, however, indicate whether all children on a school register in fact attend school even for a short time. As observed by the Education Commission "the task of universal education begins when children are enrolled in Class I. It is completed only when they are successfully retained till they complete class VIII".

The problem of drop-outs of enrolled children as well as the problem of stagnation have contributed to the unreliability of enrolment statistics as a valid measure of progress.

The National Committee on Women's Education, while admitting that these were general problems of the educational system, had indicated that the extent of wastage or drop-outs was much higher in the case of girls. The all-India average of drop-outs at the primary stage was 74 per cent for girls while that of boys was 62.4 per cent. The Education Commission reporting in 1966 found wastage at the lower primary stage to be 56 per cent for boys and 62 per cent for girls, about two-thirds of this wastage occurring in class I. At the higher primary stage wastage was 24 per cent for boys and 34 per cent for girls. A study conducted by the NCERT on the problem of wastage and stagnation in primary and middle schools also corroborates this finding. (Sharma and Sapra, 1971): The differences between the rate of wastage and stagnation for boys (62.30%) and girls (71.36%) are highly significant. The rate for boys is 37.59% between grades I and II, 10.53% between grades I and III, 7.14%

between grades III and IV, and 7.04% between grades IV and V. For girls it is 42.85% between grades I and II, 12.12% between grades II and III, 8.51% between grades III and IV and 78.8% between grades IV and V. This indicates that except for grades I and II, the differences in the rates of wastages and stagnation for boys and girls in other grades are minor.

One of the causes for this large wastage in class I is the prevalent practice of enrolling children in class I throughout the year. In spite of repeated recommendations against this practice we regret to find it to be still prevalent in many States. For example, in Madhya Pradesh an enrolment drive was undertaken just 5 weeks before the end of the session.

The economic and educational causes of wastage and stagnation are well recognized. In case of girls, however, social factors like marriage, betrothal and parental apathy to girls education also play a major part. The National Committee on Women's Education has estimated that 25 to 30 per cent of cases of wastages among girls fell under this category. In our opinion the slow progress in enrolment and the high rate of dropouts and failures in the education of girls spring from the same reasons and ultimately affect the overall progress of women's education.

Turning from enrolment to the out turn of students from the schools and the university system we find that the progress is extremely slow. The significant features are the slower rate of increase in number of girls per 100 boys at the school final examinations, viz., Matriculation and Higher Secondary and the much faster rate of increase at the university stage, particularly in the first degree. This shows that the gap between men and women is narrowing more rapidly at the higher level than at the primary and secondary stages. Since higher education in India is still confined to a small minority of the population, the impact of this trend on the educational development of women as a whole cannot be described as high.

In professional education, the only courses open to women before independence were medicine, education, nursing and law. Since very few women sought training in law, professional education for them was in fact confined to the first three. Admission to engineering and technology courses was thrown open to women only in 1948. Considering this late start, their success in these courses has been significant. Their representation in other professional fields, however, remains very slow. Similarly, women's entry into research is mainly a post independence development and the progress at this level is satisfactory. The earlier widespread belief that girl's had less aptitude and even intelligence than boys for pursuit of studies, particularly in subjects like Mathematics or Science, has been completely disapproved by their success at various examinations. At the university level in particular, the performance of girls in all subjects including Science and Mathematics has often outstripped that of boys. A general opinion of faculty members is that the average girl student is more conscientious and disciplined than the average male student.

The National Committee on Women's education had felt that provision of separate institutions of girls would help to break down the prejudice against their education, and provide more impetus to the spread of education among women. There is no doubt that in the period since 1960-61 there has been an enormous expansion in the number of these exclusive institutions. In 1947-48, institutions meant exclusively for women constituted only 10.3 per cent by 1967-68 they formed 29 per cent of the total. Out of the total number of educational institutions established during this 20-year period, slightly more than half came up between 1960-61 and 1967-68. In the case of institutions exclusively meant for women, however, more than three-fourths of the increase took place between 1960-61 and 1967-68. The process continued later.

While we welcome the growth of institutional facilities for the spread of education among women, we would like to point out certain adverse features of this rapid growth that have been brought to our notice. At the primary level, a large number of these schools are single teacher institutions, with obvious limitations on their teaching capacity. One of the reasons mentioned to us for low enrolment and high drop-outs of girls was the wide prevalence of single teacher schools which frequently have to close due to the absence of the teacher. The problems become more acute when the teacher is on maternity leave, since provision of a substitute is tardy or absent.

At the middle and the secondary levels, there is frequent criticism of the low standard of teaching facilities, particularly for subjects like science and mathematics. The students' choice of subjects is very often determined, not by their aptitudes, but by institutional limitations.

At the college level the expansion has been most rapid, from, 81 women's colleges in 1953-54 to 435 in 1971-72. Of these 250 colleges, however, have an enrolment of less than 500 (55 have less than 100), this makes them non-viable from the point of view of resources, both financially and academically. By 2001, the colleges have increased manifold.

One of the results of the policy to encourage establishment of women's institutions has been relative lack of vigilance by the public and academic authorities regarding standards of these institutions. Eligibility conditions for recognition or for financial assistance through grants-in-aid have frequently been relaxed or waived altogether.

In our opinion the spread of substandard or limited education will not help the achievement of equality of opportunities, and may in the long run damage the cause of girls education. Vigilance regarding standards is imperative, particularly at the higher levels of the educational system and must form a part of the policy of encouragement and assistance.

The need to increase the number of women teachers as an essential condition for the development of women's education has been long recognized in India. In recent years, this has been emphasized even more by the National Committee, the National Council for Women's Education and the Education Commission who recommended adequate provision for their training and recruitment. The Education Commission recommended that the employment of women teachers should be encouraged in all stages and all sections of education. In order to achieve this, the Commission suggested provisions of the following: (a) opportunities for part-time employment on large scale; (b) residential accommodation particularly in rural areas; (c) special allowances for women teachers working in rural areas; (d) expansion of condensed courses for adult women and education through correspondence courses.

In 1947, 14.4 per cent of the school teachers in the country were women. In 1965-66, they formed 21.8 per cent. The proportion of women teachers at different levels has increased very slowly.

Even in the States like Haryana, Punjab, Tamil Nadu where almost all the villages have been electrified and are connected to the cities by pukka roads, women teachers are still reluctant to serve in rural areas. The problem becomes more acute in States like Uttar Pradesh, Bihar, Madhya Pradesh, Rajasthan, Himachal Pradesh and Jammu & Kashmir where the villages are often situated in remote and inaccessible areas.

There is no public conveyance available and very often the villages can only be reached on horse back, by bullock cart or on foot. Some of the basic problems identified by women teachers, in almost all the states that the committee visited, were like this: (a) Women teachers face a certain degree of resistance from their families to their working in rural areas, partly from the general apprehension against women working away from home, and partly from a fear of personal insecurity in villages. This has been aggravated by the deteriorating law and order situation in villages. There is also a fear that rural society may be unfriendly and even antagonistic to outsiders. We would, however, like to mention that in some states we were told that rural society had now come to accept and even respect women teachers and doctors. Most of these attitudes are shared by the teachers themselves. Added to them is another cause of resistance from the women, used to life in urban areas, the life in villages would be dull and unattractive. (b) Apart from these factors, the lack of physical amenities like modern medical facilities, proper accommodation, toilets, transport and schooling for children are real difficulties that deter women from service in rural areas. Even when houses are provided, they are often outside the village, without any consideration for the problems of distance and insecurity that women have to face. If they are within the school, the teachers cannot bring their families. The problem of accommodation becomes still more acute with married women, if they have to work away from their husbands and families.

These problems need to be solved on a priority basis in order to increase the supply of women teachers in rural schools. If this is not done, then the present imbalance in the development of women's education between urban and rural areas will increase. Added to this will be yet another imbalance, that of increasing unemployment among trained and qualified women teachers, whose reluctance to serve in rural areas prevents their employment. The beginnings of this imbalance are already noticeable in many States.

The system of inspection of schools varies from State to State. The general complaint however, is that schools are not inspected regularly. In Himachal Pradesh a retired school teacher informed us that during her 24 years service she had faced only three inspections. In some states like Uttar Pradesh and Bihar, village schools to be inspected once a year are only those which are within easy reach. In most States all inspections cease during the rainy season.

There is an overall inadequacy of women on the inspecting staff. Insufficient numbers and over-large jurisdictions contribute to the general inefficiency of inspections. For women in particular, the problems of distance, and inadequate arrangement for transport and night halts create added difficulties. This leads sometimes to a reluctance to serve on the inspecting staff, and in the States where the grade of inspectors is the same as that of headmistress of a high school (e.g. Punjab), women members of the service prefer to remain as headmistresses. In Himachal Pradesh, we found that there was no women on the inspecting staff.

States like Himachal Pradesh and Madhya Pradesh do not have a separate women's cadre of inspectors, and girls schools are often inspected by male inspectors. In the case of single-teachers schools, this sometimes creates a problem. We received some complaints from teachers of misbehaviour, blackmail or exploitation on the part of inspectors.

Social attitudes to the education of girls vary, ranging from acceptance of the need, to one of absolute indifference. The Committee's survey reveals some interesting trends. A statement that girls should not be given any education received a categorical rejection by 77.8 per cent of the respondents. A small minority (16.8 per cent) did, however, agree with the view. In the case of higher education, however, we find a surprisingly hostile attitude since over 64.50 per cent responded that a girl should not be allowed to go for higher education even if she is very intelligent.

In view of the constitutional directive regarding free and compulsory education up to the age of 14, we tried to elicit public opinion on the question of making education compulsory. In response to our general questionnaire, 77.5 per cent of the respondents, male and female supported compulsory education for up to the 8th class. A separate questionnaire issued to educationists and administrators regarding measures necessary to improve girls' enrolment in schools also evoked a substantial support in favour of compulsion.

In urban areas, by and large, the acceptance of the need of education for girls is greater than in rural areas. Among the affluent there are two distinct attitudes. Some families are opposed to it for traditional reasons while others have welcomed it as an accomplishment and a symbol of modernization. Among the middle-classes the acceptance is the highest. The attitude among the lower-middle-class is more difficult to generalize because today's lower-middle-class consists of white collared as well as manual workers. Though economically one, socially they are two distinct classes, their attitudes being determined much more by their social background rather than their economic position. While an increasingly large section, conscious of economic necessity, is prepared to make substantial sacrifices for girls' education, a very large number still finds itself unable to do so for economic and social reasons. For the majority of the people who live below subsistence level, poverty is the predominant factor governing the attitude to girls' education.

Reasons for the variations in social attitudes and the consequent slow progress of women's education are both social and economic. (a) Large majority of girls, by the time they reach the age of eight, are required to do various domestic chores, e.g., collecting firewood, coal waste, cow dung, fetching water, sometimes from long distances, washing, cleaning, cooking, reaching food and water to parents in their places of work, etc. (b) Majority of girls of this age group have to look after the siblings, especially when their mothers are engaged in earning a livelihood. (c) A substantial number of girls are engaged in contributing to the family income by their own labour. The prevalence of child labour has long been admitted as the greatest deterrent to the spread of education among children of the poor. The Committee was appalled by the extent and degree of use of young girls of five to fourteen working for twelve hours a day. One 12-year old girl in Andhra Pradesh informed us that she could not remember any other pattern of existence in her whole life. Similar is the case in fireworks, matches, weaving and many other industries, mostly in unorganized sector. A very large number of girls in this age group work as domestic servants - either as helpers or as independent earners. In Calcutta, we found one 12 year old supporting a family of six members by working in a number of houses as a part-time domestic servant. This was by no means an exceptional case. These girls are too exhausted at the end of their day's labour to attend evening classes even if they could be arranged. In the agricultural sector, girls in the same age group do share the burden of field labour, but mostly in the peak seasons. Their hours of work being less, it is possible for them to attend school, if facilities were available. The school term should be adjusted according to the seasonal agricultural activities. It should be noted that the exclusion from education because of participation in labour is higher among girls than boys, as they constitute a higher proportion of the unpaid family workers. According to the National Sample Survey (1960-67), the labour participation rates for boys and girls in the age group 10-19 is on the decline in urban areas. In rural areas a similar trend is evident in the case of boys, but for girls this decline is negligible. (d) Our Survey reveals several difficulties in the way of facilities for girls' education. Nearly 53 per cent of the respondents refer to shortage of schools in general, 57.65 per cent to absence of separate schools for girls in many places. 43.57 per cent to overcrowding in schools and 53.95 per cent to distance from house to school. While 39.41 per cent point to the absence of women teachers, 40.46 per cent do not regard this as a difficulty. Other difficulties brought to our notice are the lack of adequate transport arrangements and toilet facilities, as also the prevalence of single teacher schools. (e) The irrelevance of education as imparted in schools today has been discussed at length by the Education Commission. While endorsing their views, we would like to add that this has a particularly adverse effect on parental attitude to the education of girls, especially in rural areas. Parents who have not as yet accepted the utility of educating girls find in its irrelevance a justification for their apathy. Mothers of young girls told us that except for reading and writing, which the girls could pick up in two or three years, schools taught very little that was useful. One peasant woman in a Punjab village felt that one way of making school education more meaningful would be to train girls to handle and repair tractors. Some women in the Kulu Valley wanted training in methods of fruit preservation, so that they could fully utilize the products of their orchards. (f) Education in the rural areas often results in alienation of the girls from their habitat. While this criticism was voiced in many places, the most vocal opinion was expressed by women in the villages of Himachal Pradesh. Since the development of the State and the standard of living of its people depended on the continued efforts of women in agriculture, education in their opinion was becoming an adversary of progress. Girls who completed their formal education in the villages did not want to continue living in villages or take part in agricultural activities. The problem became more accrued when, owing to absence of secondary school in the villages, they had to study outside, in urban or semi-urban areas. Many of them found village life with its hardships intolerable afterwards. This was particularly brought to our notice in Nagaland and Himachal Pradesh. Most girls who complete secondary school develop a desire for white-collared jobs, or urban life in some form. (g) While early marriage or betrothal was undoubtedly the greatest deterrent to progress of girls' education in the past, it is much less so now. Our survey indicates that only 38.1 per cent of the respondents find early marriage a genuine difficulty for girls' education while 41.5 per cent do not agree with this view. The average age at marriage has been rising steadily from 15.4 between 1941-51 to 18 in 1961-71. The national average for 2001 is 20 in urban and 18 in rural areas. The percentage of unmarried girls in the age group 10-14 rose from 77.63 to 86.21 in rural areas and from 93.01 to 95.79 in urban areas between 1961 and 2001. For the age group 15-19 this percentage changed from 14.2 to 36.91 in rural areas and 29.4 to 63.76 in urban areas. When we turn to the admittedly educationally backward States, however, we find this to be still a problem. The average age at marriage for women during 1951-61 was 14.81 in Bihar and Orissa, 13.87 in Madhya Pradesh, 14.22 in Rajasthan and 14.43 in Uttar Pradesh, when the national average was 16.3. During our tours we met a number of girls in their teens who were already married. The social restriction on girls pursuing their studies after marriage however has been rapidly breaking down. In one high school in Madhya Pradesh we found 10 per cent of the girls were married. At the higher levels of education the presence of young married women is a normal phenomenon. Nevertheless, the problem still continues to exist in certain communities and areas.

The strongest social support for girls' education continues to come from its increasing demand in the marriage market. According to our survey, 64.25 per cent of the respondents felt that education helped to improve marriage prospects of a girl. For example, when a residential school for tribal boys was started in Deomali (Arunachal Pradesh), the demand for a similar institution for girls came from totally illiterate tribal parents, as they apprehended that the boys, once educated would refuse to marry within the community if they did not find educated girls.

The influence of the marriage market is also restrictive in some ways. Since marriage within the community or caste continues to be the prevalent norm, in communities where education has not spread sufficiently among the men, the parents are reluctant to educate their girls beyond a certain level. It is taken for granted that the man has to be more educated than the woman. This has been intensified by the pressure of the dowry system which acts in two ways. On the one hand the search for bridegrooms for educated girls becomes confined to men with still higher education-whose demand for dowry is prone to be higher. On the other, the burden of the double expenditure on education as well as marriage acts as a deterrent to girls' education.

The review of the progress made by women within the formal system of education indicates its severe limitations. In spite of all the expansion, the system now covers only 10 per cent of the total female population. In the 15-25 age group however, the situation is much worse. Less than 7 per cent of the 15-25 age group and less than 2 per cent of the 25 and above age group are now covered by the formal system. The vast majority are still illiterate. As for the literate section, the skill acquired may be illusory or temporary, as many of them do not succeed in retaining literacy. A study sponsored by UNESCO on retention of literacy in Malaysia and India (1970) found that literacy is not permanently retained without four years of formal schooling, or high proficiency in adult literacy courses (designated as grade III by the Literacy House, Lucknow). Two other factors contribute to the loss of literacy:- (a) lack of use in occupation, and (b) non-recognition of the value of literacy by the community. This study also indicated that the percentage of loss is higher among women in both urban and rural areas.

As pointed out elsewhere in our Report, illiteracy remains the greatest barrier to any improvement in the position of women in employment, health, the enjoyment and exercise of legal and constitutional rights, equal opportunity in education, and generally in attaining the equality of status that our Constitution has declared as the goal of the nation. The trend of discussion in the United Nations Commission on the Status of Women and various reports of the UNESCO over the last three decades, indicate that the achievement of high educational status by a minority produces little or no impact on the status of the large mass of women if they remain outside the reach of education or other instruments of modernization because of illiteracy.

The significant point to be noted is that, unlike the enrolment in the formal educational system, literacy did not increase at such a rapid rate after independence, either in absolute number or in relation to the growth of literacy among men. The enrolment of girls in primary education increased from 20.1 per cent in 1950-51 to 68.6 in 1970-71. This indicates that despite the progress in formal education, the proper sections of Indian women, the majority of whom have to labour for living, are still illiterate. The advance of Indian women in this field can only be described as pitifully meagre.

The Education Commission had emphasized the imperative need "to liquidate adult illiteracy" and "to stop all further additions to the ranks of adult non-literates," - describing such measures as "transitional." In reality the number of illiterates has been increasing with such rapidity that the task of eradicating it is becoming more and more formidable with the passage of time.

The challenge of the widening illiteracy gap will have to be borne in mind in determining priorities in educational development in the years to come. The claims of the formal educational system which can cater to the needs of only a minority for a long time will have to be balanced against the claims of eradication of illiteracy. This stands out as the most important and imperative need to raise the status of women who are already adults and constitute the largest group.

The enrolment figures under the programmes of adult literacy for women as given by the Ministry of Education are :- 2 million in 1950-51; 3 million in 1960-61; 6 million in 1965-66, and 3.2 million in 1968-69 and above 5 million by 2001. This should not result in complacency. In the absence of specific evaluation of these programmes we have no evidence that enrolment necessarily resulted in these women becoming literate.

It is obvious that while the constitutional directive of universal education up to the age of 14 years must receive the highest priority in the formal system, the need of the large majority of adult women, illiterate or just literate, cannot be met by that system. An alternative system has, therefore, to be designed for this purpose to provide basic education to adult women, particularly in the 15-25 age group.

The sharp increase in the number of illiterate women in spite of the rapid expansion of education of women at various levels, points to severe imbalance in the distribution of educational effort and resources among different sections of the population. Education is a double edged instrument which can eliminate the effects of socio-economic inequalities, but which can itself introduce a new, kind of inequality between those who have it and those who do not.

The Education Commission had identified amongst other forms of educational inequalities, the wide disparity of educational development between the advanced and the backward classes. While agreeing with this view, we would like to emphasize another important factor which has a direct impact on the development of women's education, viz., regional differences. Imbalances in women's education and literacy are the consequences of great disparity of educational progress between rural and urban areas, between different sections of the population and between regions, which reflect, to a great extent variations in regional attitudes to women.

While the enrolment ratios shown as percentages of enrolled girls to the female population in the relevant age group have been used as a common denominator for all States, the absolute number provide some idea of the magnitude of the achievement. It is clear from statistics that while all States have been making rapid progress in the education of girls, the rate of progress has been uneven between different States. The ranking order of States for each level of education show certain variations in the achievements of the same States at different level of education. While Bihar and Rajasthan have maintained uniformly the lowest performance at all levels, States like Andhra Pradesh, Assam, Maharashtra, Karnataka, Uttar Pradesh, Himachal Pradesh, Manipur and Tripura show a higher achievement at the Primary levels during this 12 year period. The only States where both primary and middle levels show equal or similarly high achievement are J&K, Kerala, Nagaland, Delhi and Tamil Nadu. The case of West Bengal is rather unique as it seems to have merely maintained its position at the primary level and lost ground at the middle level during this period. At the secondary level only Kerala, Tamil Nadu and Delhi registered very definite progress. At the university level, majority of the States registered a distinct improvement. Enrolment in vocational and technical courses at the lower level in a number of States, however, has remained static. Some of the exceptions to this rule are Assam, Maharashtra and Delhi. For professional and technical courses at the higher level, the increase is marginal. This is not conducive to the diversification of women's education at the higher levels, or to the employment of educated women.

A statewise study undertaken at the request of the Committee found a very significant correlation between the growth of girls' education and the female literacy rate. No such significant correlation could, however, be established among the girls' education and (a) per capita income of the State; (b) density of population; and (c) sex ratio.

A recent study of patterns of literacy has emphasized the importance of population composition in determining the literacy rate. For example, cities and regions with a high proportion of Muslims or Scheduled Castes and Tribes are marked by low literacy rates while those with relatively high percentage of Christians have a high literacy rate. While there is always a big gap in the literacy rates of urban and rural population. Broadly speaking Southern

States have always maintained a higher literacy rate. It is interesting to note that the literacy of Kerala's rural population is higher than the country's city population as a whole.

Apart from the lower rate of literacy among Muslim women, the survey on the Status of Women in Minority Communities has definitely revealed that the number of Muslim Women with no formal education continues to be very high even in those States which have otherwise progressed considerably in the development of women's education.

The influence of these sociological factors on education makes it clear that the use of national or state averages in assessing educational progress are not always meaningful.

In our opinion, any plan for educational development of worker which does not take these imbalances into account will contribute to the increase of inequalities between different section of the population. Removal of these imbalances will require special attention from public authorities based on careful identification of factors responsible for them. Special programmes will need to be designed for their removal if equality of educational opportunities is to be brought within the access of the majority of women in this country.

The imbalances just pointed out make it difficult to put forward a set pattern of recommendations. Besides the general problems of education, there are certain specific issues on which it is not feasible to insist upon a uniform pattern for the whole country. One such example is co-education. This issue has been examined by various Committees and Commissions.

In 1953, the Secondary Education Commission had observed that there could be no hard and fast policy with regard to co-education as social attitudes differed very greatly in this respect. The Commission, therefore, recommended: (i) opening of separate schools wherever possible that there could be no hard opportunities for physical, social and mental development of the girls; (ii) girls whose parents had no objection should be free to use co-educational facilities in boys' schools. The Commission, however, prescribed specific conditions in the way of mixed staff, teaching of subjects, which appeal to girls such as home craft, music, drawing, etc., and separate facilities for co-curricular activities for such institutions.

In 1959, the National Committee on Women's Education had recommended that co-education should be adopted as a general policy at the primary stage, but as transitional measure, separate schools may be provided in places where there was a strong public demand for them and enrolment of girls was large enough to justify separate schools. At the middle and secondary stages more co-educational schools should be started, subject to the condition of adequate attention being paid to special needs and requirements of girls. Separate secondary schools for girls should, however, be provided specially in rural areas. The Committee while recommending alternatives in areas where co-education was unacceptable, suggested efforts to remove difficulties and apprehensions against co-education by providing right type of staff, encouraging parental visits and the appointment of women teachers and women heads in co-educational institutions.

In 1962, the Committee on the Differentiation of Curricula for Boys and Girls had admitted the division of academic opinion on co-education and recommended that: (i) Adoption of co-education as the general pattern at the elementary stage with a vigorous propaganda to overcome resistance to co-education. As a transitional measure; however, separate primary or middle schools might be provided in case of a large demand; (ii) Full freedom to management and parents to establish co-educational or separate institutions at the secondary and collegiate stage; (iii) Appointment of women teachers in all educational institutions at the secondary and university stage which are ordinarily meant for boys. Similarly some male teachers should also be appointed in secondary schools and colleges meant for girls, removing the existing ban on such appointments.

In the course of investigation there was continued evidence of this divergence of views regarding co-education. According to the survey, as many as 57.56 per cent regard absence of separate schools as a reason for not sending girls to schools. Some persons consider that co-education may lead to immoral behaviour. In Punjab, we were told that Swami Dayanand Saraswati had prescribed a distance of at least 5 miles between boys' and girls' schools. Among those communities which observe purdah there is naturally a demand for separate schools. The Meos in Haryana and Rajasthan, the Maplahs in Kerala, a large number of Muslims in Bihar, Uttar Pradesh, etc., fall in this category. It is interesting to note, however, that there was no demand for separate schools in J&K, although the majority of the population of that State is Muslim. In certain areas we found the resistance to co-education to be higher among the Hindus than Muslims. For instance, in the village Bankheri in Madhya Pradesh, not a single girl from upper caste Hindu families was attending school even at the primary level, because there was no separate school for them, while in a village with a predominantly Muslim population in Bihar Sharif there was no objection to girls attending a co-educational school up to middle level. Another respect in which our findings have been somewhat different from findings of earlier Committees is regarding the variation in urban and rural attitudes to co-education. We have found the resistance to be more of an urban middle-class phenomenon. One of the reasons for this is increasing indiscipline and rowdyism in institutions for secondary and higher education. The underprivileged classes do not seem to have such objection to co-education. In Himachal Pradesh the rural population expressed surprise at our question. In their view, if boys and girls could work together in fields there could be no reason why they could not study in same schools.

The advocates of co-education support it not only from the point of view of economy and efficiency but some of them also claim that the performance of students is better in co-educational schools especially if the sex ratio is even. Our survey of official opinion shows a clear preference for co-education. The significant point to be noted is that the support for co-education, particularly at the primary and middle levels, comes not only from the Directors of Public Instruction and Principals but from field staff working in rural areas such as Block Development Offices and Mukhya Sevikas. It should also be noted that the support from this last category is considerably reduced at the level of secondary education. During our tours we found that a large number of persons are opposed to co-education at the secondary stage because they feel that adolescent youth should be segregated.

We have been told repeatedly that boys' schools are better equipped, have more choice of subjects and have better academic standards. In one boys' school in Aligarh district there were 30 girls studying even when there was a separate school for them in the same vicinity. The quality of teaching was poor in the girls' school and therefore, the parents preferred to send them to boys' school. According to the Bihar study "most responses underlined lack of required teaching facilities as the reason for women going to men-predominated educational institutions". In other States also similar opinions were voiced.

Karnataka is the only State in the whole of India where all schools at the primary level (MV) are separate for girls; but from class V onwards co-education is the norm. The official explanation for this policy was, that separate schools made it easier to enrol and retain girls for 4 years. Once parents got used to the idea, they agreed more readily to their daughters' continuing their studies further. The Committee is not in a position to assess the impact of this policy.

Contrary to the recommendations of various national Committees, some states, e.g., Bihar, have definitely adopted a policy against co-education to the extent of discouraging it.

The considerations of efficiency, economy as well as equal opportunity require the acceptance of co-education as a long-term policy. In view of the divergent social attitudes, however, the committee recommend: (i) Co-education should be adopted as the general policy at the primary level; (ii) At the middle and secondary stages separate schools may be provided in areas where there is a great demand for them. But the effort to pursue co-education as a general policy at these stages should continue side-by-side; (iii) At the university level co-education should be the general policy and opening of new colleges exclusively for girls should be discouraged; (iv) There should be no ban on admission of girls to boys' institutions; (v) Wherever separate schools /colleges for girls are provided, it has to be ensured that they maintain required standards in regard to the quality of staff, provision of facilities, relevant courses and co-curricular activities; (vi)Acceptance of the principle of mixed staff should be made a condition of recognition for mixed schools. There is a misgiving, however, that this provision may lead to exclusion of girls from some schools. Therefore, it is suggested that this measure may be reviewed a few years after it is implemented; (vii) Wherever there are mixed schools, separate toilet facilities and retiring rooms for girls should be provided.

The need for a separate curricula for girls has been a controversial issue since the nineteenth century and reflects the ambivalence regarding the purpose of women's education. It is argued that: (i) society assigns different roles to men and women. Since women are expected to be good wives and mothers their education must be adopted to these roles; (ii) the average school life of girls being shorter than that of boys the courses for girls must also be shorter; (iii) the intellectual inferiority, lack of aptitude and physical weakness of girls call for simpler and easier courses of study; (iv) the qualities to be inculcated in girls have to be different from those of boys so that they do not become bold and independent in spirit.

These arguments received official support and became a part of the Government's policy towards women's education. Starting with the Hunter Commission of 1882, most Government committees on education accepted the validity of these arguments. This position remained even after Independence and resulted in certain subjects being regarded as specially suitable for girls. Home/Domestic Science, needle work and fine arts thus came to be regarded as exclusively girls' subjects in schools. Mathematics and science on the other hand were regarded as too difficult and unnecessary for girls and were, therefore, kept optional. Consequently, majority of girls' schools did not provide the facilities for teaching of science and mathematics.

The pace of socio-economic change, the new attitude towards women's roles in society which came with the freedom movement, and the outstanding success of some girls in subjects like mathematics and science were, however, offering serious challenges to these established views. The National Committee of Women's Education (1959) taking note of these changes, recommended common curricula for boys and girls, with no differentiation on the basis of sex. Following this, the Committee on the Differentiation of Curricula for Boys and Girls (1964), examined the whole problem comprehensively and rejected the traditional view that 'mere biological difference of sex created different physical, intellectual and psychological characteristics between men and women' which 'necessitated the provision of differentiated curricula for them'. In their opinion, the differences which men and women exhibit are the result of social conditioning, expressed through: (i) the differential pattern of division of labour between the sexes; (ii) the stereo-types of 'masculine' and 'feminine' personalities to which both men and women are expected to conform; and (iii) the unequal social position accorded to the two sexes.

The Committee therefore recommended a common course, at all levels, and advised the inclusion of home science in the core curriculum for boys and girls up to the end of the middle stage to counteract the influences of traditional attitudes which regard certain tasks as 'manly' and others as 'womanly'. The Education Commission (1966) endorsed these recommendations.

Our investigation indicates that this new trend of thought is now widely accepted. According to our survey, 69.82 per cent of the respondents agree that girls should get the same type of education as boys.

In spite of this marked change, however, a demand for differential curricula comes from parents whose sole object in educating girls is to improve their prospects in the matrimonial market. These parents often discourage girls from taking up 'difficult' subjects. Sometimes 'difficult subjects' require coaching and the parents are not prepared to spend 'that extra' on the girls, while for the boys 'it has to be done'.

The number of girls taking up science and mathematics is steadily increasing. In our tours we found girls were very much interested in science subjects. In reply to our specific question, many of them expressed a desire for science to be made compulsory up to high school. Quite a few wanted to study subjects which would give them a larger perspective. In a school in Madhya Pradesh they wanted 'general knowledge' and 'news' to be part of the curriculum.

In spite of the recommendation of the Education Commission, many States still continue to prescribe different curricula for boys and girls at the school level. This has had an adverse effect particularly on the teaching of mathematics to girls. Many girls' schools still make no provision for the teaching of science subjects. This has resulted in a lack of adequate number of women teachers in these subjects. We found in some schools science being taught by teachers who had never studied science themselves.

Home Science has for long been emphasized as a subject most suited for girls, and a large majority of girls take up this course. We are not against the teaching of home science but we feel that the courses now current in this subject require major revision. In our opinion, the present pattern of uniformity in these courses neglects the environmental factors and availability of local resources. Introducing these dimensions would make them more relevant and realistic. In one school we visited, the lesson in progress was how to decorate a room. There were two styles of decoration - 'Desi' and 'Videshi'. On enquiring, the girls told us that in 'Videshi' style the room should have a sofa set, etc., but they were not taught how to decorate it in 'Desi' style.

This course if revised and developed with proper scientific foundations, would be suitable for both boys and girls and meet the needs of general as well as vocational education.

For example, cooking should include knowledge of nutrition, dietetics, canning and food preservation, etc.

Recommendations: (i) There should be a common course of general education for both sexes till the end of class X, all courses being open to boys and girls. (ii) At the primary stage, simple needle craft, music and dancing should be taught to both sexes. (iii) From the middle stage, differences may be permitted under work experience. (iv) In classes XI-XII girls should have full opportunity to choose vocational and technical courses according to local conditions, needs and aptitudes. (v) At the university stage there is a need to introduce more relevant and useful courses for all students.

Attempts to reduce inequalities in educational opportunities must begin early if they are to have any impact. A child who has attended a pre-primary school is better adjusted to the school environment. It has been found that adequate attention at this stage can help to reduce the problem of wastage and stagnation in the first two years of primary school. It positively helps the children to overcome their environmental disadvantages. It is the best time for socialization and inculcating egalitarian values in the children as they are unaware of differences of caste, class, creed or sex and are unhampered by social inhibitions or taboos.

We were particularly impressed by the achievement in this respect of the 'balwadis' in the rural areas. The children in these institutions come from all classes of the rural population and mix freely in an atmosphere of happy cooperation. As there is no resistance to sending girls to these institutions, they also help to get parents accustomed to the idea of continuing the schooling of girls. It is felt that these institutions can make a real contribution to the changing of social attitudes in the rural areas.

Apart from the benefit that these institutions can bring to the very young, they serve another useful function, namely, relieving the mothers of small children from other works, and increasing the chances of schooling of older girls by releasing them from the responsibility of looking after the siblings.

The committee therefore recommend: (i) The provision of three years pre-school education for all children by making a special effort to increase the number of 'balwadis' in the rural areas and in urban slums. (ii) In order to enable them to fulfil the social functions discussed above, an effort should be made to locate them as near as possible to the primary and middle schools of the locality.

The problems of girls' education at this stage are mainly of accessibility of schools, enrolment and retention. There are still many areas where new primary schools need to be established. Many of the unserved villages are small and scattered, while some villages have more than one school, a position which will have to be rationalized in the interest of economy and efficiency. Though complex and difficult the magnitude of the problem is not large and it can be solved by planned and determined efforts.

Recommendations: (i) Provision of primary schools within walking distance from the home of every child within the next 5 years. (ii) Establishment of ashrams or residential schools to serve clusters of villages scattered in difficult terrains. Where this is not immediately possible, peripatetic schools may be provided for the time being. (iii) Provision of mobile schools for children of nomadic tribes, migrant labour and construction workers. (iv) Sustained propaganda by all types of persons, preferably women - officials and non-officials, social and political workers, to bring every girl into schools in class I preferably at the age of 6. They should visit local schools and involve parents and community leaders in order to promote the schooling of girls, particularly in backward areas. (v) Provision of incentives to prevent drop-outs. Since poverty is the major cause of drop-outs the most effective incentive, in our opinion, is the provision of mid-day meals. The rate of children passing the primary level has definitely gone up in States which have introduced mid-day meals. In Kerala, which has the highest literacy rate among women, this provision is one of the major factors for the enrolment and retention of children in schools today. In reply to our questionnaire, the majority has given highest priority to this incentive. The other important incentives which require to be provided to needy children are free school uniforms, scholarships or stipends and free supply of books and other study material. For girls particularly the lack of adequate clothing is a great deterrent to attending schools. For schools which do not prescribe any uniform some provision of clothing is necessary. (vi) Special incentives for areas where enrolment of girls is low. This will need to be worked out according to local conditions. We suggest special awards or recognition to the community, teachers, students, etc. (vii) At least 50 per cent of teachers at this stage should be women. (viii) Provision of at least two teachers in all schools, and conversion of the existing single-teacher ones as early as possible. (ix) Developing a system of part-time education for girls who cannot attend school on a full time basis. This system should provide education to girls at a time convenient to them. (x) Adoption of the multiple entry system for girls who could not attend school earlier or had to leave before becoming functionally literate. (xi) Provision of additional space in schools so that girls can bring their younger brothers and sisters to be looked after, either by girls themselves in turn, or by some local women.

Recommendations made for the primary stage are applicable to middle schools as well. There is a great paucity of educational facilities at this level. We would like to reiterate opening of schools and greater flexibility in admission procedure, to help girls to complete their schooling.

The gap between boys and girls is the highest at the secondary stage. At the same time, secondary education is becoming increasingly the minimum qualification for most employment, both in the tertiary and secondary sector, as well as for most professional training. Since very few girls manage to complete secondary school, this insistence debars them from most vocational training.

Recommendations: (i) Free education for all girls up to the end of the secondary stage. (ii) Improving the quality of teaching and provision of facilities for important subjects like science, mathematics and commerce. (iii) Introduction of job-oriented work-experience, keeping in view the needs, the resources and the employment potential of the region, e.g., courses leading to training as ANM (Auxiliary Nurse Midwife), typing and commercial practice, programmes oriented to industry and simple technology, agriculture and animal husbandry. (iv) Provision of mixed staff in all mixed schools. This should be made a condition of recognition. (v) Adequate provision of common-rooms and separate toilet facilities for girls in all schools. (vi) Adequate arrangements for co-curricular activities for girls in all schools. (vii) Provision of more need-cum-merit scholarships and hostel facilities for girls.

The problems at the level of higher education are general and require reform of the system to make it more relevant and responsive to the needs of society. The progress of women in this sector with all its limitations has been relatively satisfactory in comparison with the position in school education and there are no special recommendations to make.

It is, however, necessary to discuss one issue which is very often raised in this context. It is argued that a large proportion of the expenditure incurred on the higher education of girls is wasted because many of them get married and do not use the knowledge and the skills they acquire for social purposes. This argument is also used to make out a case for curtailing the opportunities now open to women in higher education. We do not agree with this view. We believe that the spread of higher education among women, whether general or professional, is still restricted, and that, for the needs of a modern society, there is need to expand it considerably. We also believe that an educated woman does become a better citizen and that the benefit of her education goes to enrich the life of her family. If her talents and skills are not fully utilized today in work outside the home, the responsibility is of the society which does not provide adequate opportunities for such women to be of greater social use. The proper policy would be to see that their talents are fully utilized for social and national development.

Recommendations: (i) Development of more employment

opportunities, particularly of a part-time nature, to enable women to participate more in productive activities. (ii) Development of employment information and guidance services for women entering higher education. Many of them suffer from lack of information regarding job opportunities and regret their choice of subjects when faced by difficulties in obtaining employment.

The greatest problem in women's education in India today is how to provide some basic education to the overwhelming majority who have remained outside the reach of the formal system, because of their age and social responsibilities as well as the literacy gap. The large majority of them are illiterate and semi-literate. Out of every 100 women in the 15-25 age group, about 7 are in some educational institution, about 18 are drop-outs from the system and 75 are illiterate. If national plans for development have to make any headway, then it is imperative to increase the social effectiveness of this most significant group of young women, even if we cannot do so for the still older group. Our review has indicated the impossibility of educating them through any kind of formal institutionalized process. Apart from the prohibitive cost that such an attempt would involve, a formal system, by its very nature and pattern of organization is limited to cater to the educational needs of only those who enter it formally and are able to stay in it for a considerable length of time. It is essentially designed for young, full-time students who are not called upon to shoulder any other major responsibility of life during their period of study.

The Government of India's efforts in the field of adult literacy and adult education since independence have been largely based on a policy of encouraging voluntary agencies to undertake this task with supporting funds and guidance from the Government. The declared objectives of these programmes were: (i) Familiarising the masses with the democratic process; (ii) Activating large-scale co-operation in the building up of a welfare state; (iii) Imparting rudimentary literacy skills as a means for self-emancipation, self-fulfilment and social justice.

These objectives, however, laudable, are extremely difficult to translate into concrete terms which would be within the grasp of both the agents and recipients of such education.

The Fourth Plan introduced a programme of functional literacy built round farmers' training in selected districts where high yielding varieties of crops were being cultivated. According to the estimates of the Ministry of Education, about 3 lakh persons received this training during the Fourth Plan, "out of whom women may be estimated at approximately 30%". This programme will be continued in the Fifth Plan, the target being 1.3 million persons. The Ministry 'hopes' that women will constitute 40 to 50 per cent of this group. It is also proposed to extend this programme to dry farming, small-scale farming, family planning, etc. Apart from this a programme of functional literacy for adult women is being formulated by the Department of Social Welfare. The curriculum will include training in vocational and occupational skills in areas like kitchen, gardening, food cultivation, poultry keeping, animal husbandry and household arts like sewing, knitting, etc., along with home management, child care and civic education. A similar programme for non-student youth (age group 6-14 and 15-25) draws a sharp distinction between men and women emphasizing family life education, health, nutrition, child care and craft and self-employment for the latter.

In our opinion, these are fields which can no longer be limited to women. Changes in family life, food habits, the control of the family, all require joint efforts of men and women and continuing this kind of artificial division between men and women may defeat the purpose of these programmes. As for vocational and occupational skills, the needs of women are perhaps greater than those of men. While we do not deny the value of crafts, women's need for vocational training cannot be limited to them. The skills will differ according to the industrial and market potentials of regions and it is imperative to relate the training to local needs, resources and employment possibilities, instead of adopting an artificial sex selective approach.

It is feared, however, that such ad hoc approaches, through a multiplicity of programmes being implemented by various governmental agencies, will lead to overlapping, lack of coordination, and ultimately to wastage of resources on administrative machinery. The problem, though of great magnitude, is an integrated one, and cannot be solved by these short-term programmes. While they may bring education to a few thousands, all the time lakhs are being added to the ranks of illiterates and drop-outs. What is needed is a continuous process, not short-term intensive courses as undertaken under existing programmes of adult education.

A formal system, designed for the young, can use certain compulsive, corrective and didactic methods which would be inapplicable to a non-formal system where the majority of students would be adults, with experience of problems of life and little time to spare for being educated. Such a system would, therefore, need to have certain definite characteristics, different from a formal system. The finding: (a) It must be useful in such a way that the usefulness is immediately perceived by the recipients; (b) It must be related to specific areas of experience familiar to the students, since educational material totally alien to their world of experience would pose enormous obstacles to understanding and interest; (c) It should aim to develop skills to acquire information and to apply it to real problems, and to understand events and happenings in the immediate environment.

The basic requirement for such a system, is a reduction of the psychological gap between those who teach and those who learn. A feeling of identity of interests and common experience are vital for such a system to overcome obstacles of low motivation and apathy. It follows that the system should be a part of the community, involving a large proportion of its members both as teachers and learners. In our opinion it is imperative to use all available educational resources in the community for this purpose, rather than import educational 'agents' from outside. The school teacher, the doctor, the ANM (Auxiliary Nurse Midwife), an agricultural extension worker and the successful farmer, the mechanic, the welfare worker, the local political representatives, and the handful of educated persons who either live in or come to the village periodically, all should be able to contribute to this programme.

Any attempt to professionalize the system will, in our opinion, defeat the purpose. The entry of professionals is likely to lead to development of (the limiting, selective and) a rigid approach, with fixed curricula and classroom procedures which generally result in increasing distance and distinction between those who teach and those who learn. This has happened frequently in adult education programmes, when they develop into 'course'. Besides, the prohibitive cost that such professionalization would involve, would inevitably limit its operation to a few selected centres. The teachers in a non-formal system must have other skills of direct relevance to the problems of the community. Without this kind of community involvement such programmes are likely to lack stability and continuity.

While it is necessary to guard any fixed or uniform curricula, certain broad areas could be identified. The object of the system should be to provide access to information and use of information for better participation in social life. Literacy would certainly have to form the core of the package, but the experience of various literacy programmes in India and abroad indicate that it is necessary to make it instrumental or 'functional' rather than the end object. It has also been suggested that in the first phase of this programme the main emphasis should be on reading and basic arithmetical skills.

The system that we have in mind is a continuous programme of learning useful things, in which members of the entire community can participate in their spare time and where the barrier that now divides the educated from the uneducated become irrelevant. Though primarily meant for adolescents and adults, the system should not excuse the young, particularly all those who for economic or social reasons have been denied any formal education. Some of the latter may even use this as a stepping stone to enter the formal system if our recommendation regarding multiple entry is accepted.

The system will need a community group to organize and sponsor it. The Panchayats and the women's Panchayats that we recommend, would appear to be the ideal bodies for this purpose, Government's role should be limited to providing technical guidance and advice, and enabling government functionaries at the local level to participate in the programme, apart from supportive assistance in the form of literature and reading material. The system can make an impact only if the access to information is available through reading material and equipment. Development of basic libraries, in villages and the slum areas in towns, is an imperative necessity for this purpose. We therefore recommend concentration of governmental effort on providing this infrastructure suggested in the discussion on the problem of formal education.

One more important matter: The deep foundations of the inequality of the sexes are built in the minds of men and women through a socialization process which continues to be extremely powerful. Right from their earlier years, boys and girls are brought up to know that they are different from each other and this differentiation is strengthened in every way possible - through language forms, modes of behaviour of labour, etc. They begin to learn very early what is proper or not proper for boys and girls and all attempts at deviation are noticed, discouraged and sometimes punished. The sissy and the tomboy are equal objects of derision. There is nothing wrong in this if it were merely a question of distinction. But it soon gets inextricably tied up with the traditional concepts of the roles of men and women and their mutual relationships which are based on inequality. The process of indoctrination affects the development of individual personalities.

The only institution which can counteract the effect of this process is the educational system. If education is to promote equality for women, it must make a deliberate, planned and sustained effort so that the new value of equality of the sexes, can replace the traditional value system of inequality. The educational system today has not even attempted to undertake this responsibility. In fact, the schools reflect and strengthen the traditional prejudices of inequality through their curricula, the classification of subjects on the basis of sex and the unwritten code of contact enforced on their pupils.

Criticisms of school textbooks in this respect have been received in many places. In Manipur and Andhra Pradesh in particular, a number of women were highly critical of the inclusion of stories of Sita and Savitri, as ideals of womanhood, since they tend to perpetuate the traditional values regarding the subordinate and dependent role of women. This results in the development of social attitudes among even many educated persons, men and women, who accept women's dependent and unequal status as a natural order of society.

Such a system of values is contradictory to the goals set before this nation by the Constitution. The concomitant of equality is responsibility and unless this is admitted by men and women equally, the desired transformation of our society will receive a severe setback. This is one area where a major change is needed in the context and organization of education.

SIX

Employment and Work

As an important factor, it would be important to analyse the changes in female work participation rates over a period of time so as to assess the impact of various programmes on female employment. The main limitations in such comparison is on account of the changes in the definition of employment.

On the basis of 'main' activity, the participation rates for rural females in 2001 were noticeably higher than in 1991, whereas only a marginal increase is evident with respect to urban females. The NSS work participation rates for females show much higher participation rates than the census for both rural and urban females. This is due to differential base figures used in the calculations. The NSS data employing the concept of modified main activity (including marginal workers) shows an upward trend in the work participation rates between the periods 1972-73 and 1977-78 The work participation rate of 1977-78 was roughly approximated in 1983 even after recording a steep decline in 1981.

There is a decline in the self-employed category and an increase in casual labour for both male and female workers except for a slight decrease in 1983 for female casual worker category. The Regular Salary and Wage Work categories, however, declined substantially for women in 1977-78 but had since shown an increase in 1983 only.

According to Census data, age specific participation rates reveal that women's participation increased for all age groups except 60+, and the increase was marked in the age group 30-39 and 40-49 for rural females. The NSS data show enhanced participation of women in all age groups, but unlike the census, do not suggest a special increase with respect to the two age groups. The Census trend data reveal that more and more women are taking up employment after completing the child bearing age. This may imply greater reliance by working mothers on older children to help raise younger children and points to the urgency of providing supportive services to working women.

The size and composition of the female labour force are a reflection of their overall submerged socio-economic status. In absolute terms, the female labour force has grown from an estimated 78.6 million in 1973 to 88.9 million in 1978 and 99.4 million in 1983 or an average annual addition of 2.1 million. In proportional terms, however, their participation rate has declined dramatically from 33.7 per cent in the 1911 Census to 20 per cent in the 1961 Census. Even following the new and broader definition of work, the female participation rate between 1991 and 2001 has registered only a marginal improvement from 12.06 per cent to 13.99 per cent.

The size of women's representation in the total labour force has also shrunk from 34.4 per cent in 1911 to 21.41 per cent in 1991, and 11.35 per cent in 2001. Sectorwise composition of women workers reveals an ever increasing process of marginalization of women, with agriculture accounting for 80 per cent of the employment in 2001 as against 73.9 per cent in 1911 and 79.6 per cent in 1961. Women workers in industry declined from 14.7 per cent (1911) to 9.5 per cent (2001) and in the service sector from 11.4 per cent to 7.4 per cent between 1911 and 2001.

In the decade 1971-81, some marginal improvement had been recorded in the ratio of female to male workers. The comparative participation rate of males and females in the primary, secondary and tertiary sectors in 1991 and 2001 reveals that the percentage of female workers to total workers increased in each of these sectors during the decade 1991-2001. Among females, the proportion of those engaged in the primary sector decreased by 1.4 per cent, whereas it increased by 1.2 and 0.2 per cent respectively in the secondary and tertiary sectors. The percentage increase in employment in secondary and tertiary sectors in case of females nevertheless has been less than that of males.

The organized sector in India (which consists of public sector and non-agricultural private sector establishments) absorbs less than one-eighth of the actual work-force of the country. Of this, the share of women as of 2000 was 12.4 per cent. Women's employment in the organized sector grew from 19.30 lakh in 1971 to an estimated 43.51 lakh in 2000. Whereas the growth rate of women's employment in the organized sector has shown a steady increase, their proportion in the total public sector Work-force has remained roughly constant.

Within the organized sector, female employment in the public sector increased steeply from 8.62 lakh in 1971 to 21.40 lakh during 2000. In the private sector too, women's employment improved, although at a slower rate. The number of women job seekers through employment exchanges rose from 11.25 lakh in 1975 to 75.35 lakh in 2000. The percentage of placements, on the other hand, increased from 1975-82, but declined in the subsequent years, i.e., 1983-86. It took place later, till 2001.

A majority of women are to be found in the vast rural and urban unorganized sector. According to an estimate by the National Commission on Self-Employed Women, 94 per cent of the total female work-force operates within this highly exploited sector. Employment in this sector is characterized by low pay, long hours of work, low productivity, low skills and lack of job security. There are few labour or trade unions/ organizations to facilitate the mobilization of women workers and knit them into a conscious work-force. This is also due to the varied nature of occupation in this sector, inadequate legislation and ineffective enforcement of legal safeguards to protect these workers, particularly, in regulating their work conditions. Traditional socio-economic relations that operate in this sector defy categorization into 'employer', 'employee', 'labour', 'capital', 'rent', and 'interest' relationships.

One of the major reasons for women's work becoming increasingly limited to the unorganized sector is that women lack the opportunity to acquire skills and training which could facilitate occupational shifts. This is related to the prevailing social relations between men and women as well as the structure of the economy. Since women have to bear the major burden of domestic chores, which in a poor household is time consuming and labour intensive, they do not have the time and opportunity to acquire skills and training for better jobs. Low skill attainment among women and their consequent relegation to jobs which are labour intensive, time consuming and arduous, is perpetuated by their unequal access to technology.

A large share of employment in the rural unorganized sector is held by women. Employment of women in the rural unorganized sector is principally, traced to nine employment systems. These are agriculture, dairying, small animal husbandry, fisheries, social and agro-forestry, khadi and village industries, handlooms, handicrafts and sericulture. The first five sectors are broadly classified as agriculture and allied occupations; the last four are categorized as village and small industries sector.

Although investment outlays in these sectors command high priority, and several government programmes exist to boost the productivity of these sectors, most endeavours are focused on men and male producer organizations. The programmes themselves are executed largely by male bureaucrats and male extension workers. Women are viewed as indirect beneficiaries through the male members of their households, and not as participants and target groups. Most of the jobs in these sectors are low paid and performed by women. It is also a recognized fact that women are gradually being displaced from some of these sectors. Structural problems have risen in the rural unorganized sector as a result of the hierarchical pattern of land ownership, the nature of land relations, and gender division of labour and the credit system. There is a strong class-caste relationship in the ownership of land which works to the disadvantage of the economically weaker sections and particularly against women.

Construction labour is a fairly large sector of casual work, employing women in substantial numbers. Though the construction labourers are engaged on a casual basis (daily or piece rate), many of them have long years of experience in this area of work. Quite a few are initiated as youngsters, moving from one project to another, often migrating to distant and alien places, constantly dependent on the contractors to hire them. The use of contractors to mobilize labour for this sector has perpetuated the age old method of recruiting by "credit tying" and "loan bondage" methods that are routinely used to mobilize migrant labour for the seasonal harvesting operation in high growth areas. The exploitation of these workers thus begins with the methods of their recruitment. Their services are hired by sub-contractors who most often obtain their labour from backward rural areas where unemployment is high. Sub-contractors obtain work from the main contractors on a piece-rate basis but make payments to the labourers on a daily basis. This enables them to keep their profit margins high at the expense of labour. Ideally, construction workers should be recruited through a workers' board or social work organizations and trade unions. There is a need to create such unions or bodies that could organize groups of migrant workers to press for enforcement of minimum work conditions like proper wages, maternity benefits, medical facilities, creches, etc.

Domestic work offers another major avenue to employment for women and girls. It is the most accessible avenue of employment for female migrants and urban poor women. This section of workers, as others in the unorganized sector, has remained grossly unrepresented in the national data systems. Of all the services in India, domestic service is the most unregulated and disorganized. The major constraints are an absence of a written contract for work and protective regulations. The highly personalized nature of the work further complicates the situation. The percentage of young unmarried girls as domestic workers, many under the age of ten, who are initiated mainly as a help to the mother has increased sharply. An estimate in 1977-78 (Sarvekshana, 1987) reported 1.68 million female domestic workers as opposed to 0.62 million male workers. The spread-over of working hours for full time living in domestic workers is reputed to be 12 to 16 hours. The immediate task is that of ensuring them dignity and security at work and regulating work conditions through organization and protective legislation. Simultaneously, they must be provided with opportunities to seek alternate employment through skill training and education.

The National Commission on Self-Employed Women in the Informal Sector has recently generated exhaustive data and analysis on these sections of women workers including specific groups such as women in the primary sector in mining, tobacco and beedi work; handlooms, handicrafts and garments; women vendors and hawkers, construction workers, and domestic workers, etc. While analysing the status of these group of workers in the framework of existing macro policies and existing legislation, the National Commission makes various recommendations for their protection and empowerment.

The organized sector accounts for approximately 10 per cent of the female labour force. Employment opportunities in the governmental and public sectors and the private corporate sector are limited in view of the general constraints on resources for major expansion and dependence on the dictates of market mechanisms which are prejudical to women. Given these realities and based on the performance in previous decades, it is unlikely that this sector can offer much relief by way of expanded employment potential to women.

Whether in the unorganized or the organized sector, women workers face several constraints which account for their low status as workers. Their lack of access to productive inputs such as raw material, credit, technology, training and markets are major impediments. Despite legislation, women's right to land deeds and *pattas* continue to be ignored contributing to their marginalization. As a result, women are increasingly compelled to migrate both, rural as well as urban areas on a temporary, seasonal or permanent basis. In addition to their lack of adequate skills and resources they may face severe adjustment problems due to differences in religion, language and socialization as well as separation from their families. The situation of migrant women needs attention.

In the Indian economy, women are concentrated in occupations which are usually at the lowest rung of the ladder. In most occupations they are engaged in the more arduous and less skilled areas of work. For example, in the construction industry men do bricklaying, while women carry bricks and mortar; women carry soil, while men do the digging; women transplant paddy, weed, reap, pluck vegetables and bundle the harvest produce while men plough and sow the seeds. In terms of access to skills, women continue to be employed in monotonous, low skilled and low wage sectors. In terms of access to credit, while low interest credit under the Differential Rate of Interest (DRI) scheme is available to women. In reality, the need for collateral, cultural and other constraints faced by women in dealing with bank staff, low priority for small loans in banks, etc., have led to a very low rate of utilization of this type of institutional credit by women workers. Unfortunately, gender differentiated data on women's use of bank credit is unavailable nationally which could yield a more precise picture.

Absence or lack of enforcement of social and labour legislation hampers women's access to basic employment benefits. Women are denied rights such as minimum hours and minimum wages, and access to maternity benefits, maternal health care, day care and legal aid. There are a number of areas in which women receive no social security benefits. These factors together contribute to the insecurity of women and reinforce their inferior status as workers.

A combination of social and economic factors are responsible for the low participation rate of women. The most critical are: (i) Segmentation in the labour market which works against women; (ii) Adverse implications of technological growth for women; (iii) Lack of unionization of female workers; (iv) Absence of a purposeful human resource development policy aimed at improving women's employability and productivity through training; and (v) Conceptual ambiguities and lack of a National Labour Policy encompassing workers in the unorganized sector.

Segmentation in the labour market leads to two major types of discrimination, viz., (i) Wage differentials between men and women; (ii) Discrimination in terms of concentration of women in particular sectors (primary sector) and in certain types of jobs or operations. In the agricultural sector, for instance, the majority of women are found to be concentrated in lower paying operations. In the informal sector, women almost uniformly get lower wages than men. In the organized sector, about 90 per cent of women are known to be engaged in unskilled or semi-skilled jobs.

A fundamental economic force that keeps women's wages low is the gap between supply and demand for female labour. In the past decades, India's overall growth rate per annum has not been high enough to generate sufficient demand for labour (particularly female labour) and to provide productive employment to a labour force which is growing at over 25 per cent per annum. Further, the capital intensive organized sector has been heavily male oriented, while many of the traditional activities which suffered from competition offered by the modern sector were those which engaged female workers.

Technological modernization has further eliminated the traditional employment activity and adversely affected women. Instances of technological modernization eliminating traditional activities are well known. Powerlooms have put about 84,000 women handloom weavers out of work in five States between 1961-71. Modeen herbicides and rice mills displaced women and eliminated their traditional incomes from weeding and milling. Apart from straight displacement of labour in the short run, there are a number of other mechanisms through which technological progress has adversely affected female incomes and opportunities. The demand from modern industry, for instance, pushes the price for raw materials beyond what traditional workers can afford (as in the case of bamboo basket weavers). Mechanized fishing displaced whole fishing communities. The rise in the water table due to increased irrigation leads to increased salinity of drinking water necessitating long trips to fetch drinking water. Conversely, increased pumping of ground water may lower the water table to such an extent that traditional wells fall dry. Increasing deforestation, linked to 'development', has often meant much longer trips for women to collect fuel, water and fodder. Reforestation has itself tended to favour cash crops over fuel and fodder and trees, entailing further hardship for women. Finally, adoption of new farming technology has significantly downgraded the input of women, largely on account of their limited education. It is therefore essential to analyse technology/ industrial/ agricultural/ environmental, policy to assess the status of women workers.

In all this, the lack of organization and unionization hampers the bargaining position of women, especially in the unorganized sector, which denies women all the benefits of collective action. Dispersed, unorganized and atomized they have no political power and no bargaining strength. The unorganized sector presents a number of difficulties in implementing protective labour laws relating to wages, conditions of work, insurance, provident fund, maternity leave, creche facilities, etc. The exploitation in this sector is only marginally under the purview of laws. Hours of work are long, wages are poor, conditions are hazardous, benefits are nonexistent and wages are below survival needs. Channelling inputs such as literacy, health, family welfare services, etc., is also difficult in this sector. As a result, there are marked disparities between women in the organized and unorganized sectors of industry. Besides, inter-state, inter-urban disparity in the nature and structure of wages and other benefits are considerable and favour the 10 per cent in the organized sector as against the 90 per cent women workers in the unorganized sector. Investment policies too continue to award low priority to the unorganized sector.

One of the major hurdles to the development of employment opportunities for women is the lack of adequate training. The purpose of training is to develop employable skills that can generate better income and improve the status of women workers. At present in most of the occupations where women are employed in large numbers, such as agriculture and construction they work as low paid unskilled labourers with little training facilities available to upgrade there skills. The existing training programmes are primarily aimed at men creating further imbalances. Though certain facilities to train women in various skills through the industrial training institutes or polytechnics and apprenticeship training under the Apprentice Act are available, there is no special focus on the training of women which is packaged along with other inputs such as credit and marketing support. Moreover, the existing facilities largely cater to urban rather than rural areas.

Currently, the nodal department for women's development in the Government of India is the Department of Women and Child Development. While it has a number of schemes such as short stay homes, working hostels, women's development corporations, it has no national programme for women's training. Further, it is evident that the mixed programs such as the TRYSEM have not reached women as effectively as visualized. Currently, there are at least 45 schemes in 17 departments/ ministries of the Government of India catering to training of women but they do not present a systematic integrated approach to women's training. It is essential that such an approach be fostered. The focus of such training should be at those who are presently the most disadvantaged, i.e., the vast majority of women engaged in the informal or unorganized sector and forming 90 per cent of the total female labour force. It should provide training to improve productivity as well as explore new avenues of employment to facilitate occupational shifts wherever possible.

Although the constraints are multifarious and real, there is difficulty in clearly understanding the problems at hand, mainly due to the invisibility and under recording of work done by women. In evolving suitable employment promotion interventions, a crucial issue has been the invisibility of women's work as well as lack of comprehension and value added to numerous tasks they perform for family survival. A conceptual framework for computing the value of such tasks is necessary. The poor data base of the extent and nature of employment of women on the one hand, and the absence of clarity on what constitutes work on the other, pose definite impediments in assessing women's actual productive participation in the economy. The low visibility of their productive worth is illustrated by the fact that only 14 per cent of the total female population in the country fell into the category of workers as per the 1981 census. Both the Sixth and Seventh Plan documents clearly attest that there are large numbers of women whose work continues to be unreported and invisible. It is this lack of adequate and accurate data which is one of the impediments to the formulation of informed policies for improving the employment status of women.

Conceptual ambiguity in assessing the employment status of women becomes a basis for a lack of appreciation of and sensitivity to the problems which women face, particularly in the vast unorganized employment sector. This, in turn, leads to the virtual absence of strategies for improving conditions in this sector. Presently, support structures, for employment such as training, mobilization of workers, legal safeguards, as well as the institutional base for identifying new avenues of employment and enhanced productivity for women are lacking.

The corrective strategies are to be viewed holistically and not as isolated piecemeal actions. In order to truly be effective, the overall employment strategy for women should be viewed as a package comprising employment opportunities, legal safeguards, training support and social services, awareness generation and mobilization. Only then will a purposeful synergy be achieved.

The corrective strategies are broadly addressed to the factors which have been reviewed earlier as constraints. Those strategies must aim to create new avenues for employment of women, upgrade their existing employment conditions as well as productivity and employment potential, make them a more articulate and conscious work-force, and assure them better status and recognition as workers.

In the organized sector, the employment potential for women is likely to grow very slowly. On the other hand, there is a considerable scope for employment in the agricultural and service sectors. Diversification in agriculture and in the other major sectors of rural employment offers enormous potential for employment. Horticulture, commercial vegetable growing, food processing, fisheries and poultry, and agro industry offer ample opportunities to rural women. Unemployed young women could be trained in extension work for imparting the necessary skills in these activities. Besides, a variety of new occupations could be created for women workers in the areas of agro-based industry weaving, textile printing, ready-made garments, production of stationery and preparation of indigenous herbal medicines and packaging, etc.

Expansion of the service sector in the rural areas is a need and reality offering scope for local women to be absorbed with the minimum training being provided. Nurseries, creches and anganwadis also offer employment opportunities for a large number of women. The areas of simple health care like immunization, diagnostic screening (testing of blood, etc.) and other health functions could be opened to intermediary levels without affecting the overall standards. These facilities are not currently available to poor families particularly in the rural areas. Middle level workers could be trained for employment in the provision of these services.

There is an immediate need to diversify the prevailing occupational base so as to promote skilled employment on a wider scale. Currently, training is imparted in traditional occupations like carpentry, welding, smithing, tailoring, book binding, etc., which is also male oriented. It is now necessary to provide training to women in such non-traditional fields as well. An area based identification of potential occupational clusters would have to be undertaken systematically in different regions of the country in order to determine the nature and size of opportunities that could be made available.

Effective linkages between metropolitan and large urban areas with the surrounding hinterlands is another modality with considerable potential for employment generation. The demand from these urban and metropolitan centres in the fields of food processing, packaging, transportation, storage and other services could open up large areas for production, processing and marketing, thereby providing employment opportunities in such areas on a sizeable scale.

Expansion of small-scale industries is widely recognized as a means of creating potential for employment. Suitable institutional mechanisms for the promotion of small-scale industry need to be developed to assist in the provision of credit, supply of raw materials, organization of marketing and creation of skills necessary for these enterprises. Two of the important areas requiring urgent attention for the expansion of cottage industries are: (i) upgradation of skills in order to raise the status of workers to that of artisans and improve the quality of products; and (ii) education, training and organizations of workers for collective action on various issues.

Appropriate technologies and modernization of their occupations would have to be inducted to increase their income potential. The role of middlemen who have been getting sizeable benefits disproportionate to their investment and efforts has to be reduced. Producer Co-operatives are one such strategy to reduce dependence.

An appraisal is necessary to examine the viability/ marketability of the trades for which training and assistance is being provided by the government. The Central Social Welfare Board (CSWB) is implementing some employment generation schemes under which voluntary agencies in the country have been availing of financial assistance. Training is also given under TRYSEM, and socio-economic schemes are undertaken under DWCRA, IRDP and the Training-cum-production scheme of the Deptt. of Women and Child Development. An attempt should be made to expand the categories to encompass new and viable trades and create necessary linkages.

A systematic human resource development strategy focused on women is essential. Three levels of training are envisaged, viz., (i) The grass roots level; (ii) The middle level; and (iii) The policy and planning level. The content of a training strategy should encompass five principal components as follows: •Organizational and extension training •Skill training •Management and entrepreneurial training •Sensitization of administrators/ implementors to women in development issues, and •Training of trainers

This component of training is to be geared to functionaries, catalysts, extension workers at the grassroots, middle and supervisory level personnel, teachers, organizers of cooperatives, etc. It should aim at conscientization on legislation, environmental health, nutrition and sanitation, education, functional literacy, paralegal training and related aspects. Effective group mobilization, communication skills, skills needed for organization and management will be emphasized in this training along with functional knowledge. Particular attention will be paid to attitudinal/behavioural component essential for reaching programmes for women at the grassroots.

This refers to skill training with special emphasis on the nine major sectors of women's employment, i.e., agriculture, dairying, fisheries, small animal husbandry, khadi and village industries, handlooms, handicrafts, sericulture and social forestry. This type of training will entail upgrading existing skills in these areas as well as training of women in appropriate technologies. It will be aimed at programme beneficiaries as well as catalysts/ functionaries, extension and supervisory workers. These skills need to be imparted on the widest scale to rural women in order to encourage them to achieve household self-sufficiency as well as supplementary income. Also included will be the skill training in the urban/ modern sector with regard to assembly, manufacturing and processing for larger industries as well as small-scale firms. Wherever possible women's employability has to be increased in the organized sector as the employment conditions in the unorganized sector indicate the need for a shift in the occupational structure. In generating such skills, care will be taken to ensure that the training imparted does not push women into sectors where mobility is limited, wages are low, health hazards are high, and worker benefits are not enforced.

This refers to training in project formulation, monitoring, evaluation, information systems, credit/ marketing management, and other skills required to administer and manage projects, as well as supervisory and entrepreneurial skills. Such training could be provided with the help of technical institutes (ITIs, Polytechnics, etc.) where special courses for training of women workers and entrepreneurs could be started. In conducting such courses, banks, voluntary organizations, and private and public sector industries could be effectively utilized to help formulate viable entrepreneurial projects for the trainees. Special training programmes to promote rural entrepreneurship in particular would need to be designed.

This type of training should seek to achieve sensitization of bureaucrats to the critical need to integrate women in development. The objective will be to develop appropriate attitudes and knowledge for planning/ monitoring/ implementing programmes and policies for women. Such training needs to be imparted through the training programmes of the Department of Personnel as well as other governmental and non-governmental agencies. A particular emphasis in this category of training must be to train the officers in charge of enforcement machineries' at the Central and State levels, workers of quasi-governmental bodies, and voluntary agencies. The Women's Division at NIPCCD is already undertaking sensitization programmes for police officers /judiciary to the issue of crimes against women.

In addition to the training of trainers within the existing institutions and infrastructures, a special effort should be made to train rural women as organizers and instructors in different sectors and trades so that they could train more women and achieve a multiple effect.

In view of the criticality of training for the development of women, setting up of a National Resource Centre for Women is imperative. By playing a coordinating/ interventionist role it would identify and strengthen existing governmental and non-governmental agencies to carry out training policy and programme research and information dissemination. The Resource Centre would provide a new thrust for training and work towards translating national developmental goals into a systematic grid of programmes and schemes for training in skill/ knowledge/ attitudes at different levels.

As a preparatory step, it would be essential to identify and classify the various types of training institutions in the country. Examples of such institutions are agriculture and rural home science centres; schools of social services, khadi and village industries, as well as vocational training centres; universities, ITIs, Polytechnics, agriculture and veterinary schools, engineering colleges, krishi vigyan kendras, etc. At present, they have no special focus on training only for women, but these should take up new courses under a coordinated effort, monitored and planned by the resource centre. In addition, newly established training and extension departments, as well as existing training institutions, agencies, management bodies, and grassroots organizations should be involved in imparting training to women.

Recommendations: 1. It will be necessary to formulate a well articulated employment generation and training policy aimed at more productive participation by women, at the same time assuring them greater employment benefits, social security and better working conditions. 2. The formulation of a National Labour Policy must receive immediate attention. The National Commission of Rural Labour set up by the Department of Labour must include in its terms of reference issues pertaining to women workers in rural areas including those in the unorganized work-force. The analysis and recommendations of the National Commission on Self-Employed Women must also be given due consideration in the formulation of such a policy. 3. The agricultural extension system currently reaches only a minimal number of women in agriculture. Special extension programmes must be evolved to create awareness and skills among women in the field of agriculture, animal husbandry and other related employment sectors. 4. Rural employment programmes and employment guarantee schemes like that in Maharashtra should be strengthened and expanded by public works programme along with the provision of social inputs such as creches, drinking water, and covered shelters at work sites. 5. The nine major rural employment sectors have high participation of women, i.e., agriculture, animal husbandry, khadi and village industries, handicrafts, handlooms, sericulture, fisheries, forestry, etc., and have large resource allocations. The mainstream sectors must integrate a woman's component into the sectoral programmes. This would need 'earmarking' programmes for the development of women along with support measures and training in these sectors. 6. Though preferential emphasis should be in favour of the unprotected women workers in the unorganized sector, keeping in view the quantum of female labour force in this sector as well as the problems and constraints. Wherever possible women's employability should be increased by diversification or provision of skill training in new or non-traditional employment in the organized sector. 7. It is expected that the next two development plans would be expanding the provision of basic services. Women should be enabled to take advantage of these opportunities for gainful employment arising from provision of basic services and to work as anganwadi workers/group organizers ANMs/LHVS, etc. The critical enabling mechanism will be requisite training and upgradation of skills. 8. While planning employment programmes, it is essential to keep in view the demand projection of employment, expansion and production projections created by different government programmes. It should, therefore, be possible to monitor the needs of the various ministries as regards women's employment and plan potential personnel needs. Similarly, income generation skills could be related to the demand created by Government programmes for specific goods. For instance, the NPE in its "Operation Blackboard" has visualized the need for teaching aids. This would be a continuous requirement for more than two decades. Similarly the supplementary nutrition need of the primary schools and anganwadis could be interlinked and provide jobs to local women that could prepare the nutrition supplement. One of the function of the District Employment Committee will be to match demand with supply and link potential areas of employment with women needing employment. 9. Employment for women should also mean household self-sufficiency with reference to nutritional and economic needs of the household as in the instance of backyard poultry, social forestry, small husbandry, etc. For example, in the social forestry programmes, certain basic types of trees rich in nutrition such as papaya, banana, drumstick, *curry patta*, etc., should be promoted. Depletion of local food resources due to food processing for export purposes must be checked at all costs. 10. Displacement of women from traditional sectors due to modernization and technology is well known, particularly in the agriculture, fisheries, textile and handloom sectors. It is essential to provide alternate skills for women displaced by new technologies. Qualitative studies of every new technology and its adverse impact on women must be undertaken before introduction of technology and formulation of policy thereof. 11.Promotion of petty trading/ manufacturing/processing small industry, employment among women should be encouraged by ensuring a reasonable share of credit and other inputs. These micro-entrepreneurs should be organized into cooperatives and other types of specialized collective agencies. 12. In the sector of wage employment, women's participation in trade union activities should be encouraged. Creation of organizations for increasing their bargaining power could be stimulated through specific programmes and schemes. In this context the recommendations of the report of the National Commission on Self-Employed Women and women in the unorganized sector must receive serious attention. 13. Organization and mobilization are critical for women to perceive themselves as 'workers' and productive contributors, not merely as 'housewives'. Special programmes for non-formal education and awareness generation of women workers should be strengthened and expanded on a national scale. For instance, the Nehru Yuvak Kendras (NYKs) provide an existing avenue to support awareness and employment generation programmes. It is urged that at least one woman NSS volunteer be employed by every NYK to assist this process. Special attention may be paid to raising employability of adolescent girls so as to provide them with alternative options to early marriage. A national programme of legal awareness for both girls and women be initiated. 14. In the organized sector, the maximum age of entry of women in employment should be increased to 35 years, with provision for job sharing, part time work and re-entry into the employment stream at a later stage. Relaxation of educational qualifications for women in specific areas of employment may be considered. 15. In the organized sector emphasis will have to be placed on the expansion of insurance cover, maternity and other benefits. 16. A Central Maternity Benefit Fund should be set up out of the contribution made by the employers, workers and Government in order to reduce the burden on the individual employers in respect of women workers. 17. Extending paternity leave benefits require serious consideration. 18. Special incentives should be given to entrepreneurs who employ more than a certain percentage of women particularly in labour intensive industries. Recognition and incentives should also be offered to employers who appreciably increase the employment of women and take up programmes for imparting functional education. 19. Avenues for part-time employment should be explored, to improve women's earning capacities; additional employment throughout the year must be available by targeting a percentage of employment in rural works for women. 20. Women should be adequately represented on all decision making bodies concerned with personnel planning and economic development like the Planning Commission, State Planning Boards and Financial Institutions such as IDBI, IFC, LIC and NDDB, KVIC, Silk Board, etc. Mahila Mandals, and other local women's organizations should be strengthened and sensitized. The local level organizations should be involved in designing suitable income generating projects depending on local resources and skills. They should be represented on the District Employment Committees recommended at point 29 here. 21. The Ministry of Labour should set up a standing committee especially for unorganized labour to promote and develop a strong organizational base to improve their working conditions. 22. In the formulation of the employment strategy, a key role has to be given to agriculture through expansion of irrigation, cropping intensity and extension of new technologies. Though the rate of industrial growth must be accelerated, it must be recognized that even a higher rate cannot guarantee a larger volume of employment for women. Therefore, massive programmes of rural development will be needed to provide larger employment. In this context, the none major rural employment sectors which have a high participation of women must incorporate a specific women's component into their sectoral programmes. This does not necessarily imply seeking higher outlays but earmarking funds and ensuring a special component for employment generation programmes for women as well as support measures, and skill training in these sectors. 23.Women should have access to productive resources such as land, buildings credit, housing and skill training. The existing loopholes in the property laws which deny women access to ownership of land should be removed. 24.Special interventions are needed to provide credit to women for production and marketing activities. Women's development banks should be encouraged at the national and local levels to provide credit, marketing and other supportive services to women's groups. Marketing is a major problem for women producers. Local producers' organizations should seek to protect their interests. In addition, marketing support for home based producers should be provided. Women's Development Corporation must play an active role in this area and the Government departments should make provision to purchase goods from organizations of women producers on a preferential basis. 25. Separate machineries at the National and State levels should be set up which can play a coordinating and catalytic role in the framing of employment policies and programmes for women. Special reinforcing cells or units in sectoral ministries should be created to enforce and monitor the policies. Annual reports of the ministries and agencies at the Central and State levels should document and review the achievements concerning the employment status of women. A special focus of such monitoring should be the enforcement of equal pay for equal work, job security and fair working conditions for women workers. There aspects should be studied in depth by the National Commission on Rural Labour. 26. Employment Exchanges must maintain separate lists for women. Every list sent to organizations /employers by the Employment Exchange should have at least 30 per cent women candidates. 27. The largest number of women work as casual labourers. They are both underpaid and underemployed. Information on employment opportunities should be widely disseminated among these groups. Avenues for part-time employment should be explored to improve the earning capacities. Additional employment throughout the year must be made available to them by reserving a certain percentage of employment in rural works. 28.Every selection board must have women in it. 29. District Level Employment Committees be set up to plan, coordinate the demand /potential of employment programmes. Line agencies, women's groups, small-scale industries be given sufficient representation. These committees should ensure 30 per cent employment for women, monitor employment opportunities, and rural training schemes, and their accessibility for women. These should become part of the agenda for the committees. 30.The National Commission on Self-Employed Women has also recommended that an advisory committee with some power of veto must be set up at the Central Government level to monitor the impact of technology on women and to identify and promote areas for research and development of pro-women technologies. 31. A small group may be set up by the Technology Policy Cell to design a format for evaluation of all proposals of technology transfer and automation in industries so that a view can be taken with reference to women's opportunities for employment. 32. It has been observed that after marriage a large number of women are forced to drop out of employment, in spite of their high qualifications and engage in household chores only. Such "post marriage brain-drain" should be stopped. Appropriate alternative measures such as part-time employment, job sharing, etc., should be accessible to these women. 33. Women workers employed in free trade zones comprise a particularly vulnerable group due to the differentials in application of labour legislation in these zones. Hence women's interests need to be protected in this area and support services provided. 34. Recognition of the critical role of training in increasing and strengthening of women's productive employment is essential. 35. A National Resource Centre for Women to provide a new thrust to training and dissemination of information backed by research, data and documentation is an urgent need. It would coordinate training efforts and identify and strengthen existing governmental and non-governmental agencies and academic institutions with resource and technical support. 36. Women must be given increased access to training in skills, management, entrepreneurship, particularly in nontraditional trades. Care should be taken to ensure that women are not pushed into low paying, monotonous and hazardous jobs where mobility is also limited. 37. Training in the nine sectors of women's employment, viz., agriculture, dairying, fisheries, small animal husbandry, khadi and village industries, forestry, handlooms, handicrafts, and sericulture must receive priority attention. 38. Special training programmes to promote rural entrepreneurship should be designed. New areas of employment should be explored for training and absorption of women workers in these rural small-scale industrial ventures. 39. Training personnel must be sensitized to local women's issues, employment needs and trades. 40. Women displaced by introduction of modern technologies must be equipped with alternative skills and employment possibilities at the same level. 41. Facilities and incentives must be provided and increased for the enrolment of women in all training institutes, polytechnics, etc. 42. Special, condensed, job-oriented training courses must be organized for women through ITIs, polytechnics, etc., utilizing existing infrastructures. Hostels for girls should be provided in existing polytechnics, ITIs so that girls can avail training. 43. There should be a separate quota for women's apprenticeship training in non-traditional skills which should be non-transferable so that women are assured entry into such programmes. 44. Planning of training programmes for women must keep in view the demands of new governmental programmes and maximize opportunities for women, e.g., the demand for physical education instructors, expansion of social forestry programmes, etc. 45. Training of trainers must lay special emphasis on group mobilization skills inter-personal and managerial skills, etc., as well as sensitization to local women's issues, employment needs and trades. 46. Training for management of cooperatives organizing and mobilizing women's groups is essential. Training women for participation in trade unions is also critical. 47. Schemes for diversification and expansion of education and skill training opportunities for women should be given the highest priority. Special training programmes should be designed to train displaced women due to modernization or introduction of technologies. 48. One diversified vocational training institution for every four or five blocks should be set up for imparting sectoral and other skills to rural women. 49. Special programmes for education (entailing functional and legal literacy and family life education) of women workers have to be evolved. 50. A nodal point should be identified to design and impart paralegal training to women workers. Legal literacy particularly in respect of, labour laws and employment benefits must be engendered widely. In this effort, CILAS (Committee for Implementation of Legal Aid Services) and similar structures should be closely involved. 51. The training programmes for rural women should be created taking into consideration their educational and literacy levels and local demands. Rural women's need for vocational training should not result in hasty attempts to extend training in a limited range of crafts, sectors and occupations considered 'suitable' for women, that have seldom resulted in providing an adequate livelihood for rural women in the past. Vocational training must cover managerial and organizational as well as productive skills. 52. The agricultural extension system (T&V) should take the women of farm families in its purview to provide the necessary information and training support. Food production, nutrition and population education should be included in the package of extension services for women. Agriculture extension for women must be expanded as a concept to truly encompass other allied fields. The system should be strengthened with adequate number of personnel at least at the rate of five per block with corresponding strengthening at the supervisory and planning levels. 53. Women's role in animal husbandry should be approached in a more pragmatic way. They should be trained in management of cattle, veterinary care and fodder production. Production of fodder collectively or individually by women is to be included as an essential ingredient in employment projects and animal husbandry. Creation of a cadre of para veterinarians from the beneficiaries themselves should be aimed at. 54. Efforts for increasing the membership of women in existing dairy cooperatives and training and other provisions to enable women to take up managerial responsibilities must be a priority. Separate cooperatives for women should be aimed at. Cooperative training institutions must provide special inputs for women. 55. Training institutions in the sectors of sericulture, KVIC, handicrafts, etc., should recognize the contribution of women to these sectors and incorporate training needs of women beneficiaries and functionaries. 56. Special efforts should be made for improving the in-service training facilities for women. 57. In case of apprenticeship, incentives should be given to employers for training of women. 58. The vital role of supportive services in enhancing productive employment should be recognized. It is essential to ensure that the drudgery of the rural women on tedious chores such as fodder/fuel and water collection, cooking, child care, etc., be alleviated. 59.Appropriate technology for reducing drudgery and enhancing productivity should be designed in close consultation with the local women. The possibility of harnessing non-conventional sources of energy such as solar, bio-gas, wind, etc., to decrease possibilities of environmental degradation and at the same time, ensure women easier access to fuel and other efficient systems of energy should be explored and pursued. 60.Besides the overall trends of economic development it will also be necessary to devise supplementary programmes to promote and strengthen employment among women in specific backward groups. 61. Greater emphasis should be placed on the provision of creche/day-care centre facilities as a support service. It is, therefore, recommended that it be made mandatory for every work site employing over 30 persons to provide for a creche facility. 62. Maternity leave benefits and family planning incentives should also be available uniformly to all sectors. 63. A maternity benefit fund should be set up, out of the contributions made by the employers, workers and Government in respect of women workers. The present obligation of employers in the formal sector to provide creche/day-care centre facilities should be replaced by a contribution of employers to a common fund to be operated at the State level. 64. Women should have access to infrastructural facilities like transport, storage, raw material and other productive material such as land, work-sheds, technology, etc. 65.Supportive services like creches, child-care centres, supply of firewood, etc., which indirectly increase women's employability should be developed jointly by the Government, the private sector and the voluntary sector. 66. In the organized sector, emphasis will have to be placed on the expansion of insurance cover, maternity and other benefits such as, creches. Universalization of creche services to reach all work sites with over 30 working people is critical. 67. Special cells /mechanisms must be created to cater to women's needs and enforce legislation on equal work, job security and working conditions. 68. Criteria for fixation and revision of minimum wage should be evolved without impinging on the right of parties to negotiate wage agreements. 69. Legal safeguards/ facilities available under various existing laws, such as the Minimum Wages Act, Equal Remuneration Act, Employees State Insurance Act, Provident Fund Act, and Maternity Benefits Act are not extended to the unorganized sectors. The possibility of extending these laws to cover the unorganized sector must be examined. The National Commission on Self-Employed Women has made specific recommendations in this regard. Trade unions and other organizations should emerge to undertake the development of consciousness among women workers about these legislative provisions. Legal aid centres, Lok Adalats should also help workers in sorting out their problems in this context. 70. There is a strong need to eliminate all forms of discriminations in employment through legislative measures, especially to eliminate wage differentials between women and men. Review of the relative evaluation of various operations in any job is called for to redefine equal remuneration for work of equal value. 71. Working conditions should be improved in both formal and informal sectors. Protective measures against work-related health hazards should be effectively implemented. Employment of women in hazardous jobs should be forbidden and suitable steps should be taken through legislative measures. 72. The Government of India is the largest employer of women. It should ensure that regulations regarding maternity benefits, provision of creches at its work sites and wage fixations are adhered to. 73. Policies should be framed to encourage women to enter managerial levels. 74. Conscientization is an integral part of organization. Presently, there is near total ignorance among women particularly at the grassroots about the various labour laws and their entitlements as well as discriminatory provisions perpetuated under these laws. Nor are they aware of the productive and social worth of their labour. Legal literacy particularly in respect of labour legislation should be widely generated. Both the Government and the voluntary as well as the private sector should come forward for setting up legal aid centres at local levels so as to develop an informed and aware female labour force. In this endeavour, effective networking with existing structures such as CILAS (Committee for Implementing Legal Aid Service) is recommended. 75. There is a need for collective action, for which purpose, organization of women need to be promoted and funded especially in the unorganized sector. Such organizations should be capable for exercising the required pressure for furthering and protecting the interest of members. 76. Although the Government has limitations in direct involvement in unionizing or organizing the female labourers, it can facilitate voluntary organizations in this task. Organization of trade unions in both the organized and unorganized sectors where such organizations do not exist at present is critical. Further to look after the problems of women workers and to improve women's participation in trade union activities, the formation of women's wings in all trade unions should be made essential. 77. Voluntary organizations, should be encouraged by Government to undertake programmes for creating awareness about the existing exploitative structures and procedures in employment concerning women. 78.Mechanisms for conscientizing producers and workers groups on a regular basis should be thought of. 79. Wide publicity should be given to training programmes and training materials focusing on women. Brochures listing crafts and other cottage and small-scale industries with potential for expanding women's participation and productivity should be prepared and made available at each district headquarters and to lead institutions for training. These brochures should also contain information on the skills and knowledge to be acquired, availability of credit, marketing facilities, raw materials, etc. The All India Handicrafts Board, Silk Board, and other agencies should have special units for dissemination of this information at various levels. They should also utilize mass media for dissemination of information, apart from conducting intensive publicity campaigns. 80. The existing information on women's employment is inadequate. Nor is it available on a regular basis. Therefore, it is necessary to improve the coverage, flow and analysis of existing statistical data. There is a need to have particularly better coverage of the unorganized sector which employs large numbers of women. It is also vital to take a fresh look at the concept and definition of 'work'. Often, statisticians and planners have ignored the 'invisible' contribution of women to the family, farm or business, and to domestic chores including collection of fuel, fodder and water. The jobs performed within the home or outside as an employee or as her own account should be included. 81. The Women's Cell in the Ministry of Labour should collect and collate available information on the employment situation of women and bring out a periodic report. 82. The annual employment review brought out of the direction of Employment and Training should furnish information of education levels, placement, and registration of women job seekers. (The survey conducted by the Directorate General of Employment and Training (DGE & T) in 1972 of graduates of 1968 gave useful information on women. There is a need to take up periodic surveys of this type.) 83.There is also the need to collate, collect and disseminate information on studies on issues concerning employment policies and programmes and their implications for women. Information on the impact and benefits of development programming on women, in view of benefits envisaged, e.g., empowerment or employment opportunities or managerial skills should also be collected. 84. The implementation of the Equal

Remuneration Act and of other labour and welfare legislation should be routinely evaluated and reported and the findings disseminated. 85. Some of the areas which require research and analysis and which could be carried out by Governmental or non-Governmental agencies are listed below: (i) Re-examination of the concept of work, and methodologies of assessing the nature and extent of employment discrimination are essential. (ii) Assessment of the extent of mechanization in selected women oriented industries and the impact of technological changes on female employment in various sectors, especially in the areas of post-harvest technology, fisheries, handlooms, sericulture and cottage industries. (iii) Studies on the non-rural employment sectors employing women. (iv) Research at the macro and micro level on the impact on women must be conducted before the introduction of new technologies associated with modernization, so that women displaced by it can be retrained or absorbed in other avenues of employment. (v) The nature and type of work performed by women in the urban informal sector and its inter-linkages with the informal-formal sector continuum. (vi) Modes and levels of wage payment for women workers with a view to identify the areas where further labour legislation should be needed and enforcement strengthened. (vii)Assessment of the existing system of hiring in both agricultural and non-agricultural works with particular reference to extra economic obligations imposed on women as conditions of employment. (viii)Evaluation of the impact of different kinds of occupations and sectors on women's economic independence, their access to employment information, their job satisfaction, and the impact of specific occupations on their health. (ix) Identification of factors responsible for the decline in women's work participation rate in the urban areas. (x) Evaluation of the impact and attitude of women working towards the family and the community. (xi) Review of the existing criteria of selection for candidates for jobs in order to identify the in-built discriminatory clauses if any against them, such as, age limit, physical characteristics, marital status, etc. (xii) Study of part-time employment to analyse whether women are engaged in full-time jobs for part-time wages. (xiii) Study of the impact of supportive service, such as health, education, child care, maternity benefits, etc., on women's work both in the home and outside. (xiv)

Study of the feasibility of introducing low-cost gadgets for reducing household drudgery. (xv) Identification of contradictions in law arising from conflict among family law, constitutional guarantees of women's rights, and protection of workers through labour legislation. (xvi) Investigative studies to identity the areas of decline in employment with a view to assess their nature and magnitude. (xvii) Identification of new areas suitable for promotion of women's employment. (xviii) The impact of national rural development programmes like SFDA, TRYSEM, EGS, Food for Work and other programmes on women's employment. (xix) The effects of young women's employment on household relations and on fertility. (xx) Development of curriculum for agricultural universities to take account of women's roles and needs in agriculture. (xxi) Credit as a crucial input for promoting women's employment. Analysis of the flow of credit to women, especially to low income group women. (xxii) Research studies should be promoted to analyse women's multifarious roles in agriculture from production to processing and marketing, and the impact of agricultural development on women. (xxiii) An inventory of available technologies in agriculture should be made. Promotion of access of women to appropriate science and technology should be aimed and research should be directed to the development of women's needs for specific technologies. (xxiv) A major area of research that has to be provided impetus, is the study of economic viability of projects, both ongoing and newly planned, particularly socioeconomic benefits/ costing. (xxv) It is also essential to study the impact of macro-policy on women, particularly the impact of agricultural policy, industrial policy, taxation, urbanization, institutional money flow as well as impact of technology policies. (xxvi) Research ought to be initiated on the impact of structural adjustment on women, i.e., analysing the relationship among women, market and the State. Particular attention has to be given to the impact on women of changes in incomes, price of consumers goods, levels and composition of public expenditure, and working conditions. (xxvii) General specific statistical inputs on development programmes, e.g., number of beneficiaries, allocations, etc., also need to be collected and made available.

SEVEN

Economic Participation

In a society, the status of any given section of population, is intimately connected with its economic position, which itself depends on rights, roles and opportunities for participation in economic activities. The economic status of women is now accepted as an indicator of a society's stage of development. This does not, however, mean that all development results in improving women's economic status.

Patterns of women's activity are greatly affected by social attitudes and institutions, which stem from the social ideology concerning basic components of status in any given period. These may differ according to the stage of economic development. For example, at certain stages of development, capacity for work may provide the highest claim to status. At other stages, when society becomes inegalitarian, leisure may substitute work as a basic indicator of status.

The debate regarding women's economic role and the need for equality of rights and opportunities for economic participation has centred round three basic arguments:

Women's economic subjugation, or dependent position is the result of a rigid distinction in men's and women's roles in society and leads to exploitation. According to Karl Marx and Freidrich Engels: The emancipation of women and their equality with men are impossible and must remain so as long as women are excluded from socially productive work and restricted to house work, which is private.

M.K. Gandhi had stated in *Young India*, 26.2.1918, that: Today the sole occupation of a woman amongst us is supposed to be to bear children, to look after her husband and otherwise to drudge for the household .... not only is the woman condemned to domestic slavery, but when she goes out as a labourer to earn wages, though she works harder than man she is paid less.

It is in the interest of the society to make full use and most effective use of its human resources. The full benefit of development can only be realized with people's participation and the economic role of woman cannot be isolated from the total framework of development. In a UN declaration on "Elimination of Discrimination against Women" in 1967, it was stated that: Discrimination against women is incompatible with human dignity and the welfare of the family and of society, prevents their participation on equal terms with men in the political, social, economic and cultural life of their countries and is an obstacle to the full development of the potentialities of women in the service of their countries and humanity.

According to Supra: To maintain the proper quantitative balance between various economic activities was one of the principal functions of the economic system, which, it was felt, should operate to give equal freedom of choice to men and women. The orientation of a society as a whole regarding the desirability that women should play an equal part in the country's development was taken as very important precondition for the development not only of the women but of the country as well.

Socio-economic and political change creates a need to extend the spheres of knowledge and activity of all members of a society. Modern trends in demographic and social changes call for a redefinition of women's roles in family and society. Changes in the age of marriage, size of families, urbanization, migration, rising costs and standards of living and the call for greater participation in the decision-making process within the family and the wider society, all lead to subtle but major changes in roles and responsibilities. These have to be recognized and provided for in order to avoid social crises. Absence of adequate opportunities and the inability of women to meet these challenges because of social handicaps present obstacles to a balanced and smooth adjustment to the process of social change.

The opposition to increasing opportunities for women's participation in economic activities springs firstly from a conservative view regarding women's 'proper role' in society; where 'proper' imposes clearly, and often rigidly defined limits to the activities that women may or may not perform. For example, the elite classes in most societies limited the activities of women to the home only. In the same societies, women of the labouring sections did participate extensively in economic activities outside the home, but their spheres were often clearly defined by a customarily accepted division of labour between the sexes. The patterns of this division have however varied, not only from society to society but among different sections of people within the same society. (Margret Meads, 1950 and Ester, 1970).

Secondly, this opposition comes from situations of chronic unemployment, or apprehensions of unemployment, where the prospects of a large-scale entry of women in the labour market is regarded as a potential cause of economic disorganization. A typical manifestation of this attitude is the theory of women's marginal role in the economy. According to an International Labour. Conference (1963) announcement: in Women Workers in a Changing World: This concept of women as a sort of balancing force in the family or national economy has a whole series of practical implications which have the net effect of making it difficult for women to become integrated as a permanent part of the work force and of rendering them particularly susceptible to unscrupulous or discriminatory treatment in the employment market.

The Report of the National Commission on Labour, Government of India, 1969 states that: In countries which are marked by labour surpluses, the need for providing employment for women when many men are available for work raises questions which cannot admit of categorical answers. It is in these developing countries that incomes by and large are low and the family requires the assistance of an additional earner. Where social conventions do not weigh oppressively against bringing women into paid employment, the family income can best be supplemented by a draft on the female population in the working age group.

In agrarian societies the family is the unit of production. The place of work being close to the home, men, women and children all participate in the production process. As a society moves from the traditional agricultural and household industry to organized industry and services, from rural to urban areas, the traditional division of labour ceases to operate, and the complementary relationship of the family is substituted by the competitive one between individual units of labour. The scarcer the jobs, the sharper is the competition. Technological changes in the process of production call for acquisition of new skills and specializations which are very different from the traditional division of labour. Women, handicapped by lack of opportunities for acquisition of these new skills, find their traditional productive skills unwanted by the new economy.

A review of the economic roles played by women in India reveals certain clearly distinct trends. The traditional village community in India consisted of the cultivators, the artisans and those performing menial services. In each of these, the women played a distinctive and accepted role in the process of earning a livelihood for the family, putting in sometimes more, sometimes less and often an equal amount of labour in both production and marketing of products of agriculture and handicrafts. Markets were mostly local or within accessible distance. By and large this pattern is still found prevalent in the traditional forms of the economy. The marketing of vegetables, processed and semi-processed foodstuffs of the traditional type (dried and pickled fish and vegetables, preparations of rice and pulses, etc.) and handicrafts mainly produced by women (baskets, hand woven fabrics, etc.) are still marketed by women in most parts of India.

Amongst most tribal and Scheduled Caste communities, the production of handicrafts as well as their marketing is mainly carried on by women. In Nagaland, Manipur and among the Galong in Arunachal Pradesh weaving is exclusively practized by women. It may be noted that handwoven fabrics constitute an important export of these States and are the most important export item of Manipur. Though weaving is a traditional industry in other parts of India also, the general pattern is for women not to weave, but to take part in other operations.

Among the agricultural classes in most parts of the country and particularly among marginal and landless agriculturists, earning a livelihood is till a family endeavour with or without division of labour among men, women and children.

The patterns of women's participation vary according to regional and cultural norms. Throughout the Himalayan region, the major role in agricultural production is played by women. In areas where the 'jhum' (shifting) system of cultivation still prevails, the men's contribution to the production process ends with the chopping down of the trees and burning the soil. The entire process of dribbling (planting) and gathering of crops is done mainly by women. With terraced cultivation the men's activities increase as they usually undertake ploughing, but women engage in all other agricultural activities. Among the Khasis of Meghalaya, women dominate the economic process and even educated women holding high positions in offices do not hesitate to do manual work in agriculture.

There is a general taboo on women engaging in ploughing but the degree of taboo differs from region to region. In Himachal Pradesh women informed us that sometimes they have to undertake ploughing in the absence of male members in the family or inability to hire male labourers. But this could result in some loss of social prestige. In most parts of the country the jobs traditionally done by women are generally transplanting, sowing, weeding, harvesting, winnowing and threshing.

The cultural norms that influence women's engaging in manual labour outside the home vary according to their position in the social hierarchy. Historians and sociologists agree that withdrawal of women from active participation in manual labour outside the home is a consequence of social stratification. (Altekar, A.S., 1963) Gradually this process of excluding women from labour outside home has itself become a symbol of higher social status. (Gadgil, D.R., 1965)

The general decline of handicrafts from the eighteenth century led to increasing pressure of population on agriculture and increase of poverty in the rural sector resulting in migrations. The Royal Commission on Labour in India attributed the migrations from village to city to three causes: economic pressure, the decay of village crafts and the social disabilities of the outcastes. The first cause, that of economic pressure was the most important. According to the Royal Commission on Agriculture, "the numbers who have no other employment than agriculture are greatly in excess of what is really required for thorough cultivation of the land." The Report of the Royal Commission on Labour (1931) states that: The driving force in migration comes almost entirely from one end of the channel, i.e., the village end. The industrial recruit is not permitted by the lure of city life or by any great ambition. The city as such has no attractions for him, and when he leaves the village he has no ambition beyond that of securing the necessities of life. Few industrial workers would remain in industry if they could secure sufficient food and clothing in the village; they are pushed, not pulled to the city.

When there was prospect of employment of the women also as in plantations, mines, jute and the textile industry, the migration was of families. Similarly the women migrated with their husbands who went as indentured labourers to other colonies in the British empire. When only men migrated the women left behind continued to depend on agricultural work as cultivators or wage labourers.

In the initial phase of industrial development, most industries continued the traditional pattern of family participation and employed a considerable number of women and children. While they confined them to certain unskilled and semi-skilled types of work at lower rates of wages, in terms of proportions of total labour employed, women constituted an important segment of the labour force in these industries.

Technological changes have affected the employment of women in these industries adversely. In the absence of training opportunities, the women, already handicapped by illiteracy and lack of mobility cannot acquire the new skills demanded by modern industry. This creates a gap in the earning power of men and women and is responsible for the widespread belief that female labour associated with backward economies is less productive (Supra).

Development has, however, opened some new avenues to women. Modernization, social change and education, have enabled some women to enter new profession, or occupations which were totally closed to them earlier. For example, the presence of women in the public services, and other jobs in the tertiary sector is now an accepted fact. For certain limited jobs, women are even preferred.

Social attitudes to women's work reflect to a great extent the current needs being faced by society. In some sections, economic pressure has precipitated withdrawal of the traditional prejudice against women working outside the home. Since this is also the class which has generally been more exposed to education and other instruments of modernization, they have benefitted more from change and development unlike the women whose world has remained confined to the limits set by tradition.

These factors pose difficulties in using any uniform indicators to assess the economic status of women. Apart from the limitations of quantitative data, a macro-analysis of women's economic participation purely on quantitative terms would not be valid for all sections of women. The heterogeneous character of the Indian economy and the uneven rates of development have had varying degrees of impact on different segments of the labour force. It would "not justify aggregation into a single dimensional magnitude". (Report of the Committee on Unemployment, 1973) The different segments need to be estimated separately, taking into account such important characteristics as region need to be estimated separately, taking into account such important characteristics as region (State), sex, age, rural-urban residence, status or class of workers and educational attainments. The relative importance of these components differ considerably between rural and urban areas.

In the Committee's opinion any appraisal of women's economic roles to be meaningful must take into account the socioeconomic status of different categories of workers. The largest of these categories consists of the women below subsistence level. We have attempted to identify some components of this vast group who are generally found in unskilled work, in both the organized and unorganized sectors. In rural areas, they are the landless agricultural labourers, members of households with uneconomic holdings, those engaged in traditional menial services performed by particular castes. A large majority of workers in traditional village and cottage industries also come within this category.

In urban areas they consist largely of migrants from villages, and members of families whose position has deteriorated due to the break down of joint families. Some of these families in previous generations, used to work in urban areas but left their families in the village to share in agricultural incomes of joint families.

A rapid rise in the population of rural areas, coupled with a steeply rising cost of living has made this difficult now, and urban workers are being compelled to bring their families to the cities along with them. The women of this class work mainly as part-time domestic servants, or in various unorganized industries. Majority of them are handicapped by lack of education or any other skills that could fit them for work in urban areas.

The second category is a most heterogeneous class. It consists of both white collared and manual workers whose existence ranges from subsistence to security. Most of them are to be found in industries, services and professions. Some are self-employed. They are mostly found in urban areas. In the rural areas, they consist of land owning cultivators and the handful of women engaged in health, education and welfare services. The level of aspiration and employment opportunities of women in this group differ with their social background and educational attainment. All of them need employment either to keep their families from starvation or to ensure a somewhat better standard of living. Some are able to achieve security by improving their earning power, others remain handicapped by lack of education and other skills.

The third category is not burdened by insecurity. It consists of the minority of women who seek employment mainly to improve their standard of living. Some do so to achieve personal independence and satisfaction. They are generally highly educated, enjoy high status both in their families and work life, and are mostly found in the higher rungs of services and professions. In recent years, a few have entered the field of commerce and business management.

The three major sources of data on employment and unemployment are the Census, various rounds of the National Sample Survey and the Employment Market Information Programme of the Directorate General of Employment and Training. The comparability of census data is limited because of conceptual differences in the definition of workers, and lack of uniformity in cross-classification of workers by sex, 5-year age groups, educational level, marital status and industry. The National Sample Surveys apart from the smaller size of the sample and shorter reference periods, do not take into consideration the sharp seasonal variations in the labour force participation rates, which are even more pronounced in the case of women, specially in the agricultural sector. Starting from the 11th Round (1956) the N.S.S. started collecting data on persons 'not seeking but available for work', which is of particular significance for rural women because of the predominance of self-employment, unpaid-family work and limited opportunities for paid employment in rural areas.

Data on women workers from these two sources also suffer from reporting bias, particularly for the large unorganized sector of the economy where the majority of women are employed and does not permit an evaluation of the total women labour potential and its relevant characteristics. A sizeable proportion of the labour input in household enterprises is provided by family workers who have only partial attachment to the labour market. While their inclusion in the labour force would be misleading, their total exclusion would also fail to reflect the reality of the economic situation. As an example, we may mention the case of women from hawkers' families, who help the family enterprises by actually producing the material for sale. As this work is done within the home it is not recorded as economic activity. Expert committees on unemployment have been repeatedly emphasizing the need to use identical concepts for collecting information on different sections of women workers to understand the complex problems of employment, unemployment and under-employment.

The Employment Market Information Programme of Directorate General of Employment and Training covers all public sector establishments and private sector establishments which employ 10 or more workers, excluding all self-employed persons and unpaid family workers engaged in small non-agricultural establishments, agriculture, small plantations and private construction activities. These estimates are useful only for assessing the employment situation in the urban organized sector. The National Employment Service has not yet penetrated the rural areas. Even in the urban areas its coverage of women is minimal. The National Sample Survey and the National Employment Service data are not comparable because they adopt different norms for classifying educational level of workers.

The long-term trend in economic participation of women indicates an overall decline both in percentage of workers to total female population and in their percentage to the total labour force after 1921. When we look at their distribution in different sectors of the economy, however, there are significant variations. Explanations of these trends have to be found in the totality of interconnected factors both (a) during the pre-1947 and post-1947 period separately, and (b) the nature of development of our economy from the first to the second period. We can only briefly describe the major factors.

Agriculture continued to receive the burden of the surplus labour force all through the period of 71 years. Variations in participation rates in agriculture during different decades mainly show a decline before 1947 and a steady rise after 1947. This is generally explained by the pattern of industrialization of our country.

The participation of women in industry, however, shows a general stagnation, and a distinct decline after 1961. One reason for this lies in the transformation of the role of household and small scale industry in the national economy. It is well known that ruination of domestic industry has been a constant factor of our history during the British period, which naturally affected both men and women. But domestic industries like hand-spinning, weaving, paper, jute articles, etc., which were relatively more female labour intensive were more effected by the process than industries like smithy, carpentry, pottery, etc., which hardly used any female labour.

In the period before 1947 both displacement of labour from small scale and cottage industry including domestic industry and corresponding increase in labour force employed in organized industries moved at a slower pace. During the 30-year period between 1917 and 1947 the total number of industrial enterprises increased from 4,827 to 11,961 and the number of small enterprises rose from 538 to 2990. Of the total participation in industry on the eve of 1947, the overwhelming majority was constituted by domestic industry.

In the post-independence period with rapid increase in the modern and organized sector of industry, the share of household industries declined rapidly. Since they constituted the biggest traditional source of women's employment outside agriculture, women were the greatest victims of this process of economic transformation. Many of these household industries like hand weaving, oil pressing, rice pounding, leather, tobacco processing, etc., had to face stiff competition from factory production.

The other reason for the exclusion of women from industry was technological change and rationalization of the processes of production which reduced the demand for unskilled labour. Since the majority of women in the modern industrial sector were employed as unskilled workers they were the main victims of this change.

According to census occupational categories, there has been a marginal increase in the proportion of women in white-collared occupations, e.g., doctors, nurses and other health personnel, teachers, office workers, etc. The effect of this has, however, been neutralized by the virtual disappearance of women from trade and commerce. With the development of modern organized markets and increase in the number of intermediaries and wholesale trade, the marketing of the products of traditional and household industry, which was one of the important avenues of earning for women in the earlier period has been gradually disappearing. As a result, the participation rate of women in the service sector has recorded a steady decline.

During the decade 1961-71 while the male and female population increased by 25 per cent and 24 per cent respectively (20 per cent and 21 per cent in the working age-group), the number of men workers increased by 15.2 per cent while that of women declined by 41.4 per cent. It has been argued that this decline is the result of changes in the definition of workers adopted by the Census of 1971. The Census basically measures the level of employment of men and tends to ignore the interchangeable roles of women as housewives and gainful workers. Since many of them participate in family enterprises as unpaid helpers, changes in the definition of workers which exclude secondary activity has an adverse effect on the recording of female employment. For example, the Census of 1971 included 2.3 million women among non-workers, whose main activity was house work but who were engaged in some secondary activity in rural and urban areas.

While the 1961 definition of workers was regarded as very liberal, according to census analysis it did not make much difference in the collection of data except in the States of Andhra Pradesh, Mysore and Tamil Nadu. It may be noted that the reported female activity rate of 27.5 per cent usually accepted as an over estimate, agrees with the rate of 27.72 per cent in the comparable round of the National Sample Survey of the same year. As for the rather restrictive definition of 'workers' in the Census of 1971 even when the figures are corrected by the inclusion of secondary workers, the fall in activity of females remains almost the same. We may, therefore, conclude that the declining trend has been a continuous one to which the 1961 figures are the only exception. The ratio of female to male workers has registered an overall decline in all categories in the rural and in most categories in the urban areas.

The other significant aspect of this decline is the variation in the order of states according to level of participation over this decade. Kerala, whose position in rural participation was the last in 1961 has improved its position to 11th in 1971 and in urban participation from the 21st position in 1961 it has improved to 5th in 1971. Manipur has also improved its position in rural participation from 21st to 4th and in urban from 22nd to 1st. Rajasthan, on the other hand, lost position from 9th to 13th in rural participation but has improved its place in urban participation from 20th to 7th. Similar is the case for Andhra Pradesh, Mysore, Tamil Nadu. Maharashtra has, however, improved its position in the rural sector but lost ground in the urban sector.

The trends vary in different industrial categories the decline of women's participation in most industries is not merely in percentages and ratios but also in absolute numbers. The distribution of women workers by broad categories shows their increasing dependence on agriculture and a decline in both the industrial and the service sector.

The variations in trends according to mode of classification of sectors confirms our opinion that the census categories are not really useful for any proper assessment of the nature and extent of women's participation in our economy. This is corroborated by the views of the expert committees on unemployment.

The number of women in the organized sector constitutes a very small fraction of the total women working force. In 1971 out of 31 million women workers 19.24 lakh only were employed in the organized sector constituting approximately 6 per cent of the total women workers. A predominant section of this group were engaged in the tertiary sector and the services alone accounted for 50 per cent. In view of the difference in characteristics and problems mentioned earlier, our classification of women workers for purposes of trend analysis divides them broadly into the unorganized and organized sectors instead of the nine industrial categories adopted by the Census. We take up the unorganized sector first as it accounts for the overwhelming majority of women workers in the country.

There are 94 per cent of women workers engaged in the

unorganized sector of the economy, 81.4 per cent in agriculture, and the rest in non-agricultural occupations. The major problems that affect them spring from the unorganized nature of all industry in this sector. They are outside the reach of most laws that seek to protect the security and working conditions of labour. Labour organizations are mostly absent. Where they do exist, they are still in a formative stage and have had little impact on women.

The gradual commercialization and modernization of the economy and the efforts made by Government to replace traditional by modern institutions of credit and marketing to stabilize ownership of land, and to maintain minimum wages, have by no means succeeded in 'organising' the production relations to control the degree of exploitation of the weaker section. Nor have they solved the problems of low productivity, poverty, unemployment and underemployment. Traditional modes of production relations which defy modern classifications into employers and employees, labour and capital, rent and interest, still prevail in most industries in this sector. The impact of this intermixture has been greater on women. Wages of women are uniformly lower than those of men, even within the low wage structure of all workers in this sector.

Many of them are unpaid family workers, both in family enterprises, and in wage employment where their contribution to the family earnings as helpers of the men earners is not always realised, or admitted. These unpaid family workers are predominantly women and children. Most of them fulfil dual roles by engaging in economic and household activity. More than half of the women who enter the labour force before the age of 15 are unpaid family workers, as compared to one-third of the men in the same category. Three estimates are available regarding the proportion of unpaid family workers in the labour force. According to the National Sample Survey (except in the 19th round based on Integrated Household Schedule) the unpaid family workers in rural India were reported to form between 15 to 17 per cent of the male-labour force and between 41 to 49 per cent of the female labour force. Despite the variation in the concepts and the timings of the survey, the proportion of unpaid family workers shows a remarkable steadiness in the various rounds.

The proportion of unpaid family workers aged 10 and over,

estimated from 1961 census, was about 14 per cent for males and 41 per cent for females. The degree of attachment to the labour force differs in the case of unpaid family workers. The NSS data from the 14th and 15th Rounds suggested that in rural India the proportion of females in the labour force and particularly of female unpaid family workers falls steadily from a peak during July August to a low during May-June.

However, taking into account all these variations the one uniform trend that emerges is that the proportion of female unpaid workers is much higher than that of males and they form an important segment of the labour force. The distribution of unpaid family workers by age groups given below, indicates that their proportion declines considerably in the case of males after the age of 24 but for females, who form a higher proportion in the age group 10-19, the decline is marginal.

Agriculture has received somewhat more attention from government agencies and experts engaged in socio-economic research. Consequently, relatively more information is available on the role and conditions of women workers in this field. The non-agricultural industries and services in the unorganized sector, however, have been neglected by most investigators, with the result that there is practically no reliable data on this field.

Census data poses several difficulties, since it does not classify workers by degree of organization of their occupations. Secondly, its classification of workers by their primary activity misses the overlapping nature of agricultural with non-agricultural occupations. Even the National Sample Survey, with its short reference periods, cannot discover fully the variety of occupations that women engage in during the course of the year.

The seasonal and fluctuating nature of their different occupations, in our opinion, is one of the main causes of large scale, short distance and short-term migration of rural women particularly agricultural labourers, who are compelled to seek work outside their village during the off-seasons.

The interplay of various social and economic factors pose difficulties in estimating employment, unemployment and underemployment of women, particularly in rural areas. In spite of such difficulties, the Committee of Unemployment found women to be a greater victim of unemployment and underemployment. The number of unemployed women in rural areas was estimated to be 4.5 million as against 3.2 million males in 1971. Thus women constitute nearly 60 per cent of the rural unemployed and 56 per cent of the total unemployed in the country.

Low labour utilization and seasonal unemployment are a manifestation of rural poverty where individuals are forced to take on extremely low productivity jobs which do not always ensure minimum subsistence. The basic problems that affect women's roles and opportunities for employment in this sector, spring from their helpless dependence caused by lack of adequate employment opportunities, limited skills and illiteracy, restricted mobility and lack of autonomous status. The occupational status of a woman worker is linked to that of her husband or father particularly so in the rural areas.

The abject poverty of these workers is the result of their lack of control over adequate productive resources. The effect of possession of marginal land or landlessness, a persistent gap between income and consumption, lack of continuous employment and low social position is further enhanced by near perpetual indebtedness. The cumulative effect of all these factors is that the worker is deprived of all bargaining power and occupational and geographical mobility. The totality of this problem results in increasing pauperization and abject poverty.

In recent years there have been various attempts to estimate the magnitude of the problem of poverty. These estimates, measured on the basis of consumption-expenditure, have attempted to calculate the number of persons below subsistence level. According to the Planning Commission, the proportion of people below the poverty line has come down slightly in the last two decades although the absolute number of people in this condition (over 220 million) is just as large as it was earlier. While the, computation of this figure is very similar in other estimates, there is difference of opinion among scholars regarding the direction of change (Minhas, B.S., 1971). While some of them agree with the Planning Commission regarding the declining proportion of persons below the poverty line, at least one has argued that in rural areas the proportion has been increasing from 30 per cent in 1960-61 to 54 per cent in 1968-69. In absolute numbers, according to this estimate, the rural people below the poverty line rose from 135 million in 1960-61 to 230 million in 1968-69. The trend continued even later, till 2000. The differences in these estimates are caused by their use of different standards for determining the minimum consumption expenditure.

It is sometimes argued that such an increase in the number of the poor is impossible in view of the rise in per capita income. This argument ignores the impact of the price increase of consumption goods, particularly of food-grains. There is some evidence that the consumer prices have risen more for the poor than for the rich.

It is difficult to estimate the proportion and number of women affected by this increase in poverty as data regarding this is not available. But the higher level of unemployment and underemployment among women leads us to conclude that their proportion below the poverty line is likely to be higher than men. The physical evidence of increasing destitution among women in recent years has been reported to us from various quarters. Unfortunately, however, no reliable data is available for estimating the size of this group. The Department of Social Welfare has estimated that about one lakh of widows become destitutes every year in the age group 20-44. For the age group above 65, this number is estimated at 48.3 lakh. It is, however, difficult to understand the basis of these calculations.

While the interrelated problems of poverty, unemployment and underemployment affect the economy as a whole, we have dealt with them in the section on the unorganized sector mainly because the overwhelming mass of women workers, both by primary and secondary activity, are to be found in this sphere. Structural changes in our economy which may decrease the share of the unorganized sector, are at present very distant objectives. The special disabilities that characterize the rights and opportunities for women's economic participation are more predominant in the unorganized sector and will require special attention and remedial measures for any economic reform, safeguarding feminine interests.

EIGHT

Emancipation and Empowerment

The status of women — social and political — can be defined as the degree of equality and freedom enjoyed by women in the shaping and sharing of power and in the value given by society to this role of women.

The Indian Constitution guarantees political equality through the institution of adult franchise and Article 15 which prohibits discrimination inter alia on grounds of sex. It should be kept in mind that this recognition of political equality of women was a radical departure not only from the socio-cultural norms prevailing in traditional India but also in the context of the political evolution of even most advanced countries at that date. With the exception of the socialist countries, no other State in the world had accepted women's equality as a matter of course.

The United States and the United Kingdom granted franchise to women only after World War 1, after decades of struggle by their women. Most other countries, Eastern or Western, conceded it only after World War II. Japan granted franchise to women in 1946, China in 1949. The exceptions were Thailand and the Philippines which granted a limited franchise, similar to the Indian case, in 1932 and 1933 respectively. Amongst the West European countries, France granted franchise to women in 1945, Switzerland in 1971.

In the case of India, the two major forces which acted as a catalyst in the achievement of political equality of women were the national movement and the leadership of Gandhi, who declared himself to be "uncompromising in the matter of women's rights." According to Gandhi in *Young India*, 17.10.1929: Women must have votes and an equal legal status. But the problem does not end there. It only commences at the point where women begin to affect the political deliberations of the nation.

The nineteenth century reform movement and the spread of education among the women had definitely initiated the process of improving the status of women. However, this process was essentially limited to improving the position of women within the traditional family structure. Prevalent social attitudes, particularly among the upper and middle-classes, continued to regard domestic life as women's sole occupation.

Nevertheless there was a minority of women who voluntarily participated in both social welfare and revolutionary movements. They were active in the cause of women's education, welfare of the weaker sections in society and relief to distressed persons during emergencies like floods, droughts, famines, etc. A still smaller group became involved in the revolutionary movement, actively participating as couriers, distributing literature, looking after various institutions and risking police repression, imprisonment, and even capital punishment.

In both these cases, the women received a certain degree of support from their families in such activities, either overt or covert. Most of them came from the affluent or middle-class families in urban areas. The social attitude to this first awakening was one of reserved acceptance, extending sometimes to admiration and pride in the heroism displayed by some of these women. But it by no means amounted to accepting this as a norm for women's role and behaviour in society.

The nineteenth century reformers professed concern for the low status of women, but their efforts were concentrated towards improving women's position within the family, for the purpose of strengthening the family as the basic unit of social organization. Raising the status of women was seen only as granting her the right to property, re-marriage after widowhood, abolition of child marriage and the right to education.

A characteristic of this movement was its elitist approach. Most of the demands were relevant only for a limited section of women, i.e., the upper and middle-classes. They did not represent the problem affecting the majority of women. The social change envisaged was a limited one of transformation within the system, rather than that of the system.

The turn of the nineteenth century witnessed some results of the dissemination of education to women, though restricted, and the impact of the ideas of the reformers in the changes taking place in the status of women. This was manifested in the emergence of women's organizations, when women entered public life in even larger numbers than before., This period saw the birth of organizations such as The Women's Indian Association (this was later merged in the All India Women's Conference), the National Council for Women and The All India Women's Conference. It also opened a new chapter in the women's movement for equality. A demand for women's franchise was initiated in 1917 when a deputation of Indian women led by Sarojini Naidu, presented to the British Parliament a demand for the enfranchisement of women on the basis of equality with men.

The constitutional reforms of 1919 left the matter to the discretion of the elected legislatures in the provinces and finally the Reforms Act of 1921 enfranchised a very small fraction of the Indian population including women. This right to vote, however, was subject to certain reservations: women could vote only if they possessed qualifications of wifehood, property and education. These qualifications, apart from making the women's right dependent on her marital status, in fact restricted it to an infinitesimal minority of women.

The gap between the radical nature of the demand and actual achievement was a characteristic of the period till independence. It represented not only the reluctance of the foreign rulers to accept the democratic aspirations of the people, but also their own political view regarding the limited role of women in Indian society. They could not believe that Indian society would ever regard women as equal partners of men. Nor could they expect women to act independently of the men, as a separate political force. Therefore, women did not feature in the framework of representation of classes, communities, and interests, which was offered by the colonial authorities as the solution of the Indian question.

A transformation of the attitude to women was precipitated by the Gandhian view regarding women's role in the social revolution and reconstruction: Woman is the companion of man gifted with equal mental capacities. She has the right to participate in the minutest details of the activities of man, and she has the same right of freedom and liberty as he... By sheer force of a vicious custom, even the most ignorant and worthless men have been enjoying a superiority over women which they do not deserve and ought not to have. Gandhi, *Young India*, 26.2.1918. Since resistance in satyagraha is offered through self-suffering. It is a weapon pre-eminently open to women.... She can become the leader in satyagraha which does not require the learning that books give but does require the stout heart that comes from suffering and faith. Gandhi, *Young India*, 24.2.1940.

Responding to his call, women of different communities and all walks of life came out to join the struggle - as political campaigners, joining protest marches and demonstrations, as constructive workers, participating in and often taking charge of the village reconstruction programmes, as workers in the cause of social and economic justice working for the removal of untouchability and other forms of social oppression. The highly educated and the not so well educated joined hands to spread literacy and develop self-reliance among the people. Women who had spent their lives behind purdah came out to fight orthodoxy, superstition and communal separatism.

Social legitimation for such activity was not forthcoming at first but the women joined the men to fight in the movement. Events proved that without the cooperation of women the freedom struggle would not have been so successful. Under Mahatma Gandhi's direction the civil disobedience movement and the salt satyagraha saw women in the forefront. The breaking of the forest laws, boycott of foreign cloth and liquor shops resulted in women suffering police repression, incarceration in prisons and other indignities. Scores of women were in the vanguard of the movement. According to Nehru in *Discovery of India*: Our women came to the forefront and took charge of the struggle. Women had always been there of course but now there was an avalanche of them which took not only the British Government but their own men-folk by surprise. There were these women, women of the upper or middle cases, leading sheltered lives in their homes, peasant women, working class women, right women - pouring out in their tens of thousands in defiance of government orders and police *lathis*. It was not only the display of courage and daring but what was even more surprising was the organizational power they showed.

This kind of participation had a direct impact on the attitudes of women also. A meeting of representative women's organizations in 1930 drafted a memorandum demanding immediate acceptance of adult franchise without sex discrimination. It was turned down by the Government, but in 1931 the Karachi Session of the Indian National Congress took the historic decision, committing itself to political equality of women, regardless of their status and qualifications.

The Government of India Act of 1935 increased the number of enfranchised Indians, the proportional suffrage rights of women and relaxed some of the previous qualifications. All women over 21 could vote provided they fulfilled the conditions of property and education.

Independence brought the promise of actual liberation and equality. The Constitution pledged the nation to achieving a just society, based on the principles of equality and dignity of the individual, and proclaimed the right to political and legal equality as fundamental rights of all Indians. The guarantee against discrimination in employment and offices under the State opened the avenues to offices of power and dignity.

It has been argued that political equality is meaningless in a country where the mass of the population suffers from poverty, continuous threat of starvation, illiteracy, lack of health, and inequality of class, status and power. It is more so in the case of women who suffer from another dimension of inequality, namely the weight of traditional attitudes that regard them as physically, intellectually and socially inferior to men. It is, however, clear from Mahatma Gandhi's statement that the equal and political rights of women were only to be a starting point to enable the society to transform itself by ending all exploitation, a process in which women would be the prime movers.

Looked at from this angle, political rights and status appear as only instrumental for achieving general equality of status and opportunities and social, economic and political justice. It, therefore, becomes important to examine the efficiency of this instrument in the practical operation of the political process. We have used the following indicators for this examination:

The readiness and willingness of the people to participate in the political process is a basic requirement for a democracy. The role of women in this field can be measured by the turn out of women voters and number of women candidates in each election.

Since attitudes play a major role in determining political behaviour, the level of awareness, commitment and involvement of women participating in politics, particularly their autonomy and independence in political action and behaviour, are important measures of their political status.

If political rights are only an instrument to achieve other goals, then this is the crucial measure of women's political status. Yet this is the most difficult to measure. Quantitative data is of little use because they may not indicate the actual reality in the political process. We have tried to measure this by looking at the women's view of their own roles and efficacy in the political process, and society's attitude to these new roles of women. This is indicated by the success of women candidates at various, elections, the efficiency of women's pressure groups, the nature of the leadership and women elites in parties and Government, and the effectiveness of campaigns for women's mobilization particularly on issues that directly concern them.

In the course of our examination we have tried to separate certain myths from the actual state of affairs, by indicating the gaps that exist between popular notions and opinions and empirical realities, between what the law provides and the policy demands on the one hand and what society actually permits on the other. The evidence for our examination has been collected by various means, from published research on Indian political behaviour, some first-hand studies sponsored by the Committee, comments of political workers and parties, and the views of the large number of women belonging to different socio-economic categories, whom the Committee met during the tours.

In a democratic system participation in politics has to be viewed at the levels of acquisition and exercise of power and rights of a citizen. The study of general elections at these two levels offers certain quantitative measures of participation of citizens both as voters and as candidates. Unfortunately the statistics for the first two general elections do not throw light on the number of women candidates or voters. Our comparison, therefore, has to be limited to the last three general elections, viz., those of 1996, 1998A and 1999. The percentage turn out of men and women voters in the last three general elections to the Lok Sabha and the overall picture of women participation indicate that the difference between percentage turnout of men and women voters has been decreasing. Between 1996 and 1998 the percentage of women who exercised their franchise increased nearly by 11 per cent but in 1991 it decreased by 7.1 per cent. This decrease is, however, nearly equal to the fall in the total voting percentage in that year. Since the difference between men and women voters does not show any substantial increase, it may be inferred that there was no significant change in the trend, which is visible when we compare the figures of 1996 and 1999. During the nine year period, while the total voters' turn out increased by only 0.90 per cent increase in the percentage of women voters was 2.25 per cent.

A comparison of the turn out in different States shows that the States of Orissa, Bihar, Madhya Pradesh, Himachal Pradesh, Rajasthan and Uttar Pradesh registered a low turn out of total voters. The turn out of women voters in these States was still lower, resulting in a high difference between men and women. Assam and Jammu & Kashmir also come under this category. These States, are generally known for the educational and social backwardness of their women. All the demographic indicators, viz., sex ratio, literacy rate, life expectancy, etc., point to a low status of women in these States. This is reflected in the low participation.

It has generally been found that there is a close relationship between literacy and political awareness. The States and Union Territories which have registered the maximum mobilization of women voters generally have a high female literacy rate. It should, however, be noted that it is impossible to establish a similar correlation between education or economic development and exercise of franchise by women. One great difficulty about the Indian political scene is that it is impossible to generalize about the interrelationship between any factor and political behaviour. Patterns of political behaviour from different regions show different relationships, influenced as they are by interrelated factors like the social status of women, their economic position, the cultural norms and the overall regional outlook towards women's participation in the wider society.

The statewise number of contestants has been generally in accordance with the total number of seats allocated to the States. The maximum number was in UP, except in 1971, when Bihar (then), the next biggest State in terms of Lok Sabha seats, took the lead by one candidate. The record of Madhya Pradesh is also high except in 1971, when it dropped. This indicates that there is no correlation between the general level of women's participation, (which is consistently low in UP, and Bihar), and the selection of women candidates, which is mostly done by the parties. Punjab, where women's participation rate has outstripped that of men in the urban areas, has fewer number of candidates. Kerala and Maharashtra show increase in the number of candidates over the years, and West Bengal a sudden one in 1971, but the most visible trend is the stagnation or even decline in the number in most States. Karnataka, though not backward in any sense, did not put up a single woman candidate in three of the general elections, and only one in the other two. Jammu & Kashmir, Nagaland and most of the Union Territories never put a single woman candidate.

Women in Manipur, Andhra Pradesh, Tamil Nadu, Karnataka and Orissa were particularly vocal in criticizing the political parties for sponsoring so few women. In their view the small number of candidates represented not the aspiration of women, but the indifference of political parties in giving them nominations.

The factors that determine the number of women candidates from different regions are obviously not related to the level of poll participation, literacy or economic and social position of women in a region. On the other hand, the States where women's position is relatively low have a record of higher number of candidates. On the whole, we have to note that the number of women seeking elections either for the Lok Sabha or for the State Assemblies, has been in no way comparable to their proportion in the population.

Apart from the election figures, our discussion with different groups of women in all the States points towards certain general conclusions. At the level of participation, women have improved their response to the political rights conferred by the Constitution. Keeping other things equal, overall development such as literacy, increased mass communication, etc., may help to draw a larger number of women into the political mainstream. The present participation of women in the political process, however, presents sharp contrasts. The overall statistics indicate that women, participation though improving, is still so small as to be discouraging, particularly when compared with that of men. Though there has been a substantial number of new women entrants. During our tours we were informed by many women that there has been a large number of drop-outs from active participation. When these are from families with long political traditions, they indicate a certain process of disillusionment. This is also corroborated by some of the State studies mentioned earlier.

Muslims and tribal women show a lower level of participation both as voters and candidates, though there are exceptions to this. A survey on Muslim women indicates that a large number of the women interviewed had voted in the previous election. The surveyor also met tribal women in Tripura, Meghalaya and Baster (MP), who, though not formally educated, have a keen interest in politics and participate regularly in voting.

Women of Scheduled Castes and other intermediary groups reveal a higher participation rate. In West Bengal, women from these groups were more aware and participated relatively more than the tribal women. Studies in Gujarat and Maharashtra have also corroborated this fact. We met a number of women from these communities in villages in different states, whose determination to participate in elections was quite obvious.

In terms of voting participation, the rural-urban difference seems to be narrowing down, though the belief in the lower participation of rural women continues to be widespread. During the general elections of 1972, the Committee had appointed some observers. The results of their investigation, as well as those of their studies indicate that urbanization per se does not have much influence on women's participation. On the other hand, the argument that domestic duties prevent them from participation is more commonly voiced by women in urban areas, particularly by the middle-classes.

In many of the villages visited by us, we came across women who have been exercising their franchise, and were fully conscious of the power that this right gave them. A group of Scheduled Caste women whom we met in a village in Madhya Pradesh had not only voted in the last elections but were very much conscious of the power conferred on them by the franchise. They were emphatic that they would hereafter vote only for such candidates who will continue to take interest in their welfare even after the election. In a village in UP, Scheduled Caste and Muslim women were very vocal, not only about their franchise, but also about the secrecy of the ballot.

There is a general consensus that the political parties have neglected their task of politically educating and mobilizing women adequately. They have also tended to ignore the claims of women in nominating candidates for elections. This criticism was voiced even by successful women legislators.

Majority of the women candidates come from relatively well-to-do families, with a sprinkling of members of old princely houses. Only one party has occasionally backed women candidates from Scheduled Castes or Tribes and Muslims. Majority of the women candidates are educated, though their levels vary. About 70 per cent to 80 per cent of the women Members of Parliament are, however, relatively better educated.

In terms of political socialization or background, the smaller group among the candidates come from families with fairly long traditions of political participation. They are, therefore, highly articulate, have a sharp perspective of politics, and have continued in the struggle for power through several successive elections. The larger group consists of new entrants. Some of them had no previous political experience but entered the political arena for the first time through elections.

The greatest deterrent to women's active participation as candidates is the increasing expense of elections. Women were emphatic that families were still not prepared to finance the elections of their women from family funds, though they would do so for the men. Since most women have no economic resources of their own, their aspirations could only be fulfilled if they were fully backed by a political party. Because of this factor, the majority of women candidates today are those who can command some independent means.

The other factors which deter many women from active participation in politics are the threats of violence and character assassinations which have increased recently. This was mentioned to us by many legislators and political workers. Some of them have a long record of political activism, but still hesitate to face candidature at elections.

It must be kept in mind that these three indices used to assess political roles are largely heuristic devices, which usually overlap in describing the empirical situation. Attitudes have a bearing on participation and impact, while attitudes in turn depend to a great extent on impact and levels of participation.

Relative differences in the political attitudes of men and women have been studied by various scholars and form a feature of most of our political literature since independence. Certain broad trends can be discerned, the most important of which are mentioned below. The point which emerges in the very beginning of our analysis is that there is no single homogeneous pattern. Levels of political awareness vary from region to region, from class to class and from community to community, and are conditioned greatly by the political culture of the area, the approach of the political parties to the women and the quality of local leadership.

It is generally held that political awareness varies with the levels of modernization in a given area, with concomitant factors such as literacy rates, education and exposure to urbanization and mass media. This correlation however seems more apparent than real, as proved by studies in different regions.

We have already pointed out the distinction in the influence of literacy and education on awareness and participation. While the former is generally found to be an important determinant for both awareness and participation, education does not command a similar influence. While a correlation can be established between education and awareness, this does not always extend to participation. We have also noted that similarly, urbanization alone cannot be identified with high political awareness or participation. In terms of urban rural variables, there is no significant difference in political awareness.

On an average, working women including professionals, indicate a higher degree of awareness, but this is not necessarily reflected in their participation. There is a uniform finding from different regions regarding the complaint of urban middle-class women that they find their family responsibilities a handicap to political participation.

There is no positive relationship between higher socioeconomic status and the degree of awareness. We may cite a few illustrations from Prof Sirsikar's study: In Gujarat, the high income group women are less aware and participate less in the political process; in Maharashtra, the higher the socio-economic status, other factors being equal, lesser is the proportion of women who participate. This is further borne out by the apathy of professionals with high socio-economic status. By and large, politics constitutes a peripheral interest for women from this strata, though a significant number of women legislators come from an affluent background.

Most studies on political behaviour have so far held that women are considerably influenced by their husbands and family wishes in political matters. During the course of our tours, however, we received ample evidence that this pattern is beginning to change and many women now exercise considerable autonomy in using their right of franchise. They emphasize their ability to do so because of the secrecy of the ballot. Many women told us that though their husbands still try to influence their judgement "they can't find out whom we have really voted for." In rural areas the influence of village elders plays an important role in determining political choice which also influence the women's behaviour. However, it would not be correct to describe this as a universal rule.

In spite of such changes, it is still evident that there is a difference in the level of political information and perception regarding implications of the right of franchise, etc., between men and women, both quantitatively and qualitatively. Most scholars have attributed this to the lack of interest shown by political parties, in improving the political knowledge of women. Some have also levelled this charge against the women's organizations and pressure groups. A study of urban voters in Rajasthan provides an illustration - 44.5 per cent of the women did not have any clear cut idea about their criterion for voting: 19.5 per cent considered the personality of the candidates, 22.3 per cent caste and family as a factor, while only 8.3 per cent and 5.5 per cent considered the party and the issues respectively.

All the State profiles indicate one common trend - that women are concerned with problems that affect their day to day lives. The issues are price-rise, non-availability of essential commodities, hoarding and black marketing, adulteration, unemployment and poverty. On several occasions during the last few years, women have organized protests against these problems.

There are indications of growing trends of disillusionment with the political process among women. This may be partly attributed to their reactions against the prevalence of corruption and inefficiency in political circles but a great deal of such attitudes is on account of their feelings of ineffectiveness in solving problems which affect their lives. According to a study conducted in West Bengal, about 25 per cent of the respondents stated that having votes has not helped women and even men. About 8 per cent stated that they would not vote on principle since it did not help in any way. Another study done in Rajasthan in 1971 showed that 42 per cent of the women interviewed including housewives and working women, supported revolution for social progress as opposed to the 'ritual' of elections. The majority of respondents in this study felt that the problems of the country needing solution in order of priority were as follows: (1) employment and poverty; (2) rising prices; (3) corruption; and (4) law and order.

The freedom movement and the period immediately succeeding independence brought the involvement and commitment of women in the political process. However, the institutionalization of this process resulted in difference in perception of goals and methods of achievement. The absence of a movement in the period after independence explains the low involvement of women in the political process. Such involvement is however always visible during national emergencies.

It was repeatedly brought to our notice that the unity between political, economic and social issues that characterized the freedom movement was one of the causes for women's high degree of participation. The divorce between social problems that affect women directly, and the political process, has been one of the major causes of women's lower participation in politics in recent years.

While the percentage of political participation and the number of women contestants have shown a gradual increase, their record of success at elections, however, presents a very different picture. The number and percentage of successful women candidates for the Lok Sabha had been declining steadily from 33 (50.6 per cent) in 1962 to 21 (25.9 per cent) in 1971. The variations in the number of contestants and those elected are uneasily accountable. The sharp decline in successful candidates in 1971 had been attributed to the sudden increase in the number of independent women candidates which increased from 10 in 1967 to 31 in 1971, only one of whom was elected, thus bringing the percentage of successful contestants down to 25.9 per cent. The trend continued in later elections, till 1999. This however, does not explain why the parties' nominations should have been so few.

A statewise comparison of successful women candidates for the Lok Sabha shows that the number of successful candidates has been greater in UP, Bihar, Madhya Pradesh and Andhra Pradesh where the number of contestants has also been greater. Orissa, Haryana, Goa, Daman and Diu and Manipur are the only areas where women contested but were never returned. Percentagewise Karnataka was the most successful. It set up only one candidate in 1962 and 1971 and elected the same. Bihar, UP, Madhya Pradesh, Tamil Nadu and West Bengal were the only States which sent women to the Lok Sabha in every election. In terms of the overall performance, however, Andhra Pradesh and Assam may also be considered satisfactory.

Analyzing the first general elections Smt. Laxmi N. Menon had inferred that the number of women candidates was in inverse proportion to the percentage of literacy among them. This hypothesis is confirmed when tested against the figures of subsequent elections in Madhya Pradesh, Bihar and UP. But Orissa, Jammu & Kashmir and Rajasthan do not substantiate this hypothesis. On the other hand, Kerala, West Bengal, Maharashtra and Tamil Nadu do not support the reverse of this view, i.e., the number of women contestants does not decline relatively with a higher literacy rate. We may infer, therefore, that literacy is not one of the facts that determine the number of women contestants or their success. The backing of the party which sponsors them, the personality of the contestants, including their family background, and the campaign strategy adopted, play a much more important role in determining the success or failure of women candidates.

Women representatives in the State Legislatures also present a varied pattern. The most significant trend, however, is either a decline or stagnation in the percentage of successful contestants. In the First General Elections (1952), Gujarat elected four out of five women candidates to the Gujarat Assembly. In 1962 the number increased to 15 out of 24 but it dropped to 8 out of 17 in 1967 and 8 out of 21 in 1972. In the case of Karnataka, except for 1957 and 1962 the ratio of female to male representatives has been extremely low, the number of successful candidates dropping to 7 in 1967 and increasing marginally to 11 in 1972. In Maharashtra the number of successful candidates improved from 5 in 1952 to 14 in 1957 but has been declining ever since. The Rajasthan Assembly, which had 24 women between 1957 and 1962 contained only 6 in 1967-68. The West Bengal Assembly had 14 women in 1962, but had only 6 in the next assembly.

The election manifestos of the parties indicate that practically all of them agree that women constitute a backward section of the society to whom special privileges should be granted to bring them on a par with men. The parties also agree that the existing gap between men and women should be reduced to the minimum possible.

The India National Congress is pledged to implement the principles of the Constitution. The recent manifestos of the party have emphasized development of education and employment opportunities for women.

The Congress has consistently maintained its position as the party sponsoring the largest number of women candidates both at Parliamentary and State Assembly elections. The number of women contestants sponsored by the Congress, however, has remained much below its stipulated target of 15 per cent of the total candidates. This percentage was initially decided by the party in 1957 and has been repeatedly reiterated since then but to no effect.

The Congress Mahila Front had been active in mobilizing women in support of the party. In recent years it has been voicing the demand of women workers within the party. In some States it is becoming very critical of the neglect of women's demands by the official leadership. There is a general feeling among women political workers that they do not have enough opportunities to develop or demonstrate their organising ability. Exclusion from the decision making bodies within the party is responsible for considerable resentment among women political workers.

The Communist Party of India believes that in the capitalist system complete equality of women is impossible. Only a socialist system can liberate women fully by ending all types of exploitation. Women have a role to play in bringing about the social revolution which cannot be achieved if they remain in a backward condition. According to its election manifesto the party stands for equality of women in every sphere of national life. The party demands equal pay for equal work, removal of all restrictions on employment of married women, extension of maternity benefits to all employed women and enforcement of the social laws that have been enacted to improve their status. The party appreciates the need for adequate financial allocation and extra facilities for women's education. It promises to achieve removal of all disabilities to secure women's equality with men in inheritance of property, marriage and divorce laws, entrance to education institutions, professions and services.

The greatest cause of women's inability to enjoy these rights was their economic dependence and poverty. Attempts to implement the equal pay for equal work principle by industrial tribunals have invariably ended in retrenchment of women workers. Poverty also prevented them from enjoying the protection of the social laws enacted to improve their status. The answer to this handicap lay in fuller participation of women in the process of social production which should not be limited to small scale and cottage industries only. They suggested specific protection against retrenchment of women and drew the attention of the Committee to a trade union demand for 20 per cent reservation of jobs for women in industry. In their opinion, this could be insisted upon in selected industries like textiles where the number of women workers has been declining. Free legal aid, particularly for women in adverse economic circumstances should also be provided to enable them to utilize the rights provided under the social laws.

Regarding education, while the party supported co-education

as the ultimate object, they noted the possible necessity of secondary schools for women. Hostel accommodation and generous provision of stipends was also essential to improve women's education.

The party believes that genuine equality between the sexes is impossible in a capitalist order, and can only be realized in the process of a socialist transformation of society. The party declares itself as opposed to any kind of discrimination against women. It is critical of the poor progress in the field of women's welfare since independence and demands greater facilities for women's education, removal of social disabilities, equal rights in matters of marriage, admission to professions and other services and equal pay for equal work. This party also holds that the nation cannot progress if its women remain in their present condition of illiteracy, limited opportunities for development and as victims of obscurantist customs and prejudices.

In a recent conference, the representatives of the party emphasized the need for economic independence of women without which there could not be real equality between men and women in any sphere of life-social, political, legal or even family life. In the absence of economic independence, women were as good as private property of men. In this context, they felt that the growing problem of rural unemployment was posing an increasing threat to the security and status of women in the rural areas. With the increase in landlessness and the decay of village industries, new avenues for employment of the vast masses of rural women were imperative. In the absence of land, basic economic security and literacy, rural women have been unable to enjoy their constitutional and legal rights to an even greater extent than their counterparts in the urban areas. This extreme poverty was also the real cause for the low enrolment of rights in schools in these areas. Their suggestions to the Committee included the following: (i) Mass employment and mass education including education of women about their emancipation. (ii) Free education of girls at all levels. (iii) Inclusion of principle of equal pay for equal work in the fundamental rights and removal of existing disabilities in the law of inheritance, marriage and divorce and admissions to profession and service. (iv) Equal shares of land and job facilities for peasant women and maternity benefits, and common kitchens for all working women. (v) Implementation of constitutional and legal rights and propaganda against orthodoxy and conservative attitudes towards women.

This party stands for advancement of women and is keen to take special steps to remove social and educational disabilities, to enable them to discharge their responsibilities to the family, society and nation, without any fundamental change in the traditionally established principles of social organisation. The party promises to enlarge and make more substantial the property rights of women, granting them absolute rights as members of their husband's family.

Some time ago, in a workshop, the representatives of the party emphasized the need to increase the consciousness and political participation of women without which the Constitutional guarantees would remain unimplemented. Their suggestion included the spread of civic and political education to foster a sense of national pride and political awareness to students, housewives and working women also who needed to be taught their civic and political rights and duties. It was their view that legislation could not improve the status of women, when society including women themselves continued to foster a sense of male superiority at all stages. In spite of outstanding performance of some women in politics, science, etc., most women are conservative, backward and wholly dependent on men. Governmental and non-governmental efforts must combine to develop not 'independence' but 'individuality' of women so that they can cooperate in family, social and national life. Illiteracy and unemployment were the causes of their low position.

They were highly critical of the present trend in advertising and films which used the female figures in very bad taste. They felt that there should be some restriction or control on the mass media as these trends were leading to immorality and degeneration, particularly amongst the youth of the country. The problem of security, particularly for working women was becoming more acute, and it was necessary to provide more hostels for working women.

Regarding social laws, they said that women who protest against polygamy receive no protection and hence were afraid to do so in public. In cases of divorce, courts should examine the reasons for a woman seeking a divorce and not go by the 'matrimonial wrong' theory.

Their suggestions included: (i) free education for girls up to the end of secondary stage, (ii) night schools for working women, (iii) vocational training in village school, (iv) compulsory home science classes in every school, (v) expansion of condensed course, and (vi) development of mobile libraries

To promote employment they suggested: (i) reservation of some jobs for women in different spheres (ii) legislation on equal pay for equal work, (iii) relaxation of conditions for employment of women, particularly rural areas.

Though only a very few women were able to reach the highest level of power and authority, those who did so were recognized for their administrative prowess and capacity to manage their affairs. Since 1952 there have been a number of women ministers in the Union Government - some of them were Deputy Ministers, while some became Ministers of State, a few attained Cabinet rank and one was Prime Minister. There is one Deputy Chair-person of Rajya Sabha and several in the panel of Chairmen of both houses of parliament. Besides this, many others have been members of various standing and ad hoc committees. About 26 of the women parliamentarians had previous experience of holding political offices in the States, either in the pre-independence ministries formed in 1937 or in the post-independence period. At the State level several women have held the office of Governor, Chief Minister, Speaker and Deputy Speaker since independence. Though only few have held cabinet rank, women have held office in most of the States. Compared to their overall number in the legislatures the number holding offices was not low.

One of the common characteristics of the women leaders in the political process during the period immediately after independence was their experience of participation in the freedom movement. The women members of the Constituent Assembly which also functioned as the Central Legislative Council in the first 5 years after independence were mostly veterans of the freedom struggle. Most of them had worked in the movement for women's welfare and development. They were the spokesmen of the women's cause in the Legislative Body and played an important role in mobilizing public opinion in support of the social legislations that changed the legal status of women within the first few years after independence. Some of them also played their part in shaping the policies and programmes of women's development that were taken up by the Government of India.

While most of the women leaders who had attained a national stature during the freedom struggle were to be found in the circles of the Central Government or legislatures, in the States a new generation of women entered the political process. The accounts from the States emphasize that experience of social work, particularly among women, while it is still considered a qualification for candidates seeking representation in local bodies, has ceased to be an important qualification for women representatives in the legislatures. As pointed out by some of the political workers interviewed by the Committee, political conflicts these days, particularly at the State level seldom reflect social differences.

The issues are primarily economic which are used by various political parties to seek power in the State Government structure. The women who have been involved in this process mostly come from the economic and political elite of the States and their entry into the political process, particularly representation, depends more on their support within the party rather than on the electorate. Their electorate campaigns are conducted by party workers among whom women form a minority. Only some women candidates have attained their position through active political and organisational work among the masses.

Women candidates and legislators have rightly seen their roles as representatives of the people. Both in Parliament and in State legislatures they have been more concerned with problems of a general nature dealing with issues of national and State importance. In the earlier years, while women participated in such general discussions, on questions relating to women, their championship of women's causes cut across party lines and evoked concerted articulation. In recent years, however, women legislators have not shown such concern or interest in problems that affect women specifically. During a recent debate in the Rajya Sabha on a private resolution on equal pay for equal work for women, not even one-third of the women members attended the discussion and only a few spoke. This lack of interest has led to criticism by women outside the circle of active politicians that the women political elite today are not much concerned with the problems affecting large masses of women in the country.

An analysis of debates and discussions in the legislative bodies indicate the very meagre attention given by these institutions to women's problems. It would appear that the political elite of the country, of both sexes, had come to believe that the problem of women had practically been solved with the measures - legal and administrative - adopted in the first few years after independence. The very articulate debates on women's problems that took place in the earlier period, in which women members invariably played a major role has not been repeated in the later years.

The reason for this lack of concern among the political elite to the problems of women is the absence of an active women's movement. While the number of political organizations seeking to mobilize women is now much higher than in the earlier period, their identification with different political parties prevents most of them from arousing women's consciousness for the solution of problems which are specific to women.

It has already been pointed out the significant gap between the degree of politicization and participation of women and its reflection in the representation of women in the legislative bodies. States which have a larger group of women representatives both in the State Assemblies and in Parliament are also States where the level of politicization among the masses of women is low. States where political mobilization of women seems to have developed more have very few women members in the legislature. It would appear, therefore, that the institutionalization of political activities has resulted in a failure on the part of women to exert adequate pressure on political institutions for solution of the problems that affect their lives. A number of women who have entered the power structure have reached it mainly through certain ascriptive channels. This, coupled with their small numbers in the legislatures as well as decision-making bodies within the parties explains their inhibition and failure to voice the problems of women in these institutions.

spouse. This lack of interest has led to criticism by women outside the circle of party politicians that the women political elite today are not much concerned with the problems affecting large masses of women in the country.

An analysis of debates and discussions in the legislative bodies indicate the very meagre attention given in these institutions to women's problems. It would appear that the political elite of the country, of both sexes, had come to believe that the problem of women had practically been solved with the measures—legal and administrative—adopted in the first few years after independence. The very articulate debates on women's problems that took place in the earlier period, in which women members invariably played a major role has not been repeated in the later years.

The reason for this lack of concern among the political elite to the problems of women is the absence of an active women's movement. While the number of political organizations seeking to mobilize women is now much higher than in the earlier period, their identification with different political parties prevents most of them from building women's consciousness for the solution of problems which are specific to women.

It has already been pointed out the significant gap between the degree of politicization and participation of women and its reflection in the representation of women in the legislative bodies. States which [illegible] women [illegible] States where the level of politicization among the masses of women is [illegible] States which [illegible] political mobilization [illegible] to have developed [illegible] very few women members in the legislature. It would appear, therefore, that the institutionalization of political activities has resulted in a failure on the part of women to exert adequate pressure on political institutions for solution of the problems that affect their lives. A number of women who have entered the power structure have reached it mainly through certain co-optive channels. This, coupled with their small numbers in the legislatures as well as decision-making bodies within the parties explains their inhibition and failing to voice the problems of women in these institutions.

NINE

Effective Mobilization

During almost all elections, it has been observed that political parties used women both as instruments of campaign and objects (women's welfare) set forth for achievement. The hand-bills, poster and public meetings emphasize the specific promises for women in the parties' manifestoes. Some local problems are also used in the propaganda. For instance, during the 1971 parliamentary elections, women of Bombay were promised copious water supply from municipal taps and abolition of prostitution.

In larger cities all the parties try to engage a number of active women workers for campaigning among women. During the 1962 elections, in one constituency in Bombay the Congress had 400 such workers, the PSP 200, the Jana Sangh 400 and the Samyukta Maharashtra Samiti 100. Housewives in urban areas were generally approached during the leisure hours of the afternoon.

Rural women, and women in smaller towns, however, generally do not get similar attention from the parties who often content themselves by approaching the heads of families or village elders. During the 1971 Parliamentary elections, villagers complained of the campaign methods of all parties. In their opinion, vehicles passing through villages, shouting party slogans or approaching only prominent persons in villages, ignored the need of explaining matters to the villagers, particularly the women. In their opinion this would be much better achieved by village meetings which the women could also attend or by house to house approach by politically committed workers. Studies on the efficacy of mass media generally agree that interpersonal contact and public meetings are more effective with women than other mass media.

The inadequate number of women party workers have sometimes led to the use of paid canvassers. This experiment has, however, not yielded very happy results, particularly in rural areas. Villagers are generally opposed to women from outside coming in for canvassing except when they are known to be politically committed workers. One study of the 1962 elections in UP noted the very critical reactions of the local community to paid women canvassers brought from outside. Their employed status was the subject of many adverse comments in private discussions.

Most parties accept the religiosity of women and make use of religious festivals to approach them by organizing religious functions. Even secular parties have indulged in this practice. It has generally been found that women attend such functions in larger numbers than men.

In spite of such occasional attempts, however, the common theme emphasized in practically all studies is that instead of approaching women voters individually or in a group, by and large all political parties and candidates attach greater importance to winning the support of the male active heads of families in the belief that their wishes would prevail with the women as well.

It is clear from the experience of all the general elections, that though the women constitute nearly 50 per cent of the electorate they are unaware of their strength nor has this source been adequately tapped by any political party. There has not been any bargaining on the part of organised women with the political parties for their support, except in Jammu where the Istri Sabha put forward a demand for reservation of 6 seats as the price of support from its members. The political parties' failure to adequately mobilize women's support indicates that they have not yet appreciated this as a source of power. In the opinion of some scholars, if a political party organizes this in half of the nation its chances of winning the elections would improve considerably.

The most important of these organizations are those which focus their activities exclusively on the welfare and liberation of women and are run by women themselves.

All India Women's Conference was founded in 1926. Recognized as a forum for voicing the problem and grievances of women, it has non-political, primarily social objectives. From its inception it has stood for equal social, political and economic rights for women. The most notable feature of such activities was its campaign for reform of marriage and inheritance laws and mobilization of support for the Hindu Code Bill. Most of the women members of the Constituent Assembly who fought for this measure in the central Legislature in the early 50's were leaders of the All India Women's Conference.

Since independence, however, the Conference has been focusing its attention primarily on the welfare and relief of women and children. The specific pressures and programmes started by the organization for this purpose include enforcement of the antipolygamy and divorce laws, development of institutional facilities for working and destitute women, liberalizing the abortion law, family planning and equal pay for equal work. The conference is mainly a deliberative body using resolutions as its main method of pressurizing the government.

National Council of Women in India was founded in 1925 it had objectives very similar to that of the AIWC. In the post-independence period it has concerned itself mainly with education, medical care and family planning. Its activities and membership are confined mainly to urban areas.

Bharatiya Grameen Mahila Sangh was established in 1955, the Sangh aims to work among and improve the conditions of rural women, to vocalize their aspirations through appropriate channels which could act as pressure groups on the government and other public authorities, for the removal of women's disabilities and to promote local leadership among rural women through constructive programmes. Its secondary objective is to assist in planned rural development, deal with agriculture, cottage industries, rural housing, etc. The Sangh has been active in organising various training programmes for farm women, for women in border areas, and in organising Mahila Mandals in villages.

National Federation of Indian Women was established in 1954, this federation has a different set of objectives. It aims at raising political and social awareness of women to fight for social justice and a social transformation, which alone can release them from their present restricted position in society. Their constructive programmes include mainly literacy but they have been active in mobilizing women's protest against all types of injustice and social evils. They have been emphatic in condemning ill-treatment and exploitation of Harijan women and women workers. The recent protests by women in different parts of the country against rising prices, hoarding, adulteration and corruption were organized as a result of an appeal from the National Federation of Indian Women. From the discussions that representatives of these organizations had with the Committee, it appears that while their broad objective and activities show certain similarities, there are certain differences in their concentration and orientation. Though the leadership of all these organisations come mainly from the urban educated middle-class, the membership of the National Federation is composed largely of women from the less affluent sections of society, particularly working women. The hard core of its workers come from this group. All of them admitted that they had not been fully successful in reaching the message of their new rights conferred by the Constitution and the Social laws to all women in the country. They also admitted that lack of consciousness among women had been a major cause for non-implementation of these laws.

Stri Shakti Jagaran is a new movement to mobilize women to fight for a just place for women in society, using Gandhian ideals and techniques. Launched by the Mahila Sarvodaya Sammelan in 1973, the movement believes that the status of women can be raised by women alone. It appeals to all women to abandon purdah, untouchability to caste or class distinctions, dowry and ostentatious expenditure during marriages, discrimination between boys and girls and to resist corruption in all spheres, both within and outside family. Apart from these bodies there are many professional or other specific women's organisations working in different parts of the country. A large number of them are engaged in some type of welfare work among women and children. The Federation of University Women's Associations has been studying problems of women and is currently engaged in exploring opportunities for part-time employment. The All-India Medical Women's Conference also has been discussing problems of women doctors, and issues arising from the present emphasis on family planning and nutrition. Though some of these organisations, like the Trained Nurses' Association, the Women Lawyers' Association, etc., are more in the nature of trade unions, some of them also take up some welfare or constructive work among women. They have not, however, undertaken any campaign to mobilize women in general. Though the trade union movement in India is not a new one, it did not involve women in any substantial numbers till later. Since most trade unions in India are associated with some political party they are normally one of the most powerful agencies for political mobilization. In the case of women, however, this part of their activity has been rather secondary. While women leaders in the trade union movement have played major role in bringing about changes in the labour laws to provide protection for women both inside and outside the legislatures, most trade unions admit that they have not made much efforts in mobilizing women to assert their legal and Constitutional rights. One of our studies found that participation in trade union activities had no direct relationship with women's political awareness. Whenever these organizations have acted in concert, to defend the rights of women, their influence as pressure groups has however been fairly effective. Their role in the enactment of the social laws has already been noted. For example, the reform of Hindu laws, the proposed amendment of the income tax law, to club the incomes of husband and wife for purposes of assessment, was protested against by most women's economic forums. It is generally believed that this protest was responsible for the abandonment of the idea.

The above findings indicate that women's participation in the political process has shown a steady increase, both in elections and in their readiness to express their views on issues directly concerning their day-to-day life. But their ability to produce an impact on the political process has been negligible because of the inadequate attention paid to their political education and mobilization by both political parties and women's organizations. The structures of the parties make them male dominated and in spite of outstanding exception, most partymen are not free from the general prejudices and attitudes of the society. They have tended to see the women voters and citizens as appendages of the males and have depended on the heads of families to provide block-votes and support for their parties and candidates.

The entire exercise of our Committee has indicated that in certain important areas and for certain sections of the female population there has been some regression from the normative attitudes developed during the freedom movement. Large sections of women have suffered a decline of economic status. Every legal measure designed to translate the Constitutional norm of equality or special protection into actual practice has had to face tremendous resistance from the legislative and other elites. Even after the promulgation of these laws, the protection enjoyed by the large masses of women from exploitation and injustice is negligible. As an example we would like to mention the cases of persecution of Harijan women that have increased in recent years. Among women themselves the leadership and the attitudes of the elites, social or political, have become diffused and diverse with sharp contradiction in their regard and concern for the inequalities that affect the status of women in every sphere.

Hence, the observation is that all the indicators of participation, attitudes and impact come up with the same results - the resolution in social and political status of women for which Constitutional equality was to be only the instrument, still remains a very distant objective. While there is no doubt that the position of some groups of women have changed for the better by opening to them positions of power and dignity; the large masses of women continue to lack spokesmen who understand their special problems and are committed to their cause, finding place in the representative bodies of the State.

From this point of view, though women do not numerically constitute a minority, they are beginning to acquire the features of a minority community by the three recognized dimensions of inequality: Inequality of class (economic situation), status (social position) and political power. If this trend is allowed to continue the large masses of women in India may well emerge as the only surviving minority continuously exposed to injustice.

The chasm between the values of a new social order proclaimed by the Constitution and the realities of contemporary Indian society as far as women's rights are concerned remains as great as at the time of independence. The right to political equality has not enabled women to play their roles as partners and constituents in the political process, because we have forgotten Gandhiji's warning not to treat political rights as an end in itself but only as a means.

Instead, these rights have helped to build an illusion of equality and power which is frequently used as an argument to resist special protective and acceleratory measures to enable women to achieve their just and equal position in society. It is surprising that in spite of the special powers provided by Article 15 (3) of the Constitution almost no efforts have been made to redress the unequal status of women in different spheres. We have frequently heard the view that the greatest indicator of the status of women in this country is that it had been ruled by a woman for many years. We are compelled to disagree with this view, because in our opinion this is not an indicator of the real status of women in this country.

Though at the public level there are a number of women who recognize and advocate the desirability of giving equal opportunities to women in economic and political spheres, the norms and attitudes regarding a woman's role in society remains traditional. In this sense, the new rights prove to be only concessional. Thus, it is clear that despite certain legal and even institutional changes, the final legitimation for a successful reorganization of society lies in a revolution in norms and attitudes in the minds of the people. The recommendations that we make are out of a desire to make the political rights of women more functional as required by the needs of a democratic system.

In the course of tours the reseachers received a demand from groups of women in some States for a system of reservation for women in the legislative bodies in the States and in Parliament. They summarized their arguments as below: (a) The difficulties being experienced by women in obtaining adequate representation and spokesmen of their cause in these bodies, and the declining trend in the number of women legislations is the result of the reluctance of political parties to sponsor women candidates. The parties reflect the established value of a male dominated society, which would be difficult to alter without certain structural changes in the socio-political set-up. The parties would continue to pay lip service to the cause of women's progress and the policy of 'tokenism' by having a few women in the legislative and executive wings of government whose minority and dependent status offer serious obstacles of their acting as spokesmen for women's rights and opportunities. (b) If this process continues over a period of time more and more women, losing faith in the political process to change their condition in life, may opt out of the political system and become either passive partners or rebels. In the present context in India the greater majority would undoubtedly follow the first path because most of them have not shaken off the feelings of subjugation and inferiority generated by centuries of subordination. (c) A system of reservation of a proportion of seats for women in these bodies would provide an impetus to both the women as well as to the political parties to give a fairer deal to nearly half the population in the various units of government. If women enter these bodies in larger number the present inhibitions that result from their minority position in these institutions may disappear faster and give them greater freedom to articulate their views. (d) A system of reservation may also increase the women legislators' sense of responsibility and concern for the problems affecting women, thus ensuring the presence of a body of spokesmen of the women's cause in the representative bodies of the States. Such a system would also help to increase the degree of political mobilization of women both in the electorate and within the parties.

Support for reservation also came from a group of scholars who undertook an examination of women's role in the political process at the Committee's request. The summarized views are given below: (a) The process of Indian women coming into their own 'politically' has been slow and halting because Indian political culture is apolitical, and force of tradition has been particularly against participation of women in politics. Improving the political status of women is an integral aspect of the overall problem of socio-economic change and 'broadening the political elite structure'. At a later stage of development changes in the socio-economic order may buttress changes in the political status of women but "it has to be the other way round in present day India". (b) The failure of Indian society to "look upon women's participation with sympathy and understanding" is an exceedingly retarding factor in political socialization of both men and women. 30 per cent reservation of seats in the legislative bodies for women will alter the very character of our legislature and will compel the political parties to change their strategies and tactics and induce them to give women their due. Reservation of seats for women cannot lead to their becoming 'isolated pockets in the nation', because "women are not marginal to society as a minority group might be". It could, instead lead to an increase in women's participation and motivate them to shoulder their political responsibilities.

If "access to policy making powers and facilities is a component of social status" then the presence of more women in the legislatures will help to direct the rate and type of changes in the position of women. Only a system of reservations, increasing the number of women representatives will help to broaden the base of women's representation in the legislative bodies.

Such a transitional measure to break through the existing structure of inequalities will not be retrogression "from the doctrine of equality of sexes and the principle of democratic representation" and may serve the long term objectives of equality and democracy in a better manner than the present system where inequalities get intensified. As compared to the situation before independence when with a system of reservation, women constituted 3.3 per cent of the membership of the central legislator, the average proportion of women in parliament since 1952 without reservation has been marginal. The existing limitations on the role being played by this minority of women legislators may increase if their number declines further with the continuation of the already recognized trend in this direction.

They however received a strong opposition to the suggestion from representatives of political parties and most women legislators. They felt that any system of special representation would be a retrograde step from the equality conferred by the Constitution. There was also some resistance to women being equated with the socially backward communities as all women do not suffer from the same disabilities as these underprivileged groups. The representatives of some parties however did not have any strong objection to reservation of seats for women in local bodies for which certain precedents were already existing.

Though they recorded that the problem of under representation of women in the representative bodies of the State both quantitatively and qualitatively was a real one, after considering the matter very seriously we find ourselves unable to recommend a system of reservation to the State Assemblies and Parliament. Their reason for rejecting the suggestion are summarized below: (a) The women's cause in India has always been championed by all progressive elements, men as well as women. A climate favourable for the betterment of women's status can best be created by their joint efforts. (b) So far women have served as representatives of the people. Separate constituencies for women would narrow their outlook. (c) There is a fallacy in the entire argument for separate representation for women. Women's interests as such cannot be isolated from economic, social and political interests of groups, strata and classes in the society. In point of fact the problems connected with status of women are linked with formulation, articulation and modalities of the realizations of the interests. (d) Such a system of special representation may precipitate similar demands from various other interests and communities and threaten national integration. (e) Experience has shown that the privilege of reservation once granted, is difficult to withdraw. This would amount to perpetuation of unequal status. (f) Women have been competing as equals with men since 1952. They must continue to do so and stand on their own merits and intensify their political and social life. A departure from this equality now will be a retrograde step. (g) The minority argument cannot be applied to women. Women are not a community, they are a category. Though they have some real problems of their own, they share with men the problems of their groups, locality and community. Women are not concentrated in certain areas confined to particular fields of activity. Under these circumstances, there can be no rational basis for reservation for women.

They did not think it would be proper for us to suggest such a major change in our political structure on the basis of the rather insubstantial evidence that we have received.

Even though we did not accept the suggestion for reservation for women in Parliament of the State Legislature, we find that in order to provide greater opportunities to women to actively participate in the decision-making process, it is imperative to recognize the true nature of the social inequalities and disabilities that hamper them. This can best be achieved by providing them with special opportunities for participation in the representative structures of local Government.

The necessity to associate women representatives in local self-governing bodies is already accepted in this country and provision for reservation on seats for women through either election, co-option or nomination in these bodies exist in most of the state legislations that govern the constitution of these bodies.

It has been experienced, however, that this association, with the exception of a few areas is mostly regarded as a form of 'tokenism.' It is felt that the time has come now to move out of this token provision for women's representation to a more meaningful association of women in the structure of local administration.

A second reason for this is the general apathy and indifference of these local bodies of women's development and change of status which has been reported to us by women's organizations and welfare and extension workers, particularly in rural areas. It may be noted that a large number of Mahila Mandals have been organized in both rural and urban areas through the initiative of welfare organizations like the Central Social Welfare Board and its state agencies, Ministry of Agriculture and Community Development and voluntary bodies like the Bharatiya Grameen Mahila Sangh. The status of these bodies is purely voluntary. Some of their members have acquired both experience and interest in developmental activities, but they are not representatives and their constitution does not result in associating or involving large majority of women in these activities. Nor do these bodies receive much recognition from the statutory local self-governing institutions. We received complaints of neglect and lack of funds for women's programmes from women workers throughout the country. This was confirmed by specialists working in the field of Community Development and Panchayati Raj.

They therefore recommended the establishment of Statutory Women's Panchayats at the village level to ensure greater participation by women in the political process. These bodies are not meant to be parallel organizations to the Gram Panchayats but should form an integral part of the Panchayati Raj structure, with autonomy and resources of their own for the management and administration of welfare and development programmes for women and children. We recommend them as a transitional measure to break through the traditional attitudes in rural society which inhibit most women from articulating their problems or participating actively in the existing local bodies. An exclusively women's body would eliminate this difficulty and provide opportunity to more women to gain experience and confidence in managing their own affairs. Their enhanced legal status, we believe, will have a direct impact on the general status of women in rural society and their increasing experience and responsibility may be expected to improve women's keenness and capacity for greater participation in the political process. Lastly, the existence of such statutory bodies would help to ensure better co-ordination of various Government services and programmes for women at the level of implementation. Like the Panchayats, these bodies could be directly elected by the women of the village and should have the right to send their representatives to the Panchayat Samitis and/or Zila Parishads. To ensure a viable relationship between the existing Gram Panchayats and the proposed women's Panchayats, the Chairman and Secretary of both these bodies should be ex-officio members of the other.

At the level of municipalities the principle of reservation of seats for women was already prevalent in certain states. They, therefore recommend that this should be adopted by all states as a traditional measure.

They also recommended the constitution of permanent committees in municipalities to initiate and supervise programmes for women's development.

They recommended that political parties should adopt a definite policy regarding the percentage of women candidates to be sponsored by them for elections to Parliament and State Assemblies. While they may initially start with 15 per cent, this should be gradually increased so that in time to come the representation of women in the Legislative Bodies has some relationship to their position in the total population of the country or the State.

They further recommended the inclusion of women in all important committees, commissions or allegations that are appointed to examine socio-economic problems.

There can be no empowerment without power. Gender gaps in development, amply supported by statistics and empirical evidence, are largely due to the absence of women from decision-making bodies. Women remain outsiders in deciding the directions of development, resulting in unjustifiable disparities. Policy making is about answering the needs of the people. What is difficult to understand is why do the other half feel that they know our needs better? What earthly justification is there for assuming that women cannot speak for themselves? Nor is there any divine injunction imparting exclusive abilities to men. It is precisely this hijacking that accounts for inadequacy, ineffectiveness and failure of many a national policy. Participatory policy-framing right from planning to enactment in legislative bodies is the democratic answer. There is no way out but partnership and interdependence between men and women in the political structures and processes.

A conceptual shift must occur where the emphasis is no longer just on women's issues but also on applying a gender perspective to all national issues. The focus in framing policies should be on how women are affected by all national problems and how they themselves can bring about solutions. This paradigm shift is possible only through women sitting at the tables of power with men. As it stands, no politician denies this framework nor its democratic logic. The problem is that what they accept in principle they violate in practice. Actions have a habit of speaking louder than words. Women have not by accident been kept as outsiders. The gatekeepers of power have ensured this imbalance. Never mind that the nation has paid a huge price by making women the most wasted national asset. Never mind that the nation has not taken full account of the interests and needs of its people. Never mind that the nation has not been denied the benefit of different values, insights and styles of governance suited to a fairer and more balanced world for all.

Women's participation in political leadership is mandated by the Constitution. Rightly fearing that the 'domination syndrome' may prevail, if 'little men' prevail, the Constitution makers had wisely provided for Article 15 to achieve participation and party in governance and to make true the preamble: Liberty, equality and fraternity. With it a balanced representation was enshrined in the constitutional vision as a fundamental right. Those who oppose 33 per cent representations for women wilfully negate the Constitution. While all oaths are taken in the name of implementing the Constitution, yet in practice their only concern has been to perpetuate themselves in power defeating the 'letter and spirit of the Constitution'. That, of course, is a matter of their political morality but it has had negative implication for women and the country.

The methodology used for sabotaging the spirit of the Constitution has been one of the brazen practice of a de facto reservation for men. And no Act of Parliament was required for that. With declining value-based politics, the statistics in 11 parliaments indicate an average of ninety-five per cent representation by men. But for our Constitution the Parliament may have been declared as a 'men only' institution! Yet you hear a few MPs even take the high moral ground claiming that merit brought them to Parliament. Women need to understand this political manoeuvring and claim their political spaces by fighting the deliberate doing-down of women. It begins with denial of opportunity, i.e., the denial of tickets to run the electoral races. In the first election in 1952 women had 4.2 per cent representation and in 1996 they had 7.2 per cent representation in the Lok Sabha. And then they had the slide-back from the 1991 figure of 7.07 per cent to 7.02 per cent.

What makes it democratically unsustainable and morally unacceptable is that women have been denied tickets even when electoral track records clearly prevail that women candidates have by far been the winners over the male candidates. For decades the myth that women are losers was perpetuated by vested interests until in 1996 Women's Political Watch uncovered the untruth in their research of about 9,000 candidates of the 1991 elections. This research brought to light the reality that women are the electoral winners whenever they are fielded. In any other true democracy winnability would be the deciding factor. Yet what we witness is fifty years of blatant exclusion of women and tons of empty rhetoric. Clearly, there is no other option but to bring the democratic balance through a bill akin to the 81st Amendment. Reservation is the only route now.

With the 81st Amendment what women are seeking is not reservation but dereservation, i.e., male representation be scaled down to 67 per cent from 95 per cent (1952-96 Lok Sabha average). It is only when women will acquire an 'effective voice' and become a legislative force will it be possible for agendas for women in terms of education, health, shelter, access and control of resources and ability to set targets for their empowerment to be implemented. The few who, understandably, fear the return to the rightful owners reclining their legislative place have put forward desperate arguments to delay the inevitable, to confuse the issuc, to deprive women longer, and to stay put to conduct business as usual. Taking a cue from the colonial political master these panic-stricken representatives follow the policy of 'divide and rule'.

They do this by raising the issue of caste. They forgot about OBCs when it came to the 73rd Amendment because it concerned only governance at the village level and there was no conflict of personal interests, between them and the women at that level. The hypocrisy of their concern for OBCs is further exposed where we note that it is in fact in the villages that caste discrimination is most entrenched. Why were the interests of OBCs not a factor then? Is anyone to believe that their hearts actually bleed for OBCs?

The last Parliament had close to 200 OBC male MPs. Why were OBC women not there if OBC women's representation was their real concern? These very OBC advocates made no attempt to promote OBC women even as late as the 1996 elections. How then can even the OBC women believe these less than honest advocates? Their talk of quotas within the quota is a blatant attempt to divide the women. What is worse is their transparent motivation to perpetuate themselves by playing divisive politics with women.

Motivated by self-interest they take another untenable position that reservation for women will benefit only urban women. It seems they need to be reminded that the rural women, with the 73rd amendment, got reservation first. What all women seek is representation at all levels of governance. In any case, what is wrong with reservation benefiting urban women? In any case a vast majority of male representatives line in urban areas and sport urban cultures.

While the country celebrates 55 years of independence yet its governance cannot even claim one per cent increase in women's literacy for every year of independence while male literacy stands at over 64 per cent. As women, we must understand that future is not given to us, it is what we do or what we fail to do which is important. The nation had two options - either to let governance be as it is and criticize from the fence or we get involved and work for changes.

The people must be prepared to commit themselves politically and organize ourselves as a political force both as an informed, organized vote bloc, and as elected representatives. Women's power was in women's 300 million votes. Every party, every MP's political destiny was in people's hands. Not one can be elected without their support. Let them use this vote power by voting for women's interests only. The change would come when they mobilize themselves right from the village, block, district, state and national level, and acquire their collective strength.

A reiteration on political empowerment of women could not have come at a better time than on the occasion of International Women's Day, and by none other than Ms Usha Narayanan, the First Lady of India.

In her public debut as the First Lady, Ms Narayanan, chief guest at a meeting organized by the United Nations Information Centre had delivered the keynote address on "Women's Rights are Human Rights."

Regretting that political representation of women in legislatures had not increased in spite of promises by all political parties to give them one-third reservation in Parliament and in state legislatures, she felt that if human rights in all its aspects were to be practically realized, political empowerment was essential.

A former national president of Karuna (an all-India organization for the welfare of women and children,) Ms Narayanan is closely associated with the women's movement in the country. "It cannot be conceived as a war of sexes, but a struggle in which the domination of man has to be challenged in every field, and the cooperation of man has to be felicitated in every field," she emphasised.

That year also marked the 50th anniversary of the Universal Declaration of Human Rights. The guest speakers on the topic included Mr Starcevic, director, UN Information Centre, Ms Indira Jaisingh, a Supreme Court advocate, Ms Kamala Mankekar.

In his address, Mr Starcevic had called for achieving a global partnership for human rights. Governments and civil society must build new forms of solidarity for the promotion and protection of the rights of both women and men. Now and in the years to come, he said, while quoting from UN Secretary General Kofi Annan's message on Women's Day.

The concept of Women Empowerment has predominantly become a focus on political participation. The latter in turn in the context of the debate on the 81st Constitutional Amendment Bill regarding reservation for women in Parliament, has become a restricted discourse on the role of women in formal representative institutions of decision-making whether it is a Panchayati Raj institution or Parliament. In the process, empowerment of women emerges as an extremely limited concept. The fact that empowerment should imply a power to participate in the decision making in all spheres of society, with no separation of the public and prenote and in all social, political, economic and cultural processes in society is completely obfuscated. This study seeks to argue that the State has appropriated the discourse of women's empowerment in order to nullify the emancipatory potential of the concept and reduced it to signify a demand for political participation defined only in terms of reservations into given set of political institutions. Hence the arena of political participation itself is in practice clearly demarcated by the State. It is further argued that the political parties with no political commitment towards struggle on women's rights not only fail to transcend the State agenda but further collaborate with the State in order to keep the patriarchal processes intact. Finally, the role of the women's movement in the sphere of political participation is analysed as a necessary step to redefine the agenda of women's empowerment.

The State response to any articulation of demands by apprised sections of society has been in the form of appropriation of their agenda and compartmentalising it within the mainstream patriarchal, upper caste/class discourse. Hence, even while using the average of "empowerment" or "rights" the attempt is to limit the scope of those terms such that they are unable to challenge the dominant structures and processes in society. Their politics of struggle against unequal power relations is sought to be replaced by a limited concept of "empowerment" which may be restricted to say even a demand for reservations. The fact that empowerment should imply a struggle at various levels of society against the structural basis of oppression is completely obliterated in the process.

The concept of women's empowerment has been a victim of this very appropriation by the State. Not only has it reduced its scope by focusing it only on political participation but it has infact made political participation almost synonymous with a demand for women's reservations. The fact that political participation may mean a democratization of various political processes and groups in society and could be linked with the various struggles for women's empowerment, is obviously ignored by the State. The politics of struggle of the women's movement is sought to be undermined not only in terms of reducing its scope but the state is also attempting to take away the agency of the struggling women by acting as the providers of the empowerment.

The right of political participation came as a result of the struggle of women within the national movement, the fact that despite 55 years of Independence women still remain a marginalized force in representative institutions which is one parameter of political participation is reflective of not only the patriarchal nature of the state but the political parties of today. Reservations then become one form of increasing political participation in the sphere of representative institutions. All political parties have committed themselves to reservations for women in their imposed struggle for gender equality. But the hollowness of their commitment is clearly exposed as well as the fact that they have never allowed women to participate in decision making within their own party structures. This is true for all parties whether it is CPI, CPM or JD, Congress or BJP. One look at the figures show that the percentage of participation in party decision making committees has ranged from 0 and 7 in CPM politburo and central committee to not more than 11 per cent or 12 per cent in Congress waving committee and BJP election committee respectively (Manushi, Sept. 19, 1996). It is also significant to note that despite the higher success rate of women in winning elections the percentage of women candidates fielded by each party has been extremely low. The CSDS Data Unit figures show that in the 1996 Lok Sabha elections, the Congress fielded only 9 per cent women while BJP and UF fielded 5 per cent women candidates each. It is therefore not very surprising that the highest percentage of women representation in the Lok Sabha has only been 8.1 per cent (1984) which came down to 7.2 per cent in 1996.

This dismal scenario in the sphere of political participation in political parties and representative institutions clearly reflects that the continuing patriarchal values on the part of all political parties have not directed there challenge towards their own parties. Infact they too have uncritically accepted their party's theoretical commitment to women's political participation despite the party's inability in increasing women's participation within its structures of decision making. The women of these parties seem content in restricting their struggle to the parliamentary arena and equating political participation with reservations for women.

In India, the autonomous women's movement emerged as a critique to the mainstream left parties and other progressive movements which had failed to articulate the specificity of the women's oppression. It was also under the influence of these autonomous women's groups that the political parties and women's movements became a heterogeneous movement. Here the autonomous women's movement is being referred to as distinct from the women's wing of parties set up separately to mobilize and organize women. If the discourse on political participation and reservations has been appropriated and distorted by the State and the political parties the role of the women's movements acquires special significance.

The autonomous movements have been organizing national conferences, on the issues concerning the women's movement at different points of time. Hence, since the 1980's when the issue of rape was taken up in the context of the Anti Rape Campaign and communalism in 1993 it had different themes in accordance with the issues concerning women and other oppressed sections. The issues have always been reflective of the turbulence in society. But interestingly the issue of political participation has never been accorded much importance in the themes of the conference. In fact the issue of reservations has never been addressed even to place it within a broader context of political participation. Some autonomous groups feel that reservation would not lead to any substantial change in the political processes. A numerical increase of women in the representative institutions may not necessarily lead to a progressive development, regarding women's rights, since women are not a homogeneous category. They are divided by caste, class, religion and as well as differing ideologies.

Although one shares these apprehensions regarding reservations one also feels that it is only by interacting with the formal and informal political institutions, that the women's movement can constantly reiterate the limited scope of reservations and broaden the agenda to link it up with other forms of political participation. Even while becoming the nature of the State and its strategy of appropriation it is only the women's movement which can subvert a limited tool by linking it up with its agenda of women's empowerment in spheres. Since it has a close relationship with mass movements of other oppressed sections, it can challenge political groups, and parties movements to fulfil their commitment to gender equality. The political participation of the women can be given a new direction by linking it up with the simultaneous struggles in other spheres of society. The women's movement has to reiterate the agency of women even in the sphere of political participation and intervene in the processes of democracy and representative institutions, despite its mistrust of the state. It has to go ahead, come what may.

TEN

Role in Politics

No doubt, the theme of political participation of women has raised a major dilemma. On the one hand, it is the fundamental right of every citizen to contribute to the decision-making process. It is in fact the citizen's duty as well and is based on the presumption that each member has adequate means and conditions to achieve a full realization of his or her personality as an entity in society. On the other hand, from a feminist perspective, an analysis of women's participation in political process has questioned the narrow definition of political participation as accepted by the mainstream of political scientists and policy makers. The New Delhi Document on Women in Development (1985) recognized that despite the rapid growth of informal political activity by women, their role in the formal political structure had virtually remained unchanged. This recognition has resulted in a serious debate on the concepts and indicators for political participation.

As a consequence of the debate appropriate indicators of political participation and fresh strategies have to be evolved, not only for formal political activities but also for full involvement and participation in non-formal mass action. It is surprising to note that there had hardly been any mention of this subject in the National Plan of Action for Women drawn up in 1976. Perhaps for the Government of India and the U.N. at that time, the issues of health, education and employment had a higher priority than political participation. However, subsequent national documents prepared at the time of the Nairobi Conference of 1985, the Non Aligned Meet of the same year and the Forward Looking Strategies after Nairobi Conference, have recognized the importance of this theme and raised issues related to the nature of political participation of women, the problems faced therein and the strategies to be evolved.

It is necessary to attempt a definition of political participation which is broader than the one covering women's participation only in the electoral and administrative processes. It includes the gamut of voluntary activities with a bearing on the political processes, including voting, support of political groups, communication with legislators, dissemination of political views and opinions among the electorate, and other related activities. Besides social relationships, there are spheres of power relationships which are generated and institutionalized by being used to encourage, control or move people's behaviour, attitudes and beliefs in specified directions. Political participation can be considered to include an involvement in any form of organized activity that affects, or seeks to affect, these power relationships. It refers broadly also to the "activities by those not formally empowered to make decisions, these activities being mainly intended to influence the attitudes and behaviour of those who have powers for decision making". In fact, protests and demonstrations against those in power also form part of political participation. Women's participation has covered a range of activities including movements, protests and support meetings on all issues connected with labour, dowry, rape, domestic violence, price-rise, food adulteration and deforestation, as also movements for the promotion of peace.

An analysis of the above terms, with particular reference to the participation of women, indicates that there has only been a limited application, mainly because of various dubious considerations of social, economic and political variables. Broad based political participation of women is severely limited due to a nexus of traditional factors. These are the domination of Indian politics by considerations of caste, class, religion, feudal and family status, etc., all of which are parochial essentially patriarchal forces that work in favour of men against women. Consequently, women are still left on the periphery of the political process, and political participation remains elusive to most of them, in spite of their voting and election, and also capture of some seats of power and influence. As amply brought out by various scholars, the most crucial problem in any attempt to measure women's political participation simply by studying official or organizational membership and voting, is the finding that much of the Third World politics occurs outside conventional political institutions. Hence, political participation seeks also to reorganize the lives of members of human society, and ensure that the participation by women is not underestimated by being branded 'non-political' and women's concerns treated as 'social' in nature.

Gender equality is a prerequisite for effective participation of women in strengthening the institutional structure of democracy. Women have been marginalized because of several socio-economic constraints. The number of women in leadership position at the local, village, district and national level is still not commensurate with the numbers in society.

Women's participation in formal elections is to a great extent dependent on the mobilization efforts of the political parties, general awareness among the community of the importance of exercising franchise, and the overall political culture. No serious effort appears to have been made to mobilize women as a political pressure group by any political party. Caste, personality and families of candidates appear to be more important to voters than party ideology or affiliations. Factors like education, religion, class and tradition also seem to affect women's participation.

One great difficulty with the Indian political scene is that it is impossible to generalize about the interrelationship between any single factor and political behaviour. Patterns of political behaviour from different regions show different relationships, influenced as they are by interrelated factors like the social status of women, their economic position, the cultural norms, and above all, the regional outlook towards women's participation in the wider society. Then again, there are some situations which are conspicuous by obvious contradictions. Kerala, which has a record of rapid growth in women's political mobilization and women's literacy, also has a record of electing very few women members to the legislature. In contrast, Uttar Pradesh, with its general low profile of women's political participation, has persistently elected a large number of women to the legislature.

Voting as an indication of political participation for women in India, has its own strengths and weaknesses. Voting has a tremendous impact for equalizing and mobilizing women. Yet, it has to be noted that voting requires the least initiative and internal motivation. Very often the woman citizen treats the day of voting as a welcome break from her dull and tiring routine and does not appear to have a notion of why she should vote for a particular candidate.

The number of women contestants in parliamentary elections has not increased significantly over the years. Political parties seem uniformly reluctant to field women candidates. The high cost of electioneering is another deterrent to most women candidates. Because of these factors there is an increasing tendency among women to contest elections as independent candidates.

Despite the general depressed picture of women's role in Indian democracy, there has been a rise in the number of women in key positions of power. For many years, India had a woman Prime Minister at the helm of affairs. There are women Ministers both in the centre as well as in the states. In the administrative machinery also, there is an increased representation of women.

The concept of participatory development, the importance of intermediaries, e.g., voluntary action groups and educational institutions were recognized as important instruments to achieve the developmental goals for women. Participatory development through group organizations has been successfully attempted in several innovative projects carried out by women's organizations. The contribution of the voluntary organizations has been considered as particularly significant in demonstrating the effectiveness of participatory development as a process of empowering women, to articulate their needs, to take part in decision making and in following their own vision. In this regard, the participation of women in the Panchayati Raj institutions, which were considered to be the most effective instruments for realizing the goals of economic betterment and social justice for the least privileged, was felt essential. The CSWI report suggested the establishment of All-Women Panchayats at village level, with autonomy and resources of their own for the management and administration of welfare and development programmes for women and children, as a transitional measure to break through the traditional attitudes that inhibit most women in articulating their problems or participating actively in the local bodies. The Empowered Committee, while examining the recommendations, suggested that the subcommittee, while examining the subjects relating to management and administration of programmes for women and children should have the power of Panchayat with earmarked funds. Participation of women in Panchayati Raj institutions has been recognized as a step towards equality.

Contrary to the normal expectation that women members in Parliament as well as the State Legislatures take little part in the proceedings and remain silent spectators, they have been very active and are found to take a lively part in the debates. Apart from subjects of direct relevance to them like welfare, child development, removal of dowry and social malpractices, education and health, centre-state relations, security, food and civil supplies and other specialized and sensitive subjects have drawn the attention of many members. There are numerous instances during the years of their participation in debates and in helping to move resolutions for legislative measures and bills. On their part, they have been feeling that the media coverage is inadequate for them as it is generally focused on men. Women have also taken part in, and in some cases initiated, calling attention notices and adjournment motions, in the Parliament and in State Assemblies, and made a mark with significant and well-articulated contributions.

On women's issues, women MPs have participated actively in the debates on dowry and influenced the government to make changes in the existing dowry laws. They have also given useful suggestions such as having a National Commission on Women, having women judges on family and special courts for hearing cases of dowry deaths. On various occasions, they have raised questions regarding the common civil code, immoral traffic in women, dowry deaths and rape cases.

Besides participation in the general elections /contesting elections is a very important dimension of participation through political party. As far as political parties are concerned, although at election time declarations are made of granting 15-20 per cent seats to women, no party has been able to achieve the target. In fact many studies have shown that before the women's decade, political parties were not even stressing on women's issues, in their campaigns or in mobilizing rallies. In the last decade all political parties have shown great interest in women's problems as a result of various developments but primarily due to the pressure of women's groups. Parties in their manifestos promise to women all opportunities for increased participation in social, economic and political life. Yet, the record of most of the parties is poor so far as women are concerned. Though exact figures are unavailable, it can be safely presumed that membership of women in parties does not exceed 10 to 12 per cent of their total membership. Parties hardly make a sincere attempt to reach out to women or to put them in positions of authority. To take the example of Congress, Mrs. Indira Gandhi and Mrs. Sonia Gandhi (present) have been the only woman Presidents of the Congress Party in the post-independence period. Sheila Dixit has been recently appointed as the Chief Minister of Delhi, strengthening the role of women in politics. Though it was stated that "women have a special role to play in the party and in the shaping of a new society", yet women have not really been able to make their presence felt at the decision making levels. There have been a few illustrations of women placed in decision-making positions as in the Congress Centenary Celebrations Committee or in the Nehru Birth Centenary Committee. In a few State Congress Committees, women have been Presidents and at the AICC level, it has been a practice to have at least one woman as the General Secretary. To protest against this continued neglect, the State convenors of the women's' front at their meeting convened in January, 1985, passed a resolution requesting the Congress President to issue instructions to include women as state convenors in the state election coordination committees and to allot at least one Assembly seat in each parliamentary constituency to women.

A number of political parties have strong women's wings spread all over the country, but advocate revival of traditional values, encourage fundamentalism, eulogize mythological women characters and generate communal sentiments. Some others struggle around issues such as economic demands, world peace, atrocities against women, secularism, national integration, price rise, etc.

On the whole, it would not be correct to state that the women's decade has forced all political parties to focus on women's problems. The major contention of the left parties that women's problems will get solved once a classless society is established, still continues. However, under the pressure of women members, at least the inclusion of women's issues in their manifestos has been feasible. Yet, access to significant decision making positions in political parties continues to elude women. Today, very few women hold crucial positions. In fact, one of the main reasons for the growth of autonomous women's groups is the disillusionment that arises, owing to a consideration of women by some political parties as peripheral elements, in spite of their involvement in day-to-day political work. This is not a problem on the Indian scene only, but is a global issue, which could only be solved with the growing awareness and rightful assertion by women.

Participation of women in the trade unions has been a topic which has acquired significance during the last two or three decades. Studies have shown that though it might be difficult to participate in day-to-day activities of the trade unions, women have provided very great strength during crisis periods, such as strikes. A recent study on the more than a year long textile strike of Bombay in 1982 proved that without the support of both women textile workers and the wives of male textile workers, the leaders would have found it difficult to continue.

A distressing fact is that the prevalence of patriarchy prevents men colleagues from accepting women's crucial role. In a recent conference on the problems of working women and their participation in trade unions, a scholar noted: "Today after more than a decade of our struggle we find to our satisfaction that the question and problems of working women and women in general are being discussed widely in our country by various organizations, individuals, press and also by the Government. The question is also being highlighted in international forums." Despite these efforts, many trade unions in the country are yet to pay adequate attention to women's issues and joint efforts have to be made to make a common cause to fight for the demands of working women. The scholar has also documented a number of struggles of women workers from different states indicating the militancy and tenacity of women who were involved in struggles of Adivasis, contract workers, women coal miners, plantation workers, etc.

A recent report also gives the picture of the women membership in the CITU and the proportion of women office bearers in some of the States. Of course, the picture is very dismal. The total membership has been around 10 per cent in 1986, and an infinitesimal proportion as office bearers.

The issues which concern women most, such as equal wages, non-provision of maternity benefits and child care facilities, retrenchment of women workers in the wake of Equal Remuneration Act, have not been taken up seriously by trade unions suggest that there are instances where they expressed their concern regarding these issues by passing resolutions and holding consultation but there is hardly any evidence that trade unions agitated or called a strike to meet these demands nor have their journals taken cognizance of these minor efforts. In this context, it has been even suggested that a separate women's cell or a union for women would ensure more participation of women. It was also strongly felt that one of the major tasks is to orient the male leaders to remove their gender bias and incorporate more and more women in the decision-making bodies.

An analysis of the problems of women working in the unorganized sector throws light on the sexist attitude of mainstream trade unions. It is well known that women constitute a majority of the unorganized labour force. The working conditions in this sector are abysmal. There is no job security, no fair wages, no facilities, and no rights to demand for the improvement of their situation. It goes to the credit of grassroots level organizations such as WWF and SEWA and the researchers who have highlighted the problems of these women, that attempts are now being made to create some kind of structure to ventilate their problems. In the absence of support from the official trade unions, the women workers are turning to some of the women's organizations for pressing their problems is a very striking trend.

Studies have shown that whenever women took up issues such as low wages, inhuman working conditions, and health hazards by organizing meetings, putting up posters, etc., women workers were harassed and victimized. They were threatened with arrest and rape, and all kinds of pressures from parents, in laws were used to demoralize the women. Employers preferred to use the 'putting out' system and 'price rate' system to enrolling women on their pay rolls. The recently published report of the National Commission on Self

Employed Women and Women in Unorganized Sector, has made several recommendations to ensure the inclusion of women in the unorganized sector in the entire gamut of trade union activities.

Political participation, viewed from a broader perspective, includes participation in any organized and deliberate activity that seeks to influence or alter the character/ function/ structure/ policies/ assumption/behaving of any institution or the power structure in any of the above spheres. In order to assess women's political participation, one has thus to look at their involvement in different types of mobilization such as movements and struggles. The question that needs to be investigated in depth is the one to ascertain women's participation in mass struggles and protest movements and not necessarily in formal political bodies ranging from village level to Parliament.

The history of women's large-scale participation in the nationalist movement is well known and in fact, one can go back to 1905 when women freedom fighters showed immense courage in fighting the British rulers. Of course, more strikingly, mass participation of women was recognized during the Civil Disobedience Movement in 1930 and also during the Quit India Movement of 1942, when thousands of women courted arrest. Some women participated in the revolutionary movement as couriers distributing literature, risking police repression, imprisonment and even capital punishment. Similarly, in the Tebhaga Movement for land reform, which took place during 1946-51 in West Bengal, it has been reported that women participated at all levels. There was a Nari Bahini (Women's Volunteer Force) which would help guard villages at night. Studies have recorded many stories of women's courage, militant spirit and innovation during these struggles. Investigations into the role of women in the Telangana and Naxalite movements subsequently have revealed that women not only gave shelter to the revolutionaries and served to liaison among various groups but also took leading part in direct political action.

One of the most significant events which dramatically brought to the forefront women's issues in the last decades has been the reopening of the Mathura rape case in the Supreme Court which triggered off a woman's protest movement. A series of rallies, campaigns, *morchas*, *dharnas* and demonstrations were held to protest against rape, wife beating, dowry deaths, molestation of women, media distortions, foeticide and other issues.

Women from various castes, communities and regions have participated voluntarily and together, to raise their voice on important issues. Current rural struggles in Bihar, Himachal Pradesh, Marathwada region and five Tamil Nadu districts centre on various issues ranging from expropriation and redistribution of the land of a Bodhgaya mahant in Bihar, the politics of liquor licensing and government water supply in Himachal Pradesh, to struggle for canal water and public lands by untouchable poor peasants in drought prone Marathwada, and struggle for self-respect, employment and justice among Tamil Nadu landless labourers.

In this narrative of women's participation in mass movements, the illustration of the Chipko Movement stands out prominently. There is a feeling that a genuine mass based women's movement can grow out of the grassroot participatory organizations of women. Through such participation will emerge political consciousness of women. The Chipko Movement initiated in 1972-74 is an example of the powerful impact that women's initiative can have on the power brokers, contractors and family members. Where women shoulder major burdens and the drudgery of bringing fuel, fodder and water from long distances, any action which affects these sources of livelihood adversely, will surely bring sharp resentment among them. In this struggle, women have not been merely supporters of an ongoing struggle but have functioned as initiators of the movement with a far reaching impact on gender relations in Garhwali society. As mentioned in the report on the State of India's Environment. "Women acting entirely on their own rose up on the spur of the moment. While in Rani (Chamoli District) the protest was against a timber contractor, in all other areas the protest was against their own cash hungry men who could not care less if the forest was destroyed while their women had to walk for many miles to collect their daily load of fuel and fodder".

Thus the record of women's participation in political processes other than the formal has been quite creditable. Of course, while women have been visible in mass movements, group upsurges and protest struggles, their presence is not felt in structured decision making institutional settings. Even in the structures where women's participation is substantial, they have not been given positions of power. However, it can be stated that protests made by women activists and scholars have resulted in their role in the grassroots level movements being recognized.

During the last decade, and particularly in the last two years, certain deliberate efforts have been made to implement some of the decisions taken at the Conference of Non-Aligned and other Developing Countries, in April, 1985 and at the Nairobi World Conference in July, 1985 as Forward Looking Strategies for the Advancement of Women. Even then, it has not been found possible by political parties to field the number of women candidates that they had planned, and by elected governments in the Centre and States to appoint the minimum number of women to ministerial positions. One significant step has, however, been the formation of the department of women and Child Development which is part of the Ministry of Human Resource Development. The Constitution of a separate Department of Women has helped in focussing programmes for women's development. Efforts are also being made to reach out to the women in the poverty sector through various welfare schemes and programmes.

The incorporation of Equality for Women as No.12 in the Twenty-Point Programme of development enunciated in 1986, and certain special schemes like Legal Literacy Programmes, Awareness Generation Programmes, Prevention of Atrocities Against Women are evidences of conscious attempts made by the government to empower women to handle complex situations. The setting of the National Expert Committee on Women Prisoners and the National Commission on Self-Employed Women are significant steps in the right direction. The most formidable hurdle in the programmes and policies of the Government has been non-implementation or very limited implementation of these measures. Before recommendations to remedy the situation are suggested, it would be useful to have a brief discussion on why women's participation in political affairs is limited.

As mentioned in the Non-Aligned Document, "understanding

of obstacles to women's effective participation in political life has generally been clouded by various assumptions regarding women's behavioural pattern, their backward consciousness, lack of interest in public issues, or biological differences in their mental make up. An assessment of the situation at the end of decade with all the shortfalls in reliable data suggests that, while the visibility of women in the political and developmental process has increased because of greater efforts to obtain first-hand information, the search has also helped to identify powerful, sometimes hidden forces of resistance that obstruct the march towards the goals of the decade."

On the question of peace, since women are one of the most vulnerable groups in the region effected by armed conflicts, special attention has to be drawn to the need to eliminate obstacles to the maintenance of peace. Women's equal role in decision making with respect to peace and related issues should be enhanced and encouraged at all levels. Women should be able to participate actively in decision-making processes related to the promotion of regional, national and international peace and cooperation. Nonetheless, it should not imply that women's ability to support causes is restricted only to pacifist issues.

One of the arguments for non-participation has been that the women wilfully place themselves in marginal positions towards matters "political". The crucial problem is that women find themselves being judged and judging themselves by two standards. One standard is of feminity, of the private world which regards them as nurturant, passive, emotional, home oriented and subordinate to men. The other standard is that of their modern role which is the standard of the public world which expects women to be rational, active, achievement oriented, ambitious and competitive. Women in such a situation have two options. Either they follow the rules of the game of politics and are called unfeminine or act in politics guided by the standards of feminity and are seen as peculiar.

A very strong reason explaining women's limited participation has been the theory of women's "backward consciousness". However, it has been seen that in non-formal mass movements, women responded with great enthusiasm and responsibility on crucial themes. Whether it is a movement against foreign government under Mahatma

Gandhi's leadership or it is a protest against vested interests in economic or political spheres or confronting the oppressive landlord or contractor, women have not hesitated; they have made sacrifices and suffered repression along with men.

The observations that women when elected do not participate in the debates or women elect those candidates whom their men wish to support, have been proved wrong with more and more research findings. Women do raise relevant issues on a wide range of subjects, and studies on voting behaviour suggest that the secret ballot system helps considerably in exercising individual preference, though these findings / revelations are underplayed by policy makers and political scientists due to gender biases.

Subordination of women in society acts as a structural constraint to their participation in political activities. Owing to the gender-based division of labour in the family, women have to bear the full responsibility of household chores. It is the woman's duty to bring fuel, fodder and water and to cook. They have to look after the rearing and education of children besides socializing. These constraints operate more or less for all classes and communities of women.

Another significant deterrent factor is that of the political culture which prevails today. Not only have the political processes become complicated but many decisions are made behind the scenes. It has also become very expensive and difficult for women, who have little control over resources. Further, the atmosphere of growing violence, character-assassination and unscrupulous struggles for power, have been a serious deterrent to women's participation in an effective manner.

In mass movements which are issue-oriented and aim at achieving concrete objectives, women are able to participate, leave the chores of the house to someone and suffer the hardships and privations of political confrontations. But when an activity requires routine, continuous work which is often complicated to follow, women find it difficult to participate due to lack of supportive structures.

Another important factor which has to be considered is that much of the political participation today requires information, knowledge and exposure to the various experiments, strategies and models. An understanding of political policies, strategies and actions requires some training, education and constant interaction. This requirement is very difficult to be fulfilled even by men in a poor illiterate society. It is a much more challenging task for women. If women's participation has to be encouraged, a more conscious and deliberate effort to educate them politically has to be made. The working of international events, the interrelationships of various systems in society, implications of political actions and policies and many such issues need to be explained to women so that they participate intelligently and consciously.

If women have to become integrated fully into political life, cultural change is necessary. In the past few centuries, the world has been divided into the separate spheres of the public and private. While women are no longer restricted to "private" activities related only to their families, their outside activities are "privatized" by men and society at large. Another prerequisite for women to be active participants in decision making activities, is the provision of facilities, like education, training, information and above all, economic security.

In conclusion, it may be said that during the Women's Decade, there has been some achievement in making women visible in the political sphere. There has been more positive action on the part of the government to integrate women in the decision-making process. It appears that the operation of larger politico-economic forces generate a political culture that women find difficult to get involved in. Women through the Constitution have been allowed to enter politics but there is a vast difference between allowing and integrating. As a scholar puts it "Toleration is not an active principle, it is a passive one. It places a premium on the elimination of tangible barriers but makes no commitment to a positive value of inclusion and membership. Political liberation of women, therefore, would mean that women would be seen not as deviants or even as welcome strangers". In short, women's real active political participation will necessitate changes both in value and in the social structure.

Recommendations: 1. It has been observed through various studies, that education of citizens not only builds up knowledge and information but also helps the citizens to understand the complexities of political process. It is, therefore, recommended that the programme of free universal education up to the age of 14 should be vigorously implemented. Further, serious attention needs to be paid to the content of education. The courses of studies and the textbooks should inculcate values of gender equality, self-respect, courage, independence, etc., which would help develop the personalities of women. 2. In order that women are able to participate fully, it is necessary to spread legal literacy not only among the general community, but also among elected representatives. Modules can be included in existing non-formal educational programmes for this purpose. 3. The working of international events, the interrelationship of various systems of society, implications of political actions and policies, economic and other such issues need to be highlighted to women. 4. Men and women in positions of power should be sensitized to women's issues. 5. Government should effectively secure participation of women in decision-making processes at National, State and local levels. This would imply use of special measures for recruitment of women candidates: •More women need to be inducted in ministries at the centre and in state governments and they must be allowed to function in areas suitable to their capacities and not be restricted to 'soft' sectors. •The Planning Commission and all ministries and government departments must have a Women's Cell. •All government delegations to international meetings must include at least one or more women members. •Wherever a Committee or Commission is set up by Government for any purpose, 30 per cent of its representation must be of women. •The Union and all State level Public Service Commissions must have women representatives. •The Planning Commission and State Planning Boards must have adequate representation of women. •50 per cent of all grassroots functionaries must be women. To facilitate its implementation, relaxation of minimum educational qualifications is needed, which can be supplemented by short training courses for women. •Reservation should be made of 30 per cent seats at Panchayat to Zila Parishad level and local municipal bodies for women. Wherever possible, higher representation of dalits/tribals, women of weaker sections should be ensured. •30 per cent of executive heads of all bodies from village Panchayat to district level and a certain percentage of chief executives of Panchayati Raj bodies at lower, middle and hi-her levels must be reserved for women. •A more effective step would be to declare a certain percentage of constituencies in the lower tier of Panchayati Raj as exclusively women's constituencies and all executive positions in a certain number of territorial jurisdictions reserved for women candidates. 6. All women members of Panchayats and other executive bodies must be trained and empowered to exercise their authority. Both men and women members must be sensitized to women's issues. A committee should be formed to look into the training needs of women Panchayat members and to help in designing modules separate allocation may be made for this purpose. Particular attention must be paid to the development of interpersonal communication skills among the trainees and community leaders. 7. Conscious efforts are needed to elicit participation of women through establishing links between the elected representatives and the development functionaries as being experimented in Rajasthan through the Women's Development Programmes (WDP). The whole experiment is based on a decentralized administrative structure. Plans of action should be formulated through frequent meetings and discussions. Further the prime need is to see that the representatives have to be made answerable to the electorate. WDPs in other States must also be linked with Panchayat/local functionaries for more effective participation of women in development. 8. Standing Advisory Committees at Central, State, District, Block and wherever possible at village level should be formed consisting of representatives of important women's organizations. 9. Executive bodies of trade unions must include more women. 10. One of the greatest hurdles in contesting elections is the exorbitant expenditure. This factor not only makes it difficult for women, who have very limited independent resources to participate, but completely eliminates women in the poverty sector from entering the arena. This situation leads to prominence of upper castes, upper classes, urban women in the political sphere. To counteract this inequitous situation, serious steps must be taken to reduce election expenditure. Further, enormous amounts needed for election, lead to corruption and various nefarious practices. If steps are taken to decentralize the political machinery, then unnecessary expenditure in reaching out to a very large electorate could be avoided. 11. A major step needed to facilitate women's participation both in formal and informal political processes is provision of support services. In all kinds of public participation as well as in seeking opportunities for self-development, the primary responsibilities of women for looking after home and children always come in the way. Unless arrangements are made for child care and other domestic responsibilities, sustained participation of women in the public sphere is impossible without the integration of men in the private sphere. This not only means that men share the familial responsibilities but a new value needs to be given to this joint sharing both in public and private spheres which would ultimately lead to a better quality of life. 12. In a democracy, political parties have a very significant role to play. The parties should take such measures which would facilitate participation of women. All political parties must be urged to ensure that at least 30 per cent of the candidates fielded for election are women till such time as women can stake their claim to nomination as equals. It should be examined if the Election Commission can be empowered to enforce this. 13. It is the bounded duty of political parties to provide political education to the people. They should organize study circles in which not only political understanding of the complex situations is provided, but controversial issues having implications on gender relations is also analysed. 14. Women members of the political groups should be vigilant about their rights and contributions. Whenever sexist attitudes are exhibited or sex discrimination is practised, women members should build up solidarity and oppose such practices. They should also press for implementing whatever has been promised to women; whether the question is of allocation of seats or of providing a creche or taking a stand in Parliament. 15. In generating a participatory political system, the role of voluntary organizations or non-governmental organizations is very crucial. There is evidence that when NGOs are active and play the role of pressure groups, the representatives also become alert. Through raising the awareness of the community, NGOs can help in fielding candidates who are responsible to the people. They can focus the attention of the people on crucial issues facing women and elect members who understand those issues and are working towards it. Organizations and grassroots women's groups have in fact effectively drawn the attention of the government to atrocities perpetrated on women, to custodial rape, to harassments for dowry, to plight of the women in the unorganized sector, and so on. NGOs can also provide training for future women leaders. They can organize legal literacy programmes and study circles for political education as well as develop participatory methods of working, and thus serve as a practical training centre for effective political participation by women. They should not adopt a beneficiary or 'welfare' approach while working with their target groups. Even if a few NGOs play their role adequately and with courage, a new climate of commitment and responsibility could be generated. 16. NGOs should work as pressure groups or political action groups to press for the fulfilment of promises. They should also provide support to the elected women representatives, when they are presenting women's cases in the deliberative bodies. In short, there should be a very strong link between women representatives and those organizations working with the community. 17. Media should play a productive role in enhancing women's participation. It should give wider coverage to various activities and measures taken by women, and should highlight the problems of women. In order to project women's issues and achievements, perhaps mainstream media may not be adequate and, therefore, it is necessary to develop an alternate media system that could portray women's struggles and experiences, help generate values which encourage gender equality and justice, and build up a positive image of women participating in public life. 18. For politicization of women, networking and creation of pressure groups representing genuine issues and felt needs are essential. 19. A massive awareness campaign aimed at eliciting the support of electors (both male and female) around causes will have to be undertaken.

The realization that real development cannot take roots if it bypasses women, who not only represent nearly half of the country's total population (accounting for 407.1 million in absolute numbers, as per the 1991 census) but represent the very kernel around which societal reorientation takes place has been the guiding principle in the formulation of our plans from the very beginning. The government has made concerted efforts towards removing various gender-biases in order to ensure women equal status in the real sense as enshrined in the Constitution of India.

The Constitution of India guarantees both rights and privileges to women through Fundamental Rights and Directive Principles of State Policy. Article 14 confers on men and women equal rights and opportunities in political, economic and social spheres. Article 15 prohibits discrimination against any citizen on grounds of religion, race, caste, sex, etc., alike. Article 15(3) makes a special provision enabling the State to make affirmative discrimination in favour of women. Similarly, Article 16 provides for equality of opportunities, Article 39 (a) mentions that the State shall direct its policy towards securing for both men and women, equally, the right to a means of livelihood, Article 39 (c) ensures equal pay for equal work. Article 42 directs the State to make provision for ensuring just and humane conditions of work and maternity relief. Above all, the Constitution imposes a fundamental duty on every citizen through Article 51(A)(e) to renounce practices derogatory to the dignity of women.

In order to safeguard the various constitutional rights, the State has enacted many women-specific and women-related legislations- such as the Equal Remuneration Act of 1976, The Hindu Marriage Act of 1955 as amended in 1976, The Immoral Traffic (Prevention) Act of 1956 as amended and renamed in 1986. An amendment brought in 1984 to the Dowry Prohibition Act of 1961 made women's subjection to cruelty a cognizable offence. The second amendment brought in 1986 makes the husband or in-laws punishable, if a woman commits suicide within seven years of her marriage and it has been proved that she has been subjected to cruelty. Also, a new criminal offence of 'Dowry Death' has been incorporated in the Indian Penal Code. The Child Marriage Restraint Act of 1976 raises the age of marriage of a girl to 18 years from 15 years and that of a boy to 21 years and makes offences under this Act cognizable. The Factories Act of 1948 (amended up to 1976) provides for establishment of a creche where 30 women are employed (including casual and contract labourers). The Medical Termination of Pregnancy Act of 1971 legalizes abortion by qualified professionals on humanitarian or medical grounds. Amendments to Criminal Law 1983 provide for a punishment of seven years in ordinary cases of rape and ten years for custodial rape cases. The maximum punishment may go up to life imprisonment. The enactments of (Prevention) Act, 1987 have been passed to protect the dignity of women and prevent violence against them as well as their exploitation. The National Commission for Women Act, 1990 was passed to set up the National Commission for Women (NCW), a national apex statutory body to review the constitutional and legal safeguards for women and recommend remedial legislation. The 73rd and 74th Constitutional Amendment Acts passed in 1992 provide for reservation of one-third of seats in rural Panchayats and urban local bodies for women as Members and as chairpersons. A new legislative Bill for 33 per cent reservation for women in national Parliament and subsequently in State Assemblies is pending in Lok Sabha. The political parties, despite all their claims for women's rights have so far failed to agree on the passage of the bill. That's the irony of the situation and the paradox of our polity.

Bibliography

Altekar, A.S., *The Position of Women in Hindu Civilization*, Varanasi: Motilal Banarsidas, 1962.

Anshen, R.N., (ed.), *The Family: Its Functions and Destiny*, New York: Harper & Row, 1959.

Asthana, P., *Women's Movement in India*, Delhi: Vikas Publishing House, 1974.

Baig, T.A., *India's Women Power*, New Delhi: S. Chand & Co., 1976.

Bhasin, K. (ed.), *The Position of Women in India*, Bombay: Leslie Sawny, 1971.

Blalock, H.M. and Blalock, A.B., *Methodology in Social Research*, New York: McGraw-Hill, 1969.

Blau, P. (ed.), Focus on Social Structure, and Introduction to the Programme of the ASA meeting in Montreal, 1974.

Blau, P.M., A Macrosociological Theory of Social Structure, *American Journal of Sociology*, 1977.

Brayfield, A.H. and Crockatt, W.H., Employee attitude and employee performance, *Psychological Bulletin*, 1955.

Burke, P.J. and Reitzes, D.C., An Identity Theory Approach to Commitment, *Social Psychological Quarterly*, 1991.

Caplow, T., *Sociology of Work*, Mc-Graw-Hill, New York, 1954.

Chaturvedi, Geeta., *Women Administration in India: A study of the socio-economic background*, Jaipur, RBSA Publication, 1985.

Cofer, C.N. and Appley, M.N., *Motivation Theory and Research,* A Wiley International Edition, John Wiley and Sons Inc., 1964.

Deckard, B.S, *The Women's Movement*, Harper and Row, New York, 1979.

Drucker, P.F., *An Introductory View of Management*, Harper College Press, New York, 1977.

Evan, M. William, *Organizational Theory Structure, Systems and Environments*, Wiley Interscience Publications, John Wiley and Sons Inc, London: 1976.

Fleishman, E.A., A Relationship Between Incentive, Motivation and Ability Level in Psychomotor, *J. Exp. Psychol.*

French, Elizabeth, G., Effects of Interaction of Achievement Motivation and Intelligence on Problem Solving Success, *American Psychologist*, 1951.

Gender Indicators of Developing Asian and Pacific Countries, 1993, Asian Development Bank.

Good, W.J., *World Revolution and Family Patterns*, London: CollierMacMillan, 1963.

Gorwaney, N., *Self Image and Social Change: A Study of Female Students*, Delhi: Sterling Publishers, 1977.

Hate, C.A., *Changing Status of Women in Post-Independence India*, Bombay: Allied Publications, 1969.

Human Development Report, UNDP, New York: Oxford University Press, 1996.

Inkeles, A. and Smith, D., *Becoming Modern*, London: Heinmann Educational Books Ltd., 1974.

Kuppuswamy, B., *Social Change in India*, Delhi: Vikas Publishing House, 1972.

Mead, M., Adolescence Issue, *UNICEF News*, 1974.

Marshall, Katherine, Employed Parents and Division of Housework, *Perspectives*, Autumn, 1993.

Mies, M., *Indian Women and Patriarchy: Conflicts and Dilemmas of Students and Working Women*. Concept Publishers, New Delhi, 1980.

Myrdal, A. and Klien, V., *Woman's Two Roles*, Routledge & K. Paul, London, 1968.

Noditch, Murray, P. and Demaw, T., Locus of Control and Competence. *Journal of Personality*. Dec. 1975.

Prakash, G., *After Colonialism: Imperial Histories and Post Colonial Displacements*, Princeton University Press, Princeton, 1995.

Rani, K., *Role Conflict in Working Wives*, Chetana Publications, New Delhi, 1976.

Report of the Committee on Status of Women in India (1974), *Towards Equality*. Department of Social Welfare, Government of India, New Delhi.

Roby, Pamela, *Women in the Work Place*, MA. Schenkrnan, Cambridge, 1981.

Rotter, J.B., Generalized expectancies for internal versus external control or reinforcement. Psychological Monographs. General Applied, 1966.

Safilios-Rothschild, C., The Influence of the Wife's Degree of Work Commitment upon Some Aspects of Family Organization and Dynamics, *Journal of Marriage and the Family*, 1970.

Taylor, Ronald, N., Age and experience as determinants of managerial information processing and decision making performance. *Academy of Management, Journal*, 1975.

Tolman, E.C., Principles of Purposive Behavior. In S. Koch (ed.)

Vitels, M.S., *Motivation and Morale in Industry*. New York: Morton 1953.

Watson, T., *Management Organization and Employment Strategy*, Routledge and Kegan Paul, London, 1986.

Whyte, F.W., *Money and Motivation*, Harper and Row. Inc., New York: 1955.

Index

❑❑❑